Plato's
Dialectical
Ethics

Plato's Dialectical Ethics

Phenomenological Interpretations
Relating to the *Philebus*

Hans-Georg Gadamer

translated and with an introduction
by Robert M. Wallace

Yale University Press
New Haven and London

The translation of this volume was made possible in part by a grant from the Translation Program of the National Endowment for the Humanities, an independent federal agency.

Set in Bodoni Book type by Brevis Press, Bethany, Connecticut. Printed in the United States of America by Vail-Ballou Press, Binghamton, New York.

Library of Congress Cataloging-in-Publication Data

Gadamer, Hans-Georg, 1900–
[Platos dialektische Ethik. English]
Plato's dialectical ethics : phenomenological interpretations relating to the Philebus / Hans-Georg Gadamer ; translated and with an introduction by Robert M. Wallace.
p.   cm.
Translation of: Platos dialektische Ethik. 2nd ed.
Includes bibliographical references and index.
ISBN 0-300-04807-6 (alk. paper)
1. Plato. Philebus.   2. Dialectic.   I. Title.
B381.G3313   1991
171'.4—dc20   91-7212 CIP

The paper in this book meets the guidelines for permanence and durability of the Committee on Production Guidelines for Book Longevity of the Council on Library Resources.

10   9   8   7   6   5   4   3   2   1

Contents

Translator's Introduction

Plato's Dialectical Ethics, now appearing in English sixty years after its original appearance, in 1931, in German, combines an essay on Plato's dialectic with a detailed interpretation of the *Philebus*, Plato's last dialogue dealing with fundamental ethical questions. It will thus be of interest to anyone concerned with Plato, with the relation between Plato and Aristotle, or with ethics in general. In addition, it has a special importance for those interested in the influential conception of hermeneutics that Gadamer later presented in his *Truth and Method* (1960, trans. 1975 and 1989) and, indeed, anyone wanting to understand twentieth-century German thought in general. For it shows Gadamer coming to grips simultaneously, and for the first time, with two major challenges: the hermeneutic challenge of Plato and the philosophical challenge of Heidegger.[1] The way in which he met these challenges is crucial to the interpretation of the entire subsequent trajectory of his thought—of which, I think, we do not yet have a comprehensive or an adequate understanding. And since these two challenges (if we take the problem of interpreting Plato as repre-

1. Gadamer's later publications on Plato that are available in English include a collection of papers under the title *Dialogue and Dialectic: Eight Hermeneutical Studies on Plato* (New Haven, 1980) and *The Idea of the Good in Platonic-Aristotelian Philosophy* (New Haven, 1986), both translated by P. Christopher Smith.

sentative of the problem of interpreting the history of philosophy in general) have constituted the matrix for the greater part of German philosophical work since the 1920s, Gadamer's trajectory, and this book in particular, can also teach us a good deal about the process of German philosophical thought as a whole in this period.

The most influential philosophical interpretation of Plato in Germany in the early part of this century was that of Paul Natorp, who was a leading member of the Marburg school of Neo-Kantian philosophy. In his *Platos Ideenlehre* (1902), Natorp took Plato as, essentially, a precursor of Kant and thus of modern scientific thinking, summed up in the concepts of natural law, hypothesis, and method. After the First World War, the growing opposition to this unhistorical (optimistic, liberal) view of Plato took the forms of a less tendentious examination of his theory of the Ideas (Julius Stenzel), a more sophisticated literary analysis of the dialogues (Paul Friedländer), and an interest in questions of development and cultural context (Werner Jaeger et al.), all of which made Natorp's innocent modernism look somewhat one-sided.[2]

Gadamer's break with Neo-Kantianism was informed by most of this work (he studied under Friedländer, as well as under Natorp himself), but found its primary inspiration elsewhere.[3] In Martin Heidegger, under whose supervision he wrote *Plato's Dialectical Ethics* as his *Habilitationsschrift*, or "second doctorate," Gadamer found a spe-

2. Natorp himself moved toward a more mystical interpretation of Plato and Platonism in the appendix to the second edition of *Plato's Ideenlehre*, published in 1921.

3. Gadamer has provided valuable autobiographical sketches of this period of his intellectual formation in his *Philosophical Apprenticeships*, trans. Robert R. Sullivan (Cambridge, Mass., 1985). Another early influence on Gadamer was the George Circle, a group which formed around the poet Stefan George at the turn of the century and which produced a couple of Plato books that Gadamer respected (those of Kurt Hildebrandt and Kurt Singer). But the text of *Plato's Dialectical Ethics*, from the preface on, acknowledges and exhibits the influence of Heidegger in a way that puts these others in the shade.

cifically philosophical inspiration that went beyond what textual interpretation and historical and literary criticism could provide. In *Being
and Time* (1927), Heidegger broke with the Cartesian tradition of
subject–object thinking with which Kant—at least as the Neo-Kantians understood him—was still involved. Arguing that human thinking
could never start from scratch but was always already involved with a
"world" and with language, Heidegger cast doubt on the modern assumption that by means of scientific method, objective reality could
in principle be thoroughly clarified and thus subjected to the will of
the subject. In place of this bipolar subject–object conception of truth
and knowledge, Heidegger suggested (roughly) that the remarkable
thing was that truth "happened" at all: that conditions existed in which
human beings were *able* (hubristically) to imagine that they had the
powers that modern, Cartesian philosophy attributed to them.

　　This was the change of focus that Gadamer brought to bear
in his study of Plato. His concern is not with the Ideas, which the
Neo-Kantians wanted to interpret as scientific hypotheses (generated
by the subject in pursuit of knowledge of objects), but with the Platonic
dialogue itself and the "dialectic" that it embodies: with the way in
which Plato (inspired by the example of Socrates) describes truth as
happening, as coming about, among human beings. This is not
through rigorous deduction or methodical interrogation of the object
but through a questioning openness that allows itself to be guided, in
the back and forth of conversation (which may be actually, or only
potentially, *interpersonal* conversation), by reality—*die Sache*, as Gadamer calls it: the "facts of the matter"—rather than by one's own
(individual or collective) "vested interests."[4] Gadamer describes this
openness as being achieved, paradigmatically, by the "knowledge of
his own ignorance" that Socrates claims, and as being preserved,

4. To avoid excessively clumsy constructions I have translated *sachlich* and
Sachlichkeit sometimes as "substantive" and "substantiveness," sometimes by the less potentially misleading "oriented toward the facts of the
matter," etc. An overview of translations adopted for significant terms is
given in the Translation Key.

despite Plato's development of "theories" of Ideas and so forth, by the institution of the dialogue, which continually undermines any tendency to dogmatism (so that Aristotle's main criticisms of Platonic doctrine, for example, are already forcefully presented in Plato's own dialogues).

It is possible to put Plato, or Socrates/Plato, on a pedestal and view the dialogues as so exemplary that the rest of the philosophical tradition can be dispensed with, in effect. Gadamer has not done this. For one thing, he finds doctrine in Aristotle—in particular, the analysis of *phronesis*, or practical judgement—which cannot be found in Plato and which he considers extremely valuable. Likewise Hegel, Heidegger, and many other thinkers make contributions that cannot be found in Plato. Someone who takes the concept of dialogue seriously, as Gadamer does, cannot place any one contributor, however important, on a plane above the rest.

However, among philosophical texts, Plato's dialogues have been Gadamer's single most continuous preoccupation throughout his career, precisely because of the way in which they embody and exemplify the process—which is Gadamer's most persistent and fundamental intellectual concern—of truth's "happening" in dialogue among human beings. This affinity was even strong enough to enable him to resist as mistaken the fundamental critique of Plato mounted by the later Heidegger.[5] The conception of truth that had been inspired by Heidegger withstood, in Gadamer, the conception of the "history of being" to which Heidegger himself moved on.

This interest must have been an important factor in Gadamer's choice of the *Philebus* as the topic for his Habilitationsschrift. For this dialogue contains some of the most explicit discussions of the nature of dialectic to be found in Plato's later works and thus provides an occasion not only for a comparison and synthesis of material on this

5. "In the background was the continuous challenge posed for me by the path Heidegger's own thought took, and especially by his interpretation of Plato as the decisive step toward 'metaphysical thought's' obliviousness to Being" (*Idea of the Good*, p. 5).

subject from most of the major dialogues but also for a presentation of Gadamer's own systematic phenomenology of "Conversation and the Way we Come to Shared Understanding" (*Das Gespräch und die Vollzugsart der Verständigung*) which is, in effect, an account of the way in which truth can "happen" in human conversation.

I will mention a few of the high points of this deceptively simple forty-page analysis. Gadamer's intention, he says, is "to make intelligible the derivation of the Greek concept of science (which reached its mature form in Aristotle's apodeictic) from Plato's dialectic by showing its substantive origin in the specific form of the Socratic conduct of conversation" (p. 21). The reference of "substantive" (*sachlich*) here is to the human *experience* of knowledge, as one of the "primordial motives of human Dasein" (same page, n. 4) that phenomenological analysis can reveal, and which a proper understanding of the Socratic conduct of conversation will also reveal. Gadamer cites Aristotle's *Metaphysics* to the effect that knowledge involves access to the "why," the reason (*logos*), and that "the primary sense of logos is *being answerable,* giving an account" (p. 27). But this answerability already implies the possibility of speech and other people who are (or could be) spoken to. (Hence the extended use of *logos,* which originally meant "word," for "reason" as well.) But the kind of conversation that is directed at reasons and is based on a "shared willingness to question" is only one kind of "being with one another." It is equally possible for us to seek, in conversation, not so much understanding of reality as understanding of *each other* (as participants in the conversation); and it is possible to use such understanding of each other as an excuse for *limiting* what we are prepared to question, in our own position as well as in the other person's. Gadamer writes, "When one 'understands' the other person's disagreement—that is, explains it as a result of the difference between his assumptions and one's own undiscussable assumptions instead of (precisely) making those assumptions the subject of the conversation—one *excludes the other person in his positive function,* as someone to whose substantive agreement and shared understanding one makes a claim" (p. 40; emphasis added). By contrast, Gadamer observes that "the inherent tendency of the intention of coming to an understanding is to want to do this precisely with the person whose prior opinion contradicts one's thesis most sharply" (p. 41).[6] The earnestness of this analysis is underscored by the penultimate section, "Degenerate Forms of Speech," in which Gadamer discusses the "specific possibility of inauthenticity" to which Plato points over and over again: *phthonos*, the desire to "come out ahead" in the argument, which leads to the use of sophistic means to win agreement for oneself or to refute others.[7]

In the final section of this systematic account, the section

6. *Verständigung*, the term that I render "coming to an understanding" or "coming to a shared understanding," has the convenient (for Gadamer) characteristic that it *suggests* a sharing between two or more people but does not entail it. In the absence of a correspondingly suggestive term in English, I have had to settle for a vacillation between these two equally inadequate renderings.

7. In this section and the following one, the Heideggerian term *Verfallen* ("falling"), together with *uneigentlich* ("inauthentic") and, in the analytical index, *Gerede* ("idle talk"), is prominent. Robert R. Sullivan's ascription of the image of "falling" to the influence of Biblical tradition (*Political Hermeneutics. The Early Thinking of Hans-George Gadamer* [University Park and London, 1989], p. 101) is probably not entirely mistaken, though he overlooks the more immediate source of this group of terms, for Gadamer, in Heidegger's *Being and Time*. The dualism of authenticity versus falling does gesture toward an explanation of something (in this case, why the same individuals are, at different times, more or less free to engage and interested in engaging in candid inquiry into the "facts of the matter," as opposed to manipulating one another or killing time), an explanation of something that the Greeks seem not to have formulated as a distinct issue and that the Biblical/Heideggerian imagery suggests a way of looking at, if not understanding. It is interesting to observe, in n. 10 to this section of the book, how this way of looking at the matter replaces, for Gadamer, the usual modern interpretation of what he calls the "sceptical turning in the theory of the logos," an interpretation in terms of inevitable purely theoretical problems.

entitled "The Socratic Dialogue," Gadamer interprets Socrates' endeavor as not merely destructive—aimed at exposing the ignorance of his interlocutors—but, in line with the "positive function" of the other person that was referred to in the quotation above, as a project of bringing about a constructive "shared search" for the knowledge that (both as "agreement with oneself"—that is, self-knowledge—and as agreement with others) Socrates takes to be necessary for virtue and thus for the good.

The remaining three sections of this chapter, on dialectic in the *Phaedo, Republic, Sophist,* and *Parmenides,* show the permutations of this effort of Socrates' in Plato's thought. Gadamer sees no demarcation point at which a "Platonic" dialectic replaces the Socratic one. The *Republic,* for example, for all its political and cosmic dimensions, is very much a continuation of Socrates' search for (self-) knowledge as virtue in Gadamer's view. ("Just as it is part of the essence of the ordered constitution that the individual orders himself in relation to this order, so the order of the individual's own self (the *psychē*) is not something commanded by others, in the form of a customary ethic; rather, it produces itself through the unity of Dasein's self-understanding" [p. 80].) The doctrine of the Ideas, in the *Phaedo* and the *Republic,* and the doctrines of *sunagōgē* (bringing together) and *diairesis* (division), in the later dialogues, are articulations of the same project.

In fact, what Gadamer wants to show, in the light of his own phenomenology of speech and knowledge as an intersubjective endeavor, is that the "dialectic" of Plato's later works is continuous with the "ethics" that Socrates pursued, because dialectic (that is, conversation, in its genuine form) *is* ethics, in that a "shared search" for both agreement with oneself and agreement with others is both the means to and a leading *instance of* aretē, which is what ethics is about—hence the title of Gadamer's book, which, as he says in his preface, is not about a Platonic "ethics" that happens to be dialectical, but about the question of "whether and in what way Plato's dialectic *is* 'ethics'" (emphasis added).

In the light of this intention, his choice of the *Philebus* as his primary text makes sense in several ways. The *Philebus* addresses an "ethical" question: whether pleasure or thought is the good in human life. At the same time it includes two major detours into considerations regarding dialectic as such (the one and the many, sunagōgē and diairesis, the "four genuses" of reality), detours whose overt contents are important for any study of Plato's dialectic but whose role in this dialogue is itself a significant problem for such a study. There are, of course, substantive connections. The conclusion reached by the dialogue is that the good in human life is a "mixture" of pleasure and thought, but one in which thought is more closely related to the "cause" of the whole (that is, to the good), because it lacks pleasure's tendency toward "boundlessness," which is contrary to the "measure" that is necessary for a good mixture. All the terms given in quotes in this sentence get elucidated in the so-called digressions. But the transitions by which Socrates introduces and moves on from the "digressions" have left some commentators with the impression that Plato may have simply thrown together several separately composed sections without taking the trouble to integrate them into a coherent development. This might seem consistent with the view that in his "post-Socratic" phase, when he had worked-out doctrines to expound, Plato no longer found the dialogue form as important as he had previously; which might lead one to wonder whether the relation between dialogue, dialectic, and ethics is as close as Gadamer suggests. So the *Philebus*, like other later dialogues, is a challenge to Gadamer's thesis.

He responds to this challenge in several ways. First, he helps us to see what a key role Protarchus (Philebus's designated stand-in) and Philebus himself actually play in the discussion, despite the fact that the great majority of the words spoken are Socrates'. For Socrates has to go to considerable lengths to procure their acquiescence (or, at any rate, Protarchus's acquiescence) in what he proposes. Secondly, Gadamer ties the content of the digressions closely to the logic of the unfolding discussion. And finally, in what may seem a paradoxical move, he undercuts the picture of Plato as "expounding doctrine" in the later dialogues, by emphasizing the extent to which the *Philebus* anticipates characteristically *Aristotelian* ethical ideas—specifically, that of the "mean" between extremes, the acceptability of "appropriate" pleasures, and (above all) the necessity of asking not what is "the good" but what is good *for human beings* (who, as such, are neither beasts nor gods). Ultimately, as Aristotle himself made clear, this kind of thinking undermines the Socratic identification of knowledge with virtue—and thus of dialectic with ethics—by pointing to the irreducible complexity and concreteness of the situations in which human beings have to make decisions as to what is good. If knowledge cannot "tell us what to do, in advance," dialogue and dialectic both become less central to human existence than Socrates has made them seem. But if Plato himself *recognized* this (and he may have done so in earlier dialogues than the *Philebus*), then to make a division between the early, Socratic Plato and the later, didactic one is clearly to oversimplify. The later Plato may have had more modest expectations of what dialectic could achieve, but that awareness may in fact have made it easier for him to remember what it *can* achieve and not to abandon it when (and if) he began to have doubts about the identification of knowledge and virtue.

In *Truth and Method,* his magnum opus, Gadamer's modestly hermeneutic side—as in the connection he draws between Aristotle's *phronēsis* (nondemonstrative, practical judgment) and interpretation—is more evident than his ambitiously "scientific" side. Perhaps this was inevitable, since the purpose of the book (which was ambitious enough, under the circumstances) was only to draw together from various sources the elements of an account of interpretation and understanding that would make it clear that an alternative to modern scientific "method" exists. But the unintended consequence, given the inevitable ambiguity regarding the relations *between* modern science and hermeneutics (how could there be such an "alternative" approach to what was presumably the same, sole reality? or, if there were "two" realities, how should we understand the relation between them?), was that a reader could get the impression that Gadamer was interested only in "understanding," not in knowledge as such (perhaps in line with the supposed dichotomy between "explanation" and "understanding").[8] This misunderstanding of Gadamer's intentions becomes considerably less plausible on acquaintance with the phenomenology of knowledge presented in *Plato's Dialectical Ethics*, which takes precisely Aristotle's conception of (demonstrative) *science*—that is, knowledge—as its point of departure (see chapter 1, section 1). This makes it clear that the accusations of antiscientific relativism that have been leveled at the author of *Truth and Method* do not, in any case, apply to all his work.[9] In which case, given the absence of any evident consciousness on the author's part of a "break" between his earlier and later work, it behooves us to do our best, in the first instance at least, to interpret it as a consistent whole.[10]

8. Gadamer sought to ward off this kind of interpretation of his project in the foreword to the second (German) edition of *Truth and Method*, where he wrote that "the difference that confronts us is not in the method but in the objectives of knowledge [*Erkenntnisziele*]" (2d rev. Eng. ed. [New York, 1989], p. xxix; 1975 ed., p. xvii). But he did not elucidate this latter formulation or make clear the relation between knowledge and the "understanding" which, following Heidegger, he described as "the mode of being of Dasein itself" (1989 ed., p. xxx; 1975 ed., p. xviii).

9. See, e.g., J. Habermas, "On Hermeneutics' Claim to Universality," in *The Hermeneutics Reader*, ed. K. Mueller-Vollmer (New York, 1985), pp. 294–319; and E. D. Hirsch, *Validity in Interpretation* (New Haven, 1967), pp. 245–264.

10. Throughout his hermeneutic inquiries, which critics like Habermas and Hirsch suspect of having subjectivist or relativist consequences, Gadamer has never accepted those labels and has always drawn a line against what *he* calls "sophism." Although he shows much more sympathy for "the tradition of rhetoric" in *Truth and Method* and subsequent works (see, e.g., "Hermeneutics as a Theoretical and Practical Task," in his *Reason in the Age of Science*, trans. F. G. Lawrence [Cambridge, Mass., 1981]) than he does in *Plato's Dialectical Ethics*, with its strong Platonic line against sophism (see sec. 4 on "Degenerate Forms of Speech"), he always ties this sympathy firmly to what he calls "Aristotle's *philosophical* rhet-

I cannot go into the later work in enough detail, here, to suggest how this might be done and the difficulties that would be encountered. What I want to suggest, however, is that Gadamer's resistance to the modern conception of knowledge as the product of "method" will be better understood when it is seen that what it is really based on is the Platonic-Aristotelian "effective unity" (as he has called it)[11] more than anything else. It is the existence of this great precedent that makes it plausible to Gadamer that access to truth may not depend, in every case, upon a "method" in the modern (Cartesian) sense of an instrumentarium, a specifiable set of procedures for generating and controlling intersubjectively valid results, and that the "true method," rather than being "alien to the thing" in that way, might instead be "an action of the thing itself," in which "certainly, the thing does not go its own course without our thinking being involved, but thinking means unfolding what consistently follows from the subject matter itself."[12]

Both the attractiveness and power of Gadamer's resistance to the Cartesian concept of method and the difficulty of making that resistance stick in the conditions of the modern age (in which the

oric," as part of a "practical philosophy" (rather than, say, as a necessary *alternative* to philosophy in its central, Socratic/metaphysical strand, as Blumenberg, for instance, presents it in his "An Anthropological Approach to the Contemporary Significance of Rhetoric," in *After Philosophy. End or Transformation?*, ed. K. Baynes, J. Bohman, and T. McCarthy [Cambridge, Mass., 1987], pp. 429–457, esp. pp. 431–432).

11. *Wirkungseinheit*; see *The Idea of the Good in Platonic-Aristotelian Philosophy*, pp. 1ff.

12. *Truth and Method*, 1989 ed., p. 464 (compare 1975 ed., p. 421). Gadamer appeals here to Hegel as well as to the Greeks; but of course Hegel too, as Gadamer presents him, is harking back explicitly to Plato (and, not incidentally, resisting Newtonian physics [see *Truth and Method*, 1989 ed., p. 460; 1975 ed., p. 417]). (Gadamer goes on to distinguish his hermeneutics from Hegel's dialectic, but this distinction does not imply any difference between them in regard to the critique of Cartesian method.)

intervening experience of Christianity, in particular, seems to have intensified problems that were perhaps only latent for classical Greek thought and thus call for solutions that the latter may be unable to provide)[13]—both of these follow from this relation between Gadamer's project and his Greek predecessors. An informed reader no doubt senses this situation, in outline, from Gadamer's other books; but it is nowhere made as clear as it is in (especially) the first chapter of *Plato's Dialectical Ethics*, in which Gadamer establishes—one might almost say, "founds"—the "effective unity" between Socratic dialogue and the conception of knowledge that he had constructed under the influence of Heidegger.

In view of the important role played by Gadamer's hermeneutics in contemporary discussions of rationality, relativism, the cultural sciences, and so forth, a clearer understanding of the genesis and nature of that hermeneutics would be very useful. As Gadamer would be the first to agree, his hermeneutics needs not only to be evaluated

13. It seems, e.g., that the issue of our control or lack of control over nature—together with the "alienness to the thing" which the perception of such an issue necessarily presupposes—is much more serious and central for modern thought than it was for the Greeks. It also seems reasonable to suppose that Christian notions of divine creation, power, and providence have played a key role in (at least) making such a perception possible. In my view, it is probably Gadamer's reliance on the Platonic-Aristotelian "effective unity" (together, of course, with Hegel— or, indeed, perhaps *including* him) that has made it seem unnecessary to him to try to come to grips, in a systematic way, either with this issue of the control of nature or with the question of its genesis. Deferring, then, to the "specialists" who have addressed themselves to these issues, Gadamer gets caught in the crossfire when they disagree with each other (as in the Löwith–Blumenberg debate; see Löwith's and Gadamer's reviews of Blumenberg's *Die Legitimität der Neuzeit* [Frankfurt am Main, 1966], in *Philosophische Rundschau* 15 [1968]: 195–209, and Blumenberg's response to Gadamer in *The Legitimacy of the Modern Age* [Cambridge, Mass., 1983], pp. 16–17).

for its truth value, as a doctrine, but also—and initially—to be *under-stood*, as a response to a specific, historically urgent question. The more clearly we understand the question—which, I take it, is (roughly) the question of what, if anything, could take the place, for us, of the Cartesian subject–object model of man's relation to reality—the more clearly we will understand the doctrine that we are trying to evaluate and the more we will learn from the whole exercise.

As I suggested at the outset, such an understanding could also be very useful for those wanting to understand the course of German thought since the 1920s. For in many of its leading person-alities—Karl Löwith, Leo Strauss, Hannah Arendt, T. W. Adorno, and Max Horkheimer, for example—the radical break that Heidegger carried out, or at least came to represent, has left behind (even among those who are determined opponents of Heidegger in other respects) the same fundamental doubts that Gadamer expresses about the role of the Cartesian tradition and of modern science in our thought and action. Consequently, these philosophers have all been driven to en-gage (in one way or another) in historical interpretation; and at the same time many of them have tried, like Gadamer, to establish a connection with Greek thought which would go beyond mere historical interpretation.[14] Gadamer's distinctiveness lies in two things, primarily: first, the philological care and historical sophistication with which he (as the only fully trained philologist among the figures just mentioned) has interpreted the Greeks, and second—and this is what *Plato's Dialectical Ethics* makes especially evident—the philosophical radi-calism of the trans-historical connection that he has tried to establish with them. The conjunction and contrast between these two charac-teristics of his work make especially vivid the task that post-Heideg-

14. It would also be interesting to compare Gadamer's post-Heideggerian recourse to Plato and Aristotle with the revivified interest in the same subject among post-positivist Anglo-American philosophers—e.g., Ter-ence Irwin (who shares Gadamer's interest in the underlying continuity between the two great Greeks; see his *Aristotle's First Principles* [Oxford, 1988], pp. 177 and 547, n. 62, e.g.).

gerian German thought has had to confront: that of doing full justice to the specificity and differentness of forms of consciousness, modern and nonmodern, despite having abandoned (the naive self-confidence of) the Cartesian tradition, while, at the same time, maintaining a lively relation to the truth about the world (*die Sache*, the "facts of the matter"). Gadamer's emphasis, in this context, on the role of "the other person" and thus of dialogue in our access to that truth—an emphasis in which his personal and scholarly practice have shown a remarkable degree of harmony with his doctrine, from *Plato's Dialectical Ethics* onward—is surely one of the more admirable and instructive responses to this task.

Translator's notes are flagged with upper-case letters. Interpolations in square brackets in the text are also the translator's. Interpolations in square brackets in the author's notes (including several entire notes to his Introduction), on the other hand, are material added by him in the reprinting of this work in the *Gesammelte Werke*. (The few exceptions to this last statement have "RMW" appended.)

The original, very helpful analytical table of contents (of which the Contents in the front of this book constitute an abbreviated version) has been included as an appendix. A list of works cited in the text by author's name only and a brief translation key are also included.

The text betrays a certain lack of (fully implemented) system in its references, in the section headings in chapter 2, to sections of the *Philebus*, and in the relation between these sections of chapter 2 and the analysis of "The Structure of the *Philebus*" given at the beginning of that chapter. I have not attempted to smooth out these rough edges, though I have corrected a few evident specific slips.

I have retained the masculine form of the pronoun ("he," "him") in impersonal constructions throughout the translation, since the alternative would have been to introduce usages that are anachronistic in relation to the original text.

I would like to thank Tom Bennigson and Bruce Krajewski for helpful comments on and objections to my introduction and Karsten

Harries and Jean van Altena for helpful comments on and suggestions for improving the translation. I would also like to thank the National Endowment for the Humanities, an independent federal agency, and Inter Nationes, an agency of the Federal Republic of Germany, for grants that made the translation possible.

Preface to the First Edition (1931)

This book's two chapters do not form a whole. Its title should not disguise this fact. The title does not promise an answer; rather, it poses a question: in what sense Plato's dialectic poses, and—in general—can pose, the problem of ethics. I do not assert that Plato's "ethics" is dialectical; rather, I ask whether and in what way Plato's dialectic is "ethics." This question guides the interpretation of the *Philebus* which I undertake in the second chapter. In the service of this interpretation, the first chapter tries to show that the theory of *dialectic*, in Plato, is the theory of the objective possibility of *dialogue*.

The task was to bring the things themselves (the facts of the matter) that are discussed in Plato freshly into view, so as—through their conceptual explication—to make the horizon of Plato's philosophizing stand out. This task is limited, then, to making available, for the use of historical research on Plato, a way of understanding Plato which is invigorated by contact with the matter that is in question. I am aware that this attempt at invigoration was undertaken in a very partial way, and, above all, that even within its consequent limitations it has not been uniformly successful. The closer these interpretations adhere to Plato's text, the more distant they are from their task of clearing the way toward that text. The more distant they are from the world of Plato's language and thought, on the other hand, the closer I believe they come to performing their task.

The nature of the undertaking made it seem appropriate to

cite only a very frugal selection of passages as evidence. The proposed interpretations are meant to produce conviction not through the rich and explicit confirmation of them that can be found in Plato's text but rather through the fact that they can be helpful in interpreting Plato. They assume that the reader is "acquainted" with Plato. Beyond that, the second chapter requires continuous reference to the text of the *Philebus*. The only reason it does not have the form of a uniformly thorough explication of details is that I wanted it to carry with it as little as possible of the burden of what has long since been known.

Only occasional reference is made to recent Plato scholarship. It goes without saying that this scholarship in fact determines to a large extent what is emphasized in the interpretation. The continual relationship to Natorp's and Stenzel's interpretations of Plato and to the research on Aristotle by Jaeger and his students occasionally becomes explicit. But since the work was completed some time ago— in the spring of 1928 (whereupon it was submitted to the philosophical faculty of the University of Marburg as a *Habilitationsschrift*)—all the literature that has appeared in the meantime has either not been taken into account or has been taken into account only by way of supplementary notes. I discuss in detail the methodological bases of the recent books on Plato by Friedländer, Reinhardt, Singer, and Stenzel in a review that will appear soon in the journal *Logos*.[1] That discussion may indirectly illuminate the method that has been employed here. Only in the case of Friedländer's interpretation was I already familiar with (and thus able to learn from) the author's method before his book appeared.

What I owe to the teaching and research of Martin Heidegger is revealed by many references, both explicit and tacit, to his book *Sein und Zeit* (*Being and Time*) and still more by the whole methodological attitude of my work, which tries to extend what I have learned from Heidegger and above all to make it fruitful by practicing it in a new way.

1. *Logos* 23 (1933) [:63–79; now in the author's *Gesammelte Werke*, vol. 5 (Tübingen, 1985), pp. 212–229—RMW].

I am indebted to the Emergency Association of German Scholarship (*Notgemeinschaft der deutschen Wissenschaft*) for a research stipend that enabled me to write this book. The book's publication also was made possible (in addition to private help) by a grant from the Emergency Association, as well as by the publisher's obligingness.

H.-G. Gadamer
Marburg, April 1931

From the Preface to the
Second Edition (1967)

I have hesitated for a long time to reprint my long since out-of-print Plato book from 1931. Of course, it was clear to me that the book of one who was then a beginner could not be revised so much later; but I would have preferred to merge its results with the intensive interpretations of Plato that I have been engaged in for a long time and that I hope some day to present in book form. However, the alarming acceleration in the rate at which my later years are going by serves as a warning not to postpone the reprinting any longer. If the 1931 book appears here in unaltered form, this may be excused by the modesty of its ambition. My intention in writing it was really only to apply the art of phenomenological description, which I had just learned, to a Platonic dialogue. The fact that this exercise also produced results that were relevant to the central questions regarding Plato's dialectic could not license any pretense that these questions had been dealt with adequately, even within the interpretation of the *Philebus*.

However, I eagerly continued my Plato studies during the thirties and was aided by (among others) the work of Jakob Klein ("Die griechische Logistik . . . ," *Quellen und Studien zur Geschichte der Mathematik, Astronomie und Physik*, vol. 3, no. 1) and Helmut Kuhn (*Sokrates* [Berlin, 1934]); by a more careful study of the English scholarship (see my review of Hardie's *A Study in Plato* in *Deutsche Literaturzeitung* 59 [1938]; and later also by the work on Plato of

Gerhard Krüger (*Einsicht und Leidenschaft. Das Wesen des platonischen Denkens* [Frankfurt am Main, 1939]), Heidegger (*Platons Lehre von der Wahrheit* [Bern, 1947]), and Szilasi (*Macht und Ohnmacht des Geistes* [Freiburg, 1946]); but it was especially my deeper acquaintance with Hegel that contributed to my Plato studies. The importance of Aristotle's account of Plato and the central position of the doctrine of the two principles in Platonic philosophy, as well as the function of number as a model for that philosophy, already became clear to me then. This allowed me, starting from Aristotle, to get the Platonic position into sharper focus.

So as to indicate the direction in which, today, I would want to improve my own essay of 1931, I have appended to the new edition, together with two older essays that extend the original Plato book in particular directions, two newer studies.[A] In this way I hope to put the reader sufficiently in the picture that he or she can make use of my novice's work within its limits. In general, my interpretations of Plato try to show that in the unique and still only insufficiently appreciated harmony of *logos* and *ergon* (word and deed) that distinguishes the dialogues, they contain a great deal more of the Platonic philosophy than all the later testimony, even if, without that testimony, and especially that of Aristotle, we would hardly be in a position to gather, from the dialogues, Plato's ultimate philosophical intentions.

H.-G. Gadamer

A. "Plato and the Poets" (1934), "Plato's Educational State" (1941), "*Amicus Plato Magis Amica Veritas*" (1968), and "Dialectic and Sophism in Plato's *Seventh Letter*" (1964), all translated in *Dialogue and Dialectic* (New Haven and London, 1980).

From the Preface to the 1982
Reprinting of the First Edition

As a result of continued requests for the now more than half-a-century-old book, of which the second, expanded edition of 1968 had also gone out of print, the publisher approached me regarding a reprinting.

Now, after I had become an emeritus, in 1968 (the year in which the second, expanded edition had appeared), I had continued my studies of Greek philosophy and had accumulated—in many scattered locations, but especially in the *Proceedings of the Heidelberg Academy of the Sciences*—the components of a longer work on Plato, a work whose foundations have been laid. So it made no sense to withdraw from the planned collective work the essays that had been appended to the second edition of this book, so as to publish them along with it once more. Over against them, the book stood, and stands, entirely by itself.

Like all first books, it was a first step into a field whose dimensions were not yet at all clear to its youthful author. Thus, the book had its own distinctive character precisely because of the circumstance that it sought, with conscious one-sidedness, to stand out against the patterns recommended by its predecessors and teachers. Scholars like Paul Natorp, Nicolai Hartmann, and Julius Stenzel and classical philologists like Werner Jaeger, Karl Reinhardt, and Paul Friedländer (at that point hardly any writers in other languages, except for Léon Robin) stand behind this first attempt, although it does not expressly connect up with them. On the contrary: I felt like a first reader of Plato, one who sought to try out on a classical text the new immediacy of thinking access "to the things (the facts of the matter) themselves," which was the watchword of Husserl's phenomenology. The fact that I dared, then, to do this, was due, above all, to the deep and decisive influence that Martin Heidegger's teaching during his years in Marburg had on me. In the force and radicalism of the questioning with which the young Heidegger fascinated his students, there lived on something that was inherited not least of all from phenomenology: an art of description that devoted itself to the phenomena in their concreteness, avoiding both the learned airs of the scientific fraternity and, as much as possible, the traditional technical terminology, thereby bringing it about that the things (the facts of the matter) almost forced themselves upon one. Should it not be possible for me too to see Greek philosophy, Aristotle and Plato, with new eyes—just as Heidegger was able in his lectures on Aristotle to present a completely uncustomary Aristotle, one in whom one rediscovered one's own, present-day questions in startlingly concrete form?

In those days classical philology, the craft of which I had been privileged to learn under Paul Friedländer's guidance, had arrived at such a refinement of the sense of history that in Werner Jaeger's school in Berlin numerous concepts from Aristotle's ethics and rhetoric were increasingly appearing untranslated in scholarly discussions— as though such mere taking-over guaranteed historical appropriateness! Did that not involve an evasion of the real task of expressing by means of one's own linguistic materials, employing the conceptual potential of those materials, the way in which, in Greek thought, the things themselves, the facts of the matter, presented themselves?

So I tried to lay aside all scholarly knowledge for once and to take as my point of departure the phenomena as they show themselves to us.

Since the second edition (1967), fifteen more years have passed, years in which I have continued my work and in which the way in which the problems present themselves has changed once again in many respects. True, I cannot see at all that the priority of the Platonic dialogues that have survived down to our own day—as opposed to the indirect tradition—can be disputed. We would be poor readers of Plato if we did not allow his dialogues to lead us to the things, the facts of the matter, themselves, rather than reading them as mere material from which to reconstruct Plato's doctrine of principles. What, then, was Plato's term for what Aristotle called a "principle" (*archē*)? Even Porphyry, who still had before him a copy of the lectures on the Good that are the origin of the indirect tradition, acknowledged, after all, that he would not have been able to understand them without the help of the *Philebus* (see K. Gaiser, *Platons ungeschriebene Lehre* [Stuttgart, 1963], Appendix, Fragment 23B).

But this same remark of Porphyry's indicates, on the other hand, the one-sidedness of my youthful effort where the interpretation of the relevant parts of the *Philebus* is concerned. After all, the book's second chapter merely reproduces, in a sort of phenomenological transcription, the course of the discussion in the *Philebus*. This still seems to me to hold its own as far as closeness to the text and convergence between description of the phenomena and textual interpretation are concerned. Even where I have learned in the meantime to draw further conclusions from textual observation and interpretation—for example, in regard to the recasting of the Pythagorean "causes," the unlimited and the limit, into a trinity and a quaternity of "causes"—the authority of the initial work, proceeding from the textual observations on which I based my analysis, has not been undermined. However, I was not yet up to the task of explaining the dialogue in terms of its position in Plato's work as a whole and, in particular, of interpreting how it runs parallel to the *Timaeus*—that is, the correspondence between the conversation about ethics and the conversation about physics. But that was, after all, the phenomenological limitation of this, my academic firstborn and journeyman's qualifying piece: to show that I had learned to use the tools of the phenomenological trade.

On the other hand, the first chapter, which undertakes—also by phenomenological means—to clarify the connection between Socratic dialogue and Platonic dialectic, sketches out, to a large extent, the whole of my later Plato investigations (including those still to be published). While fully acknowledging the methodological primacy that the Aristotelian art of concepts possesses in relation to the interpretation of Plato, phenomenological interpretation leads more and more to an important hermeneutic insight: that literary creations, products of art like the Platonic dialogues, on the one hand, and working papers like the texts that are collected in the *corpus aristotelicum*, on the other, cannot be measured by the same standard and cannot be related to each other at all unless hermeneutic precautions are taken.

Thus the two chapters of this, my first book, may still be able to teach two things: first, that phenomenology is not so much something that one talks about (which happens too much nowadays, rather than too little) as something that one has to practice and to acquire as a skill (which certainly happens much too little these days); and second, that in dealing with philosophical texts one may never dispense with hermeneutical reflection, which teaches one how one is to hear what the most differing forms of philosophical talk—dialogue and dialectic, myth and logos, the art of dramatization and the exertion of the concept—have to say. And in its widest extension, that includes the lesson we should have learned from German Romanticism: that while of course one should not mix up the revelations of art and the results of philosophical thought, one should continually measure the one against the other; indeed, one should rub them against one another until the sparks fly. By this I do not mean to imply that in writing this, my first book, I myself paid adequate heed to these two lessons that can be drawn from it; but I do mean to say that I tried to do so, and that they represent something from which no thinker can purchase his freedom. What Socratic-Platonic giving an accounting is, and to what extent we are able, starting from modern thought, to approach it, without falling into the one-sided procedures of modernity (that is, without misunderstanding self-consciousness as self-assertion and without reducing comprehension of something to calculating and gaining disposition over it)—these are things that I did not yet see clearly enough.

H.-G. Gadamer

Plato's
Dialectical
Ethics

Introduction

The investigations that follow include a detailed philosophical interpretation of Plato's *Philebus*, preceded by a general discussion of the structure of Plato's dialectic. The *Philebus*, in particular, was chosen as the object of interpretation because of (for one thing) the central importance of this dialogue in the history of ancient ethics. But above all, a need for a philosophical interpretation of the problems of the *Philebus* has existed since W. Jaeger attempted, in his *Aristoteles*,[A] to apply the perspective of a history of development to Aristotle's ethics. This is because the substantive context in which Jaeger placed the *Nicomachean Ethics* when he proved the authenticity of the *Eudemian Ethics* and demonstrated the Platonism of Aristotle's *Protrepticus* is laid out with a view to the late form of the so-called Platonic ethics, which the *Philebus* exhibits.[1] Crucial to the interpretation of the *Philebus* (which thus presents itself as a task in view of studies of Aristotle's ethics) is the fact that the *problem* of ethics is really seen here, but is not taken hold of, in itself, as a task. The fact that the *Philebus*'s position in regard to ontology is identical with the general Platonic position that we call the doctrine of the Forms cannot conceal

A. See "Works Cited."

1. [See my essay "Der aristotelische 'Protreptikos' und die entwicklungs-geschichtliche Betrachtung der aristotelischen Ethik," *Hermes* 63 (1927): 138–164; *Gesammelte Werke*, vol. 5 (Tübingen, 1985), pp. 164–186.]

the distinctive concentration of the *Philebus*'s inquiry on the ethical problem—that is, on the good in *human* life. The goal, after all, is to argue from the general ontological idea of the good precisely to the good of actual human existence. In the context of this substantive intention we are given a thorough dialectical analysis of *hēdonē* (pleasure) and *epistēmē* (knowledge), an analysis whose positive content and methodical attitude both make the *Philebus* the proper basis for an interpretation of the specifically Aristotelian problem of a science of ethics.

At the same time, I take it absolutely as a premise that Plato does not teach a philosophical ethics any more than he teaches any other philosophical discipline. Plato is a follower of Socrates, and Socrates is the figure through whom Plato expresses his own philosophical intentions, precisely because his literary works repeat, with the explicitness of literature, Socrates' entirely unliterary and undogmatic existence. Plato's dialogues are no more philosophical treatises than the elenctic disputes, by which Socrates made himself partly laughable and partly detested by his contemporaries, were philosophical treatises. The dialogues are comprehended in their own intention only when one understands them as serving to lead the reader toward the existential ideal of the philosopher: toward life in pure theory. The fact that this existential ideal is not an extrapolitical one which would relinquish all *praxis* (the latter being something that for the Greeks, of course, never meant the banausic activity of work but, rather, concerning oneself with political matters) now stands in the foreground of the modern view of Plato. But it is crucial to realize that the first-person testimony of the *Seventh Letter*, to which this modern view properly appeals, itself teaches us that for Plato, the matter-of-course directness with which one took up "politics" has been deflected, by Socrates and by the Athenian state's failure in relation to Socrates, into *the detour that is philosophy*. For that detour decisively changed the concept of the statesman for Plato: Socrates himself and his elenctic, disturbing existence now appear to Plato as performing the true political task. Thus Plato's *Republic* is not a reformed constitutional structure that is supposed to have a directly political effect, like other proposals for political reform; instead, it is an educational state.[2] This constitution is not meant, as a better-designed institution, to reform an existing state but to found a new state—which, however, means to form human beings who can construct a genuine state. Plato's *Republic*, as an educational state, is a design for man, and the founder of the republic is someone who forms men. And if Plato hoped throughout his life for political efficacy and tried his hand at it, it was always through philosophy. Politics, in particular, set him the task of leading people to philosophy, because it is only people who have been led to philosophy who in turn can order others—and that means a whole state—in a way that relates to what true understanding aims at: the idea of the good.

But this by no means involves undertaking what philosophical ethics is properly concerned with—namely, developing *aretē* (virtue), a specifically human potential for and intelligibility of *Dasein*, into an available and repeatable possession, by means of the *concept*. The reason it does not mean this is not that the praxis and aretē that are connected to the state have the higher aretē of a life of pure theory above them; for that would not distinguish Plato's position from the general Greek ideal of philosophical existence. Rather, it is because for Plato actual human existence and the concept of the good in this human reality are not in themselves treated as objects to be defined and held in safekeeping but instead are defined as referring to something else that alone really "exists" and is really "good"—and they are defined as something that really exists only in this referring, that is, as something depending on what they refer to.

Plato's philosophy is a dialectic not only because in conceiving and comprehending (*im Begreifen*) it keeps itself on the way to the concept (*zum Begriff*) but also because, as a philosophy that conceives and comprehends in that way, it knows man as a creature that is thus

2. [See my essay "Plato's Educational State" (1942), in *Dialogue and Dialectic* (New Haven, 1980), pp. 73–92.]

"on the way" and "between." It is precisely this that is Socratic in this dialectic: that it carries out, itself, what it sees human existence as. This is where philosophy's name comes from: it is not *sophia*—the knowledge that gives one disposition over something—but a striving for that. As such, it is the highest possibility for man. And if Socrates is a philosopher, and Plato also, in Socrates, then Plato's philosophy is not the act of comprehending this highest possibility and keeping it safe but precisely the act of implementing it. But this means that being human involves not having disposition over oneself and that philosophy, as a human possibility, also has a dialectical existence in this dialectically questionable state in which it knows itself as a human activity. Socrates says at one point, most significantly, about his sophia, that it is *amphisbētēsimos hōsper onar* (as equivocal as a dream) (*Symposium* 175e3)—that is, that it is contestable and ambiguous; that one does not know whether one has it, just as one can debate whether what one sees in a dream exists or not; and this can be seen from the contrasting image of a better sophia that *pollēn epidosin echei*, that is continually enhanced, because what is known in the latter is no longer equivocal. In contrast to this, Socratic wisdom is not confirmed by its step-by-step growth, but instead its nature is to resemble the isolatedness and unrepeatability of a vision in a dream: it is not something one possesses and on which one can confidently rely when confronted with someone who disputes it. It is true that philosophical ethics will also be a doctrine of the ideal life and thus, indirectly, protreptic (persuasive)—everyone knows that Aristotle's ethics, too, culminates in a sketch of theory as an existential ideal, and in such a way that the whole breadth of the phenomena of human ethos is included in this ideal as the highest possibility of human existence. Nevertheless, the center of gravity of Aristotle's effort, in his ethics, lies not in leading us to and exhibiting the theoretical ideal as such (as in Plato) but in analyzing the specifically human possibilities and the human manner of existence, to which pure theory is added only as something extreme and never fully attainable. It is true that for Plato, no less than for Aristotle, this

unattainableness of the ideal of pure theory is an essential characteristic of man's humanity; but Plato always sees man's existence, and
thus the true relations between ethos and praxis, in the light of this
characteristic—which means that he presents them as defined by the
process of going beyond them. Man is a creature who transcends
himself. Aristotle, on the other hand, sees both the reality of human
life and also this extreme possibility of theory—that is, both what he
is destined to strive to surpass and what that striving is directed
toward—in himself, in his own possibilities of perfection. Alongside
the first, true life, he sees a second, second-best life, which still is
a "best" life, however; for this human life, too, is capable, in itself,
of an accomplished completion, even if one limit of this completion is
the new, fundamental incompletability implied by the ideal of pure
theory.[3]

So this is what makes Aristotle the originator of a philosophical science of ethics: not the fact that he was the first to make this
second-best life, this life in the ethos, which shows the imprint of
affects and passions, into the object of philosophical inquiry—for Plato
did this, no less explicitly, in the *Philebus*—but the fact that, for the
first time, he undertook to define *ethos* and *aretē* not privatively, from
the point of view of and in relation to this thing (pure theory) which
is beyond what is human, but rather positively, in themselves. But just
this makes him the first theoretician: that his philosophizing is no
longer the carrying out of a shared philosophical process, and his
literary works are no longer the protreptic presentation of the kind of
philosophizing mode of existence for which, as in Plato's works, something like a "doctrinal content" was only an indirect result of the
process that the works pursued and portrayed. When philosophical
teaching, in a purely conceptual understanding of its subject matter,
expresses only that subject matter's problematic and not its own, words
for the first time acquire the real task of the concept: to analyze the

3. [See my essay "Über das theoretische unk praktische Lebensideal,"
which will appear in vol. 7 of my *Gesammelte Werke*.]

structure of the subject matter of thought and to make it available in the logos. The concept becomes the true language of philosophizing, and each area of its subject matter articulates a system of concepts that are specifically appropriate to that subject matter. The fact that, even after Aristotle, philosophical ethics does not refrain from making practical claims is not an objection to this. For the peculiar character of this field is that the concepts that are appropriate to it grasp it in such a way that in doing so they are also useful to ethical experience. Philosophical ethics always makes this claim in one way or another— which is not to imply that ethical action depends upon philosophical concepts but is definitely to imply that it is essential for ethical concepts and comprehension to take their orientation from ethical experience and to come back to it. Thus the concepts of ethics must essentially include a recognition of the distance between (on the one hand) the generality and the "average" quality of their comprehension and (on the other) the unique character of each situation where it is a question of action. But this means recognizing that the dependability and the power of disposition that are achieved in the concepts of ethics do not represent a complete disposition over each real situation of action but only a certain help in that regard, and a help that is not even that if it thinks it is more than a mere help. Thus this restriction on the sense in which concepts, here, allow one to take possession of the object at all is part of the semantic claim of a concept that is appropriate to the object.[4] But it is fundamentally different from the protreptic provisionalness in which Plato's ethical dialectic is suspended. For the latter does not take possession, even in a restricted

4. The scientific claim made by the *Nicomachean Ethics* is determined, throughout, by a methodical consciousness of this restriction. An interpretation of that work in relation to this problem of its scientific character is much needed. [In pursuing this problem I finally drew philosophical conclusions that led to my work in hermeneutics (*Truth and Method* and the further development of this philosophical hermeneutics in the direction of "practical philosophy": texts that now appear in vols 1 and 2 of the *Gesammelte Werke*).]

sense, but points, precisely, away from all supposed possession and toward the possibility of a possession which is always in store for it, because it always slips away from it.

But this contrast between Platonic dialectic and Aristotelian conceptual investigation itself is necessarily understood on the level of the concept if it is supposed to be understood philosophically. On this level, Aristotle necessarily wins the argument with Plato. The meaning and the justification of Aristotle's critique of Plato are still a controversial problem. What I have been saying was meant to make it clear that this problem is not accidental—not a result of the state of our comprehension—but represents a necessary state of affairs, not something that could in principle be resolved like any other interpretive problem. The conclusion that Aristotle misunderstood Plato is rightly felt to be impossible. But it is equally certain that in this critique what is truly Platonic does not make itself felt in the positive character that it still has even today, for us. Aristotle projected Plato onto the plane of conceptual explication. The Plato who presents himself in this explication is the object of Aristotle's critique. What makes this critique problematic is that this projection cannot also catch the inner tension and energy of Plato's philosophizing as they speak to us, with such incomparable convincingness, in his dialogues. The unique importance of this critique is that it is not a historical riddle presented by a radical misunderstanding in a one-time situation in the history of philosophy but an expression of the systematic problem of philosophy itself: that the part of lived reality that can enter into the concept is always a flattened version—like every projection of a living bodily existence onto a surface. The gain in unambiguous comprehensibility and repeatable certainty is matched by a loss in stimulating multiplicity of meaning. That Aristotle's critique of Plato does not evince a historically incomprehensible misunderstanding of his great teacher is something that we can absolutely take for granted. The projection that he offers us is an eminently accurate projection. But, like every projection, it has the effect of something completely dissimilar and different to the extent that one remains in this projective plane itself and takes its shadow lines as the thing itself and not as referring to a form having completely different dimensions.[5]

So much can be foreseen, both historically and philosophically, regarding the problematic of Aristotle's relation to Plato. But just as all reflection on the relation between concepts and what is living can itself be grasped only in concepts, so the Platonic existence of philosophy can be grasped philosophically only if one repeats, oneself, the same kind of projection onto the conceptual plane that Aristotle undertakes. All scientific philosophy is Aristotelianism insofar as it is conceptual work, and thus if one wants to interpret Plato's philosophy philosophically, one must necessarily interpret it via Aristotle. The historical realization that this will always be a projection cannot be made productive by trying to dissolve or avoid this projection. The firsthand discovery that Plato is more than what Aristotle and conceptual analysis can extract from him cannot, itself, be conveyed secondhand. It stands at the limit of all Plato interpretation, just as there stands, at the limit of all conceptual work in philosophy, the realization that all interpretation makes its object univocal and, by providing access to it, necessarily also obstructs access to it.

Philosophy, for Plato, is dialectic. Dialectic, as effort directed at the *logos ousias* (word or reason of being), is determined by the meaning of being. The original motive of the Platonic Idea is the question of the good, which asks, simply, what an entity has to be, on the strength of which it can always be understood as the same. This determination of the concept of the good is a universal ontological one. With it, everything that is determines itself, uniformly, in terms of what it has to be. But this means that the world, as the universe of entities, is determined in an ontologically uniform way, irrespective of whether the entity that is determined in this way itself determines

5. [I have discussed these questions further in writings that will appear in vol. 7 of the *Gesammelte Werke*, especially in the essay prepared for the Heidelberg Academy of Sciences: *The Idea of the Good in Platonic-Aristotelian Philosophy* (New Haven, 1986).]

itself to this being and thus is human or is an entity that is not capable, itself, of determining itself to something. The true being of everything that exists is the being of the Idea. The expectation of ontological intelligibility, which is thus directed at everything that exists, has the consequence that the latter—inasmuch as it is involved in coming-to-be and in change—cannot be met with, positively, at all; which means, however, that, like changing nature, man, in his factual conditionedness and finitude, is (from the point of view of ontology) null and exists and is comprehensible only in what has true being: the selfsameness of the intellect that cannot be affected by coming-to-be and perishing, the *apathēs nous*, the selfsame contemplation of the selfsame. However, Plato does think it is possible to ask how this being that really is shows itself and is encountered within human Dasein—or better, whether and how that which is encountered as "good" in factual human existence and consciousness is related to that which the good really is—or, to put it differently, how man, when he thinks he understands himself within the possibilities that are in fact attainable by him, does not obstruct and conceal what is really good, and how in this understanding of his factual possibilities he possesses an orientation toward what really is and can be, which thus also represents his ownmost possibility of being. It is with this goal in mind that Plato asks in the *Philebus* whether man should understand himself in terms of pleasure—of well-being—or of his capacity to understand being. That is, he can understand himself in terms of both. But the question arises, in which way he understands himself better, in which of the two types of understanding he is open for that which is "the good" or, in other words, which of them also provides, for the other one, that in which this other one is itself, in the true sense, understanding.

So this is what one must pay heed to in connection with talk about "late Platonic ethics." It is not as though actual human existence and the human good (*anthrōpinon agathon*) were not under discussion here. The question is, for what methodological purpose are they under discussion. Is it with the goal of seizing the "good" that man encounters—both pleasure and cognition—in its highest potential and thereby developing man's factual understanding of human existence further, by working it out conceptually? This is evidently not Plato's intention. Insofar as it does occur, it is not an end in itself for the investigation. That end is, rather, to read off, from the contents (observed and arrived at) of the accomplished possibilities of human existence, what constitutes (what is the universal ontological structure of) their being good, and on that basis to reach a final judgment and decision as to which fundamental possibility—pleasure or cognition—has precedence over the other. But this means, in relation to which of these possibilities is factual Dasein turned toward being and being good: Is it in the loss and forgetfulness of self which goes with enjoyment and with passion or in the state of being conscious, which retains itself in everything and expects itself from everything? But the detailed analysis aimed toward this question that is carried out in the *Philebus* culminates, characteristically, not in the firm conceptualization of an accomplished comprehension of the phenomena under discussion but rather in a conceptually vague, but protreptically vivid, decision of the central question on the basis of a preliminary notion of the good itself.

Consequently, the present interpretation will be concerned to allow the conceptual means by which Plato grasps the phenomenon that he has in view—and, in general, the ontological fore-conception with which he approaches, especially, the problem of the affects and their "truth"—to emerge, first of all, from the positive insights into the subject matter which he formulates by these means. The conception (which guides the whole discussion) of bodily pleasure and displeasure as oscillations around a state of equilibrium, the understanding of the affective element in desire and hope as based upon an opinion about things to come, and especially the view of the "mixture" of pleasure and displeasure as a simultaneous existence of both—all these formulations of substantive insights must be "liquified" again, so that the uniform key to these analyses and their universal ontological fore-conception can become visible. For the interpretive method that is appropriate to the *philosopher* Plato is not that of clinging fast to his definitions of concepts and developing his "doctrine" into a uniform system, in relation to which the individual dialogues might be criticized in terms of the objective legitimacy of their assertions and the validity of the logic used in their proofs; instead, it is to retrace, as a questioner, the course of questioning that the dialogue presents and to describe the direction in which Plato, without following it, only points. It is only on this assumption that Plato can be said to have a "doctrine" at all, whose investigation can be an object of philosophical and historical research. The *Philebus*, in particular, is a problem that will never be surmounted by an interpretation that clings to its specific verbal contents; and that is not only because of, say, the unreliability of the transmission of the text but because what Plato has done here is to take up the most disparate preliminary conceptions—which he encountered in this area which was much discussed by theorists at the time—not in order to reconcile these conceptions into a uniform, consolidated set of concepts but in order, by discussing them, to form our view of the subject matter.

Moreover, the logic of the connections in Plato's analysis is even more concealed here than it is elsewhere and can be uncovered only by having recourse to the logical order of the subject matter itself.[6] It is obvious from the above suggestions regarding the relation between

6. An illustration of this state of affairs, and one which is instructive on account of the naive and unreflecting way in which it carries out a dogmatic, logical, and substantive critique, is A. Bremond, "Les Perplexités du Philèbe," *Revue neoscholastique*, November 1911. This "Essai sur la Logique du Platon" would be even more instructive if it did not mix with its dogmatic-logical critique a dogmatic-substantive critique from the standpoint of Aristotelianizing Scholasticism. [In the meantime there has appeared—stemming from the viewpoint of modern logic and "analysis" and representing another extreme ("we know better") in terms of method— an extremely learned, painstaking, and shrewd commentary on the *Philebus* by J. C. B. Gosling (*Plato: Philebus*, translated with notes and commentary [Oxford, 1975]).]

Aristotle and Plato that such a substantive interpretation must take into account, from the very beginning, the dialectical provisionalness to which Plato's philosophy adheres as a matter of principle; but it is also obvious that this taking into account should not mean letting this dialectical provisionalness stand as it is, but that, on the contrary, one must try to develop, conceptually, the fore-conception that is implicitly at work in it. A genuine conceptual reception of Plato's investigation necessarily involves a terminological fixation of what Plato's dialectic makes visible in the reality in question and how it makes it visible, just as much as it involves a thoroughgoing freedom in relation to Plato's own means of linguistic presentation. Since the latter do not undertake the terminological univocity of the concept, they give us this freedom toward them, which makes terminological univocity practically an obligatory task for philosophical interpretation. Here the modern philosophical interpretation of Plato does not simply repeat what characterizes Aristotle's critique of Plato, which takes as terminologically fixed what in Plato was still not meant to be terminologically binding at all. Instead, a substantive interpretation of Plato tries to work out also, within Plato's loose linguistic dispensation, the tendencies of meaning which escape Aristotle's conceptual standard; that is, we do not criticize Plato on the basis of Aristotle, but instead we try to let him show us how all the Greeks looked at the phenomena that are of interest here. That is, in the explicit disagreement between Plato and Aristotle we seek the identical fore-conception that links them together. It is not as though the disagreement does not exist for us, but that our own distance from the Greek interpretation of life and the world allows us to see Plato not in the perspective of the progress in conceptual differentiation that Aristotle presents and applies as his standard but, rather, in terms of the unchanging view of the reality in question which everywhere moves Plato together with Aristotle as soon as one dares to go beyond the provisionalness of Plato's dialectical explications.

This kind of philosophical interpretation of historical philosophemes is not too refined to submit itself to the scrutiny of historical scholarship. It cannot claim to be measured by the special standards of, as it were, a second truth. At the same time, it has goals that are different from those of historical scholarship. No more than it can evade contradiction by historical criticism (when the latter has to contradict it) is it defined, as such criticism is, by the claims of historical investigation. Its relationship to historical criticism is already a positive one when that criticism, thinking that it gets no assistance from such interpretation, finds what it says a matter of course. The endeavor of this kind of philosophical interpretation has always been to construe matters of course; and this is also the case when it is confronted with historical texts. One can put this paradoxically: as an interpretation of historical texts, it wants to understand, by construing, that in them which is understood as a matter of course. In this understanding which it wants, which to the historical researcher seems (in relation to his own research) like a preliminary that can be taken for granted, this kind of philosophical interpretation finds difficulties, and thus a task. What is understood as a matter of course, as something self-evident, is always something that strives to evade the explicit grasp of comprehension. It continually loses itself, as it were, in all the other things to which it is related and with which it goes together to form a phase of the history of the spirit—rather than presenting itself with the urgency of its substantive content.

Thus, what is understood as a matter of course is a positive feature of the opinion contained, historically, in a text itself. An elucidation of it indicates the matter-of-course, yet difficult and easily lost path of an interpretation that conceptualizes what we understand in a historical text when we proceed from a substantive understanding of our own of what is discussed in it—but not with the intention of misusing history in order to promote this understanding of our own but rather (in reverse) solely to understand what was understood there. It is clear that this path will not make understandable everything that could be understood, but also that what it does make understandable will have an immediate evidence that is superior to all roundabout historical deduction and investigation, precisely because its claims are modest.

Accordingly, the interpretation of the *Philebus*, which is given in what follows remains indebted to historical research for the elucidation of the historical connections that come together in the puzzling structure of this dialogue. What it seeks to do is to clarify the immanent meaning-content of the dialogue, and to do so, specifically, by elucidating the problems of its mode of composition. In one respect, admittedly, its performance of even this task is incomplete: by taking seriously what Plato speaks of here, it takes his speech as well with a degree of seriousness with which it is precisely not meant to be taken. The suspended, ironical quality that characterizes Plato's writings, not only where everyone perceives the irony but continually, is entirely disregarded here,[7] which is a burden that has to be accepted by an interpretation that does not stand still where Plato's philosophizing is dialectically tentative but goes beyond that tentativeness, interpretively. For when it does that, it suspends the distance which is a necessary precondition for reflecting the totality of a literary creation. Its attitude is that of a humorless listener to the conversation, a listener whose report may be worth attending to, but only because he tries, in all seriousness, to make comprehensible the means by which Plato plays his serious game.

The sketch of Plato's dialectic, which I have placed first, was originally intended as an excursus on the theory of dialectic which the *Philebus* presents. It was entirely arrived at from the *Philebus*'s prob-

7. Paul Friedländer's new work (*Platon* [Berlin and Leipzig, 1926–30] = *Plato*, trans. H. Meyerhoff [Princeton, 1958]) takes on this basic theme of Platonic irony in a vivid and appreciative way. Therein lies not only the fertile importance of this book but also, in general, the standard by which it must be judged. Here for the first time, as it seems to me, an attempt has been made to approach the problems of form in the Platonic dialogues from the point of view of this central motive of their distinctive literary character.

lematic and is intended to demonstrate, by characteristic examples from Plato's other writings, the derivation and the philosophical coherence of the unity of dialogue and dialectic which *only* the *Philebus*, out of all Plato's literary works, presents in this way. The recognition of this unity turns out to be the precondition that makes it possible to understand the integrated structure of this dialogue. Therefore it may be a good idea to read this chapter alongside or after the interpretation of the *Philebus*.

1

On Plato's Dialectic

Part I: Conversation and the Way We Come to Shared Understanding

Section 1: The Idea of Science

The process of reaching a shared understanding of the matter in question through conversation (*Sachliche Verständigung im Gespräch*) is aimed at knowledge. Both its idea and the way we implement it are derived from the idea of knowledge and of science that Greek philosophy developed. It must be possible to gather from their developed form what the productive moments in their origin—what the dialogical aspect of this origin meant. It might seem strange that the problem of Plato's dialectic is approached here from (of all things) the angle of the strict Aristotelian concept of *epistēmē* (knowledge), which is *apodeixis* (demonstration). The opposite might seem to be the natural thing to do: to start with the Aristotelian concept of dialectic, which, after all, is unquestionably related back—albeit in the manner of a radical revaluation (in fact, devaluation)—to Plato's dialectic and to practical exercises of the Academy. Nevertheless, it is already a recognized fact that the historical line of development runs directly from Plato's dialectic to Aristotle's apodeictic. It is less clear, however, *why* Plato's dialectic, with its indubitable genesis in Socratic dialogue, is the intermediate stage, historically, in a development that leads precisely to Aristotle's epistēmē, which leaves behind it both dialectic and dialogue. For Aristotelian science is characterized by its lack of need for any explicit agreement on the part of a partner: it is a showing, based on a necessity, which is not concerned with the actual agreement of others. Dialectic, by contrast, lives from the power of dialogical coming to understanding—from the understanding of others who go along—and is sustained every step of its way by making sure of the partner's agreement.

The following analyses do not trace the historical course of the development of the concept of science, which has its parallels, seen in terms of the history of forms, in the transition from the oral, Socratic conversation, by way of the Platonic dialogue, to the Aristotelian discussion dialogue, and which terminates in the Aristotelian *pragmateia* (treatise). Instead, they attempt to make this course intelligible on the basis of a substantive analysis of what links Socratic and Platonic dialogue, in a unitary way, with Aristotelian apodeictic.

The point of departure here must be the realization that, among the Greeks, dialectic is not a uniform phenomenon but can appear in diverse forms. What Plato calls "dialectic" (and connects with the figure of Socrates) does not by any means coincide with the whole extent of what was alive among the Greeks as dialectic. Its origin from the Eleatic critique of the senses is well known, as is Gorgias's relationship to this. As such, dialectic has an essentially negative sense. It does not present the reality itself but seeks out what speaks for it and what speaks against it; which is to say that it takes up its position not by explicating the seen object by progressively approaching it, while keeping it always in view, but rather by developing in itself all the sides of the explications through which it encounters the object and by embroiling them in contradictions, so that its distance from the object comes to the fore. In other words, it takes these explications as its point of departure; that is, it states a hypothesis and develops it into manifestly impossible consequences and then makes the opposite assumption and develops this, too, to the point where it cancels itself out. The goal of this exercise (*gymnasia*; see

Parmenides 135d) is, by displaying what speaks for the one assumption and for the other, to make the object itself accessible. Dialectic relates to a seeing of the object which is supposed to be prepared for precisely by unfolding *ta dokounta* (the appearances)—that is, the forms in which we already encounter it in the public explications embodied in language—in order to dissolve them. That is, through refutation it succeeds in laying bare the object field, but in itself it does not have at its disposal any means by which to prove *ta dokounta* positively by reference to the object.

Now in this essence of dialectic, which can be characterized in this way on the basis of Aristotle's reports and with an eye to the Eleatics (see also Plato's *Parmenides*), Plato discovers a characteristically positive quality; and this, precisely, is his accomplishment.[1] It seems, after all, that Zeno's refutation of multiplicity and of the unity corresponding to it finds a universal application to every logos. The fact that a single creature (for example, a human being) can be addressed as such, and as such in many ways—in respect to its color, figure, magnitude, character, and so forth—makes it a many (*Sophist* 251a). But this does not put in question the possibility of addressing an entity as something; rather, it sets us the task of giving a positive justification of the possibility of addressing it. For the fact that this capacity of the logos for multiplying the one is a positive capacity is shown by the fact that the logos enables people to reach shared understanding. There is a kind of speech that progressively discloses the object, continually addressing it as something different, despite the contradiction between the one and the many which is inherent in so doing. This is the crucial fact. It is from the perspective of this positive capacity that dialectic in the Platonic sense receives an unusual scope. For everything that is defined by logos, and is thus within the realm

1. To avoid misunderstanding, let me emphasize explicitly that the dialectical tentativeness of Plato's writings, which I described at the beginning, is perfectly compatible with marking his accomplishment in this way. For what Plato means by "dialectic," and the dialectical tentativeness with which he holds this, like all his other views, are two different things.

over which a knowledge has disposition, gets its binding certainty from dialectic. *All science and all technē* (art, skill) *is this kind of positive dialectic.*

But this means—however paradoxical it may sound—that Platonic dialectic does not embody the contingently given dialectic of discussion, the questioning and answering *synousia* (being together, meeting), with its animation, which is specific to the situation. The fact that it is portrayed by literary means in the dialogues does not mean (even in the case of Plato's later dialogues) either that the dialogue form becomes a barrier constraining Plato's tendency toward positive exposition (as Stenzel thinks) or, conversely, that the Platonic dialogue took the character that dialectic exhibited in the Academy—the character of practical discussion—and gave it a certain stylized uniformity (as Solmsen thinks). The decisive fact, rather, is that Plato, in his efforts to disclose the facts of the matter, recognized in Socratic dialogue itself the means—and the only means—by which to arrive at a really secure stance toward the things. Socratic dialogue, in particular, is distinguished from all disputation technique by the fact that it is not a disorderly disputatious talking back and forth, which takes up and plays off against one another whatever arguments happen to come to mind. Rather, Socratic dialogue itself has a stylized uniformity. It embodies, for the first time, what fundamentally distinguishes the logos of science, which is speech that exhibits the facts of the matter in a logical sequence (*folgerichtig sachaufweisende Rede*). Despite the change in its negative/maieutic character, it is not contrary to its own nature but precisely as a development of the positivity already inherent in it that the elenctic style of Socratic conversation became the container of Platonic doctrine. Hegel characterizes this brilliantly when he says that Plato presents "youths and men of such a temper who would calmly suppress *their own* reflections and opinions in which thinking for oneself (*Selbstdenken*) is so impatient to manifest itself . . . [and] who would attend only to the matter at hand."[2]

2. G. W. F. Hegel, *Hegel's Science of Logic*, trans. A. V. Miller (London

So the intention of the sketch that follows is to make intelligible the derivation of the Greek concept of science (which reached its mature form in Aristotle's apodeictic) from Plato's dialectic by showing its substantive origin in the specific form of the Socratic conduct of conversation. The problem of the historical Socrates is entirely separate from this question. It is not necessary for me to take a stand in regard to Stenzel's attempt at demarcating the Socratic realm within the Platonic,[3] since my endeavor here is to make the connection between dialogue and dialectic fruitful for the understanding also, and specifically, of the late form of Plato's dialectic.

To proceed, then. At the beginning of his *Metaphysics* (A 1–2) Aristotle describes the genesis of the idea of science and the way it is rooted in an original motive of Dasein. This recourse to a motive that is located in Dasein itself has neither the character of a historical explanation of science nor that of a justifying argument in support of it. It makes the "fact of science" intelligible merely as a fact; that is, it shows how it is the case that one thing for which human existence contains the potential is science.[4,A] The unexpressed horizon of this exposition is the following: all Dasein is in a world and is so in such

and New York, 1969), p. 40, translation slightly revised. Original: *Wissenschaft der Logik*, ed. G. Lasson (Leipzig, 1923), vol. 1, p. 20.

3. Art., "Sokrates," in *Paulys Realencyclopädie der classischen Altertumswissenschaft*, ed. G. Wissowa (Stuttgart, 1894–), vol. 3A (1926), col. 871ff.

4. As a result of this recourse to primordial motives of human Dasein, the interpretation that follows has a "phenomenological" character. Its possibility, in principle, is based on the assumption that "factical" (*das faktische*) human Dasein is the origin of all meaning and thus must be the point of departure of all philosophical reflection—an assumption that the work of Heidegger has opened up in both its fundamental-ontological and its historical-hermeneutic importance.

A. The "fact of science" was the Marburg Neo-Kantians' description of their point of departure in epistemology.

a way that it "has" its world, that is, that it is always already in an understanding of itself and of the world in which it lives.

This world in which Dasein lives is not just its surroundings; it is more like the medium in which it implements its own existence. This world is that in which Dasein implements itself, which (however) means that it is the world in which it has itself. All understanding of itself is given to Dasein from its understanding of the world in which it lives and which "makes up" and determines its Dasein. Dasein's most primordial care is to establish itself in its world. But implementing this care does not have the character only of a practical performance that makes provision for something and of the circumspect care included in that; Dasein has also included in its care, equally primordially, the pure seeing of what is. Thus it is not the case that Dasein, as becoming at home in its world, implements itself, primordially, only in practical circumspection—simply in a dissection of the whole surrounding world which, by manipulating that world, elucidates and classifies it in regard to its usefulness for something (ultimately, its usefulness for Dasein itself). Rather, if Dasein is at home in its world, it is always already equipped with a knowledge of where it stands with everything, not only in relation to a future manipulation of it for purposes of providing for something but also entirely apart from that, merely to ensure that nothing unknown or unfamiliar is within the horizon of its vision.

This primordial tendency toward knowledge as a removal of all disconcerting unfamiliarity around one is revealed with varying degrees of clarity in Aristotle's analysis. Aristotle says explicitly that the pre-eminence of vision over the other senses is due not so much to its superior functioning in the circumspection that guides the performance of tasks as to its superior accomplishment in merely making us familiar with what exists and the manifold differences therein. No other sense equals vision in this respect, because, after all, all things have color, so that in seeing the common characteristics like figure, magnitude, number, and motion are always part of what is seen (*De sensu* 437a3). Thus vision does the most to make things familiar.

The same tendency toward knowledge as a mode of Dasein's care which is independent in relation to the ability to perform everyday tasks is expressed in the characteristic capacity for *technē* and *logismos* (art and reasoning), which is reserved, among all other living creatures, to human Dasein. Dealings with the world which make provision for things involve a way of seeing that develops, by virtue of retention in memory, into *experience*. In making repeated provision, by performing the same task, the object, seen each time in a circumspect way, is retained and recognized as the same in each new instance of performance. Thus from the multiplicity of memories the unity of an ability, a state of having experience, emerges. So the essential thing about having experience is that through our retention of what is the same in every case, our having made something many times before leads to a wider circumspection. But the tendency of the development of this kind of circumspection is toward arrival at a way of seeing which not only proves itself, in fact, in each new case of everyday task performance, as the circumspection which guides such performance, but which knows in general, *in advance*, what is to be done in every possible case of the performance in question. This enhancement, or raising, of experience to the level of technē is already *no longer aimed at the performance as such*. This is because for the purpose of making provision in individual cases, it is no enhancement at all, since it does not develop further the circumspection that governs the process of making provision itself. After all, it is possible for a person who draws only on his experience to be the better practitioner; and even someone who is master of the technē cannot dispense with experience when it comes to practice.

So what is excellent about technē, by comparison with experience, does not become apparent in the execution of an individual performance. Rather, it consists in the fact that technē is knowledge in a new sense. This knowledge does not consist in the capacity, in line with experience, to choose (when faced with the task of producing something concrete) the right means and the right time at which to execute the process; rather, it is already to dispose over the execution in advance, and with sureness in advance, for every possible case of the performance in question—which, however, means that this past discovery and this disposition have discovered and put at one's disposition something *general*, in a stricter sense than that in which experience too is a general ability, that is, a single thing that, deriving from many retained things, has become an ability. For the generality of this ability that goes with experience is proved in each case only by the concrete production. In seeing an individual thing in the present, its being of the same kind as (not being different from) many other things seen previously is seen at the same time. So experience is based on retaining things that are past and recognizing what was retained in what is present as the same. But in technē an anticipatory disposition over the process of production is achieved, as a *general* disposition that precedes all concrete task performance and does not have to be demonstrated through it. Someone who has the technē not only knows what is the case (for example, that this sick person here can be cured by this means, in the same way as in previous cases) but also why it is the case (why all people who are sick in this way can be cured by this same means). In other words, one has disposition over the production of these things because one's knowledge extends beyond the question of how one should act in each case.

It is not as though the practitioner who lacks technē could not also arrive at his course of action in the light of the result that he seeks and, in doing so, be equal or even superior in practical self-confidence to the person who knows; but this personal self-confidence and his objective reliability in hitting the mark still do not mean a free power of disposing over the thing to be produced. True, the experienced practitioner knows how to do the job, but he does not have the power to justify what he knows in any way except precisely by success in doing it. The fact that the experienced person's advice is right becomes evident only when one tries it out. For his knowledge, too, proves itself by being tried, just as it was gained in the first place by trial and error. What he does not know is the reason or cause that would support the action to which his experience directs him and would justify the confident expectation of its success.

The practitioner acts like a doctor. He sees what the sick person lacks—and this includes an anticipation of the person's health, of the way the person ought to appear. The real doctor does not act differently, but his understanding of this connection is different. For the doctor, health—what and how it is—is the reason or cause on which his action is based. He knows what always constitutes being healthy and, based on that, tries to identify what the sick person lacks. That is, he makes a picture of the illness for himself: what kind of bodily event it really was that led to the disturbance. Then, on the basis of this understanding of what the illness is, he chooses a remedy; that is, the doctor chooses a remedy for the patient on the basis of his understanding of the nature of the illness and the nature of the particular remedy. At any rate, it is only to the extent that the doctor acts on the basis of such an understanding that he acts as one who knows— that is, that he has an anticipatory certainty that his action will make the patient well: because he knows about what health always is and from this anticipatory knowledge gets the ability to identify disturbances of it and possible ways of restoring it. Thus this disposition over the reason or cause is primarily a knowledge of what one performs the task "for the sake of"; but this reason or cause also contains the cause in the sense of the *eidos*, or form (the appearance of what is to be produced), the cause in the sense of what it is to made from (the material), and the cause in the sense of the beginning of the process of production (where one must begin in this process). It is precisely one's anticipatory disposition over the reason or cause that is unfolded in these four senses that makes up the general and necessary character of one's disposition over the process of producing things.

A more detailed analysis of this subject, which Aristotle develops repeatedly (*Metaphysics* A 3 and elsewhere), is not needed here, where our only object is a general characterization of the concept of knowledge and the motives for it that are in keeping with Dasein. The important thing to remember is that the concept of technē is already governed by an idea of knowledge which, in its most characteristic sense, goes beyond what technē accomplishes in producing things and performing tasks, so that technē already represents a new mode of Dasein's care. In establishing itself in the world, Dasein has included in its care the *certainty* of its disposition over the world. This care about certainty manifests itself primarily in technē, as an anticipatory disposition over what is to be produced, a disposition that is characterized in its execution by knowledge of the reason or cause unfolded in the fourfold way. The very being of what is produced is under our disposition through this disposition over its reasons or causes. Now part of the tendency of this care is to get disposition in the same way over the being of everything that exists—that is, having discovered, and knowing, the reason or cause, to understand entities on the basis of that reason or cause as what they always and necessarily are. Thus the really scientific concept of being arises within the primary horizon of production through technē. In the comprehension (which is inherent in Dasein's disposition over it) of what it is produced from and as, the being of what is produced is independent of its factual presence in sense perception at any given time. The same tendency of Dasein toward certain disposition over the world in which it lives gives rise to the idea of *theoria*, knowledge of the world based on the reasons or causes of its being. In the flight from ignorance, the motive of knowledge reveals itself, independently of any practical use, as the separate and governing motive of a special care, even if the latter depends in fact, as a precondition, on all Dasein's practical needs being satisfied. In any case, the possibility of lingering which this factual precondition creates—the possibility of leisure, which in its turn is a prerequisite for the practice of theoria—should not be interpreted as simple freedom from care. Science, theoria, is itself a specific way in which the care of being-in-the-world is put into effect. Its precedence over the *technai* (arts) is due to the fact that the knowledge sought in it is not sought for the sake of anything else at all, but purely for the sake of its ownmost accomplishment of discovery and knowledge, because it is not applicable in any practical performance.

But technē too is not characterized in its most primordial motive by what distinguishes it from the theoretical sciences (that is, by its relation to its practical application) but by what it has in common with those sciences, which is its capacity to account for why something should be done and why it should be done in a particular way (with this material, by this means) (*kata to logon echein autous kai tas aitias gnōrizein, Meta.* 981b6). Thus, the primary sense of logos is *being answerable*, giving an account in the sense of stating the reason or cause. Command of a technē is characterized, in its execution, by anticipatory disposition over the thing to be produced, in the form of understanding and (in explicative speech) explaining the thing to be produced in terms of its reasons or causes. This disposition over the things has the character of universality and necessity insofar as the reason or cause (or the reasons or causes, when the system of them is analyzed) is universal and gives necessary reasons applying to every possible case of the performance in question. For example, for the sake of health (whose appearance, or universal eidos, is what the art of medicine has in view) a sick person who has such and such a type of illness is to be treated with remedies that restore his health. In the execution of the technē, this connection is evident—that is, it can be exhibited in speech. Correspondingly, in the cases in which Dasein's care relates to making visible and having disposition over entities that do not need to be produced but are there of their own accord, it is the exhibition of the reasons or causes that explain why an entity of this kind always and necessarily is the way it is which gives one disposition over the entity. In discovering and appropriating the reason or cause, by stating it, the entity is addressed as something that necessarily is as it is.

It is in the possibility of addressing entities as things that are necessarily the way they are that the characteristic *teachability*, which distinguishes technē and science from practical experience, is rooted.

For the being of something that is known on the basis of its reason or cause can be put at the disposition of other people as well, by stating the reason or cause. Thus the being toward the object that is arrived at in knowledge necessarily claims to be communicable, and it is thereby also claimable, in the reverse direction, by the other person, in such a way that when the reason or cause is stated, the entity is intelligible, in its being, for everyone. So here speech, as a form in which knowledge is put into effect, has the character of making the entity available by exhibiting it to oneself and to others, and in such a way that the thing thus exhibited is held fast in its discovered state. All giving of reasons or causes presupposes an acquaintance with the entity for which the reasons or causes are given. The "that" has to be established before one can meaningfully ask for the "why." Thus the care that goes with knowledge is a care that has to do with giving reasons or causes. As such it presupposes the primary understoodness of the entity as something that is given together with the understanding of the world which is part of our understanding of Dasein itself. So giving reasons or causes is a way of appropriating this kind of acquaintance. The thing for which the reasons or causes are given is at the disposition of the knower, whether in the certainty of always being able to produce such a thing or in the certainty of always encountering such a thing when the reasons or causes for it are present. A thing is appropriated as something that has been understood insofar as it is shown that what it is understood as belongs necessarily to the thing that is understood in this way (see *Meta.* Z 17). Whatever does not belong necessarily to an entity is also not comprehensible by the logos of science (compare the investigation of the *kata symbebēkos* [the accidental], *Meta.* E 2). When it presents something together with reasons or causes for it, talk makes the distinctive claim to assert something universal and necessary about an individual entity. In doing so, such talk is, in a distinctive way, *a speech that lets the other person speak too.*

So in what follows, the structure of scientific assertions, which give reasons or causes, is to be contrasted with pre-scientific assertions. Using as its clue the function of the other person in speaking with one another, the analysis tries to clarify how scientific talk is carried out as a way of coming to a shared understanding about reality, and in that way to grasp more precisely the structure of scientific assertions—of assertions that give reasons or causes. At the same time, by doing this, the basis is prepared for bringing out the historical horizon in which the development of the idea of science among the Greeks reached theoretical clarity. In this way also the use of Aristotle's explicit concepts of science and technē to clarify Plato's doctrine of the logos will be justified.

Section 2: Conversation and Logos

Speech, in its primordial form, is part of a shared having to do with something. As an articulating declaration about something, it makes the thing it speaks about manifest as something; but its goal is not that the thing addressed in this way should be discovered. Rather, the real point of this making manifest has to do with carrying out the shared process of making provision for something. The declaration that is made in such a situation is itself part of the carrying out of the circumspection that governs the process of making provision. The thing that is made manifest as something in this case is interpreted in terms of an involvement which it is thus going to help to provide for, although this relation to an involvement is not itself stated. Structurally, then, the situation is no different from the constant practice, in circumspect making provision, of silently understanding something *as* something. What one understands it "as" has the character of a "for what." To understand something as a hammer means to understand it as a tool for hammering, which is a "for what" in which it is most primordially accessible and understood in the act of hammering itself.[5] Thus the making of a declaration that the hammer is heavy is

5. Compare Heidegger, *Being and Time*, trans. J. Macquarrie and E. Robinson (New York, 1962), pp. 95ff. (= *Sein und Zeit* [Halle, 1927], pp. 95ff.).

itself circumspectly motivated. The point is not to bring the other person, to whom this is said, to an understanding of the fact that the thing possesses the characteristic of heaviness; rather, in understanding what is said to him, the other person follows the reference in it to something that he (as part of the shared activity of making provision) should do—for example, look around for a lighter hammer. Insofar as the other person does not understand what he is really meant to gather from the declaration, the person is a poor helper. One is so little concerned in this situation with the understanding of what is said as such and (likewise) with the other person's understanding as such that, if necessary, one calls someone else who understands one better, or one helps oneself. The sole, circumspect aim of what one does or says is that of getting the job done.

Even if, in the production of something, the other person (in his being toward the thing to be produced) is explicitly included in one's care—for example, as an apprentice—the character of the declarations that are made in this context is not that of a scientific presentation that gives reasons or causes; so the claim to intelligibility which one's declarations make has a different foundation. For the transmission of understanding which is going on here proceeds most primordially not in speech and the understanding of what was spoken but in showing and having the other person imitate, as, for example, if one wants to help someone who is learning a craft to acquire a circumspect understanding of a tool with which he is not familiar. No matter how thoroughly one examines the tool visually and no matter how thoroughly it is described as a thing that is present-at-hand, this does not make one familiar with it. For it is not as a thing that is present-at-hand that it is unfamiliar; indeed, it must be, precisely, familiar in this way (through vision or description) in order to confront us as something puzzling. Furthermore, as something puzzling it is always already seen in relation to a particular kind of understanding. If we encounter it in the context of a workshop, it is already understood as meant for use in producing things—that is, as a tool. And it is precisely as a tool, understood in this way, that it is unfamiliar and puzzling in its "for what." This "for what," in turn, is not really understood when someone states the purpose for which it is intended, but only when we actually use it. Only the ability (from now on) to use the tool, as demonstrated by one's actual use of it, shows the extent to which the statement of its purpose made it cease to be puzzling. The declarations made by the teacher in the course of didactic demonstration or of having the apprentice do it are only a linguistic "commentary" on the practical circumspection itself. How far this is from being natural can be seen from the fact that a special effort is required not to fall back into the activity of making it oneself, following the natural course of making provision for something, without regard for the learner. Here, too, the declaration itself is not meant to be understood through what it says in words but gets its meaning and its claim to intelligibility from the tacit but present context, into which it fits, of making provision. (This state of affairs is what makes possible the kind of practical joke in which the wag takes what one tells him literally—that is, intentionally *mis*understands it.)

In both cases, the speech, as a circumspect interpretation of the circumstances, has the character of giving direction; that is, it serves to direct the other person not to what it exhibits, as such, but to an actively productive use of what it exhibits. As a mode of circumspection, then, the declaration reveals the entity in the existential mode of being ready-to-hand in a way that is plain to circumspection. As a moment in the carrying out of circumspection, the declaration does not constitute a self-contained process of making provision which is completed by our making provision for the declaration.

Nor is this altered by the ontologically important detachment of vision from practical circumspection. When entities are merely looked at and regarded from a distance, they are understood simply in their appearance—which is to say, ontologically, as things present-at-hand that have such and such an appearance.[6] This carefree regard

6. Compare Heidegger, *Being and Time*, p. 216; *Sein und Zeit*, p. 172 and repeatedly.

is also a mode of the care of being-in-the-world. It originates in taking a rest from the care of producing. As a resting tarrying in regarding entities that do not have to be provided for as things to be produced, this attitude has the character of ridding oneself of the immediate tasks of making provision. As a resting, however, it continues to be connected to the productive process of making provision, from which it takes a rest. This connection is not to be understood as though, in taking a rest, one kept in view the things for which provision is to be made. On the contrary, one seeks, precisely in being toward other things for which one does not have to make provision, to forget the former things. But this being toward other things (in the attitude of regarding) has a more specific character, which is, precisely, that this is a being toward something other than the tasks of making provision which await one.

The nature of this specific character is clearest in a special way of taking a rest: in games. For games, it is essential that the players be "involved"—that is, that they allow themselves to be carried along by the tasks of the game, without keeping in mind that it is not in earnest. This does not prevent its being the case that the only purpose of the game is recreation—which is to say, that it is pursued for the sake of a later activity which it makes possible. (See *Nic. Ethics* K 6, 1176b35.) Thus in playing a game one's being toward the matter at hand is peculiarly neutral. Although the matter at hand must be taken seriously, the purpose of one's playing is not that matter but the manner of one's being toward it—that is, the fact that something becomes the object of care and effort without being something that would be the object of such care "in earnest." The object of the player's effort is something that is of no concern in itself: the game exists for the sake of playing. (See *Nic. Ethics* K 6, 1176b6.)

The same specific neutrality is characteristic of the resting attitude of regarding. It is true that, in allowing itself to be carried along by the world's appearance, the attitude of regarding always discovers entities in their presence-at-hand in the manner of appearance; but this having discovered does not, in the first instance, become a separate care directed at this discoveredness; that is, it does not take care to hold fast to what is discovered. Thus the speech, also, that communicatively explicates what is understood in such regarding is not intended to hold fast to what is discovered as something discovered; rather, in communicating with others, it presents the entities to them for them to consider in the same resting and tarrying way, whether by their listening or through the suggestions that the communication conveys for their own seeing. In its resting and tarrying, this attitude has a characteristic tendency to want to be with others. Speaking with one another, which is a way in which this being together can be accomplished, is not so much one's being toward the object (taking that as something to be communicated) as the sharing of this being toward the object. Thus speech is essentially expressing oneself; that is, it is communication of how one is faring. (In sections 35 and 36 of *Being and Time,* in the context of a fundamental-ontological analysis of Dasein's everydayness as "curiosity" and "idle talk," Heidegger exhibits the tendency to degenerate that is implicit in such a resting allowing oneself to be carried along by the world's appearance and in the kind of talking with one another that goes with it.) In this way of explicating the world by only regarding it, speech and expressibility do not have an importance that modifies one's comprehension itself; nor does one avail oneself of the other person with whom one speaks in the special function of someone who shares in constituting the explication and its implied claims.

Only when the discoveredness of the world for its own sake is placed in Dasein's care does the linguistically articulated explication of what is discovered acquire a peculiar function, which reveals itself, at the same time, in the constitutive role that is assigned to the person who is addressed by the speech. As was shown earlier, the care directed at our secure disposition over the world (a care that is rooted in a dependence, which is inherent in the constitution of Dasein's being, upon the world) constructs the idea of an advance disposition which is sure of itself. This is the idea of both practical and theoretical science. This care directed at security of disposition is implemented through inquiry into the reasons or causes (*archai* or *aitai*) of entities. Inquiry, then, is the search for reasons or causes. Dasein finds this sought-for understanding of the world and itself laid out spontaneously, as it were, in language.[7] In scientific inquiry, this understanding becomes the object of a special explicative and appropriative effort. As a search for the reason or cause, scientific inquiry is guided by an understanding of what is sought (of the reason or cause) as that from which the being of entities proceeds. Scientific inquiry aims at a peculiar ability of talk not only to make an entity visible as something but to exhibit it, in light of what makes it the way it is, as necessarily being that way. It is only in this idea of determining something by giving reasons or causes that declaration is consummated as a way of implementing the theoretical attitude. It is true that all speech about something addresses what it speaks about as something; but the fact that a declaration as such has been made need not mean that circumspect understanding has been leveled off into an explication of entities as present-at-hand, nor is an attitude of mere regarding enough to ensure that one's declarations will have the theoretically determining character that goes with such an explication. Rather, it is *only* when speech plays the role of exhibiting [that is, exhibiting reasons or causes] that the predicative judgment lays claim to speech in the distinctive function of "determining"—that is, of making the thing that is addressed available, subject to disposition. This idea of the logos as something that secures by determining points to the real existential motives of Greek ontology, which understands Being as something present-at-hand in the present. The development of this ontology into logic continues, up to the present, to govern the idea of scientific declaration. Thus the real motives of logic are operative not in judgment but in *inference*. It is only the recognition of the "individualizing" sciences, with their distinctive methodological character—and beyond that, the exhibition of the idea of an ontology of Dasein—that put in question the universal claim made by the struc-

7. Hence the Socratic turning to the *logoi*; see pp. 70ff. below.

ture of predication as an account of scientific assertion.[B] In any case, the Greek ontology of the present-at-hand is connected in the closest possible way with the Greek idea of science and determines, on that basis, the theory of the logos. It is not an accident that, for the Greeks, "logos" means what is enunciated, just as much as it means the reason or cause; for what one is looking for is a logos that places at one's disposition what gives the reason or cause of an entity in its being. Thus the substantive content of the logos that one seeks is the object's reason or cause (the *aitias logismos*, as Plato says).

Section 3: The Motives of a Concern for the Facts of the Matter in a Shared World (Logos and Dialectic)

The scientific speech that I have been discussing involves a specific claim to understandability. In itself, all speaking has the character of "speaking with someone" and, as such, intends that what it speaks about should be understood as the kind of thing that the speech makes it visible as. Even where, in fact, no one else is present to hear my words, the assumption inherent in what I say is still that it is understandable by others. Even when we do not reach the point of audible enunciation—that is, when we "think"—we think in a language which, as a language, refers to possible others who speak the same language and who therefore would understand my thoughts if they could "read" them. In the same way all "speaking with some-one" speaks to the other person with a view to a corresponding response from him, although that response need not itself have the character of speech. But even if the other person does in fact answer— if he "has something to say" in response to what was said—the logos of science makes an additional, specific claim to understandability and to a corresponding response, a claim that makes up the speech's characteristic way of relating to the facts of the matter. Every scientific

B. Heinrich Rickert (following Wilhelm Windelband) distinguished "individualizing" (also "idiographic") from "generalizing" ("nomothetic") sciences. The "ontology of Dasein" is, of course, Heidegger's.

statement is an assertion that either does not need to be supported (with further reasons) or does need such support, and it has, itself, the character of a provision of such support, insofar as it does not simply assert that a state of affairs exists but exhibits it as necessary for a reason. So it is only when it asserts a reason that a scientific statement at the same time asserts the necessity of what the reason grounds. This claim to necessity involves, at the same time, a claim to evidentness (*Einsichtigkeit*). But in that case a claim is made to the other person's agreement, purely as something that follows from his going along with the reasoned presentation of the previously discovered reality. Part of the sense of such giving of reasons, however, is that if the other person takes the speaker up on it, he does so freely—that is, not only by agreeing with it but also possibly by contradicting it. In accordance with the dual character of what is asserted, the contradiction can be directed either at the evidentness (which was presumed not to need support by further reasons) of the state of affairs that was given as the reason or (and this is the real contradiction) at the claim that this state of affairs is in fact a reason for the previously recognized matter of fact—that is, it can be directed at the adequacy to reality of the reason-giving explication itself. In the first case, the contradiction gives the speaker the task of providing reasons to support the supposed reason itself and thereby gaining acceptance for the reason-giving explication, while in the other case it gives him the task of finding a more exact reason (the *oikeios logos* [proper, fitting logos]) for the matter of fact. The important thing, however, is that the contradiction is directed not at the matter of fact itself but at the reasons given for it—that it takes the roundabout path of reasons. Accordingly, the fulfilment of the claim to evidentness, when there is agreement, means that the reason-giving explication is passed back to the speaker by the other person and is confirmed in its claim. Both speech and contradiction, as scientific actions, are subject to the same guiding idea of concern for the facts of the matter, which gives their claim to necessity and evidentness its character.

This subordination to the idea of simply opening up access

to the facts of the matter entails a characteristic restriction of the function of speech itself. For in speaking about something, Dasein always expresses *itself* at the same time. Even more than the words actually spoken, the speaker's intonation and gestures express his mood and his inner state at the time. In understanding what is said and meant, the other person always understands this inner condition of the speaker as well, and it modifies his understanding (which, after all, has one mood or another) of what was meant. Thus the matter of fact that was meant and made evident by the speaker's speech is conceived and understood not only in itself but also in what the speaker gave expression to in his speech, what he intentionally or unintentionally said and suggested by it. Accordingly, the other person does not really reply to what was said, as such; instead, he replies to the speaker's self-expression and does so by expressing himself about it in a responsive way. This pattern of mutual self-expression constitutes a specific possible way of being with one another. The idea of shared understanding which guides this activity is not one in which agreement is reached about the matter under discussion, and its motive is not to secure the disclosure of this matter, but, rather, to enable the participants themselves to become manifest to each other in speaking about it. Thus, at bottom, such a conversation is made no less fruitful by the participants' inability to come to an agreement about the matter, as long as it enables each of them to become explicitly visible in his being to the other. Of course the question as to whether this way of understanding the other person represents a genuine way of being with one another is an important one, which constitutes a key problem of existence in a shared world. For, even ignoring the turning away from the task of gaining access to the facts of the matter, one wants to know whether this kind of understanding of other people through self-expression about something is not a degenerate form, made possible by self-reflection, of being with one another. For a person who thinks that he understands another person who contradicts him in some way and that he understands him without agreeing with him has by that very means protected himself from the other person's contradiction. That is, in understanding oneself—an understanding that essentially always involves contrasting oneself with others in this way—one rigidifies oneself in ways that make one, precisely, unreachable by the other person. Genuine being with one another can hardly be based on an understanding that pushes the other person away like this but must be based on a way of being with him that refrains from claiming this kind of understanding of the other person and of oneself.

To this idea of coming to a shared understanding, which arises from a specific tendency of self-reflection in being with one another, we must contrast the idea of coming to a purely substantive shared understanding and the way in which that idea is implemented in scientific conversation. Of course, scientific talk's concern for the facts of the matter does not prevent it, too, as speech, from being a self-expression of the speaker's state. But the claim that scientific talk makes to understanding and to a corresponding response demands precisely that we disregard what is also expressed about Dasein when it speaks about the facts of the matter; and the one who responds, likewise, demands a similar disregard for the unsubstantive aspect that is also expressed in his answer. The attitude that is part of this manner of conversing is not even adequately characterized by the merely negative quality of disregarding what also gets expressed while attending to the matter of fact to which the speech refers. For in this kind of conversation, which seeks to gain access to the facts of the matter, we find expressed not only the things that are to be disregarded in accordance with the idea of a concern for the facts of the matter but also a characteristic positive disposition of Dasein, which does not need to be disregarded, because it is shared by the other person with whom one is speaking, and which also *cannot* be disregarded, since it makes up the actual human basis of the conversation's concern for the facts of the matter. This positive disposition is the shared willingness to question. As a characteristic shared state, it constitutes the kind of coming to an understanding that insists on reasons and listens to reasons.

This kind of coming to an understanding is aimed entirely at the substantive agreement that is to be achieved. Within this pure self-abandonment to the facts of the matter, the real potential of speaking with others consists in letting the other person help one in the process of gaining access to the facts of the matter. After all, the speaker shares with the other person an antecedent understanding of entities and claims, by addressing these entities, which he does by exhibiting reasons for them, to support this same understanding with reasons. So the extent to which this claim is justified in a particular case is essentially decided by whether the way the matter of fact is understood really is supported by the reason that is given—that is, whether the matter of fact is addressed in what makes it, necessarily and always, what it was previously understood as. But in conversation, that is decided by the other person's agreement or disagreement; in other words, it is decided precisely when one lays one's assertion open to the other person's response. For if it is possible to contradict it, one's claim is refuted; but at the same time, each contradiction contains a new insight and thus a pointer to a correct account. The substantive productivity of conversation consists in its letting such contradictions indicate the direction of its search. Understood from the point of view of conversation's most characteristic tendency, an inability to come to a shared understanding is never a final outcome but indicates only that one has been unable to bring the process of understanding to a conclusion, and therefore requires resumption of the conversation, whose characteristic sense is that it is repeatable and is capable, precisely by being repeated, of being moved forward toward gaining access to the facts of the matter and thus toward agreement.

The fact that failure to reach a shared understanding, even in conversations that are concerned with the facts of the matter, is sometimes interpreted in such a way that the contradiction that has emerged is taken as a positive result—that is, as showing a difference in assumptions that are not open to discussion—does not cast doubt on what has been said about the guiding concern for the facts of the matter but instead confirms it. For such an "interpretation" involves forsaking speech's intention of gaining access to the facts of the matter.

One asserts the irreducibility of a difference of opinion in order no longer to be faced with the other person's contradiction as something that was meant to be substantive. When one "understands" the other person's disagreement—that is, explains it as a result of the difference between his assumptions and one's own undiscussable assumptions instead of (precisely) making those assumptions the subject of the conversation—one excludes the other person in his positive function, as someone to whose substantive agreement and shared understanding one makes a claim. Then the conversation ceases to be what it was: a process of coming to a shared understanding about the facts of the matter.

The same forsaking and the same exclusion also take place on the side of the other person if he contradicts one's statement without being willing to answer for his contradiction or if he presents only an appearance of agreeing with one's statement—so as to be released from the conversation—without really agreeing with the way one develops the facts of the matter. In these cases it is the other person who excludes himself from the shared intention of reaching an understanding about the facts of the matter, by not accepting what is said as the substantive opinion that it is and making it the object of his answer, but instead tacitly keeping his eye on assumptions made by his partner, which he thinks he "understands"—by doing which he precisely shuts himself off from his partner's substantive opinion.

The positive thing that this makes clear is that, in scientific conversation, the other person is needed solely for the sake of coming to an understanding about the facts of the matter—which is to say, he is needed insofar as he is able and willing to listen to reasons and to respond with reasons. Insofar as he shares one's antecedent understanding of the matter at hand and possesses this readiness to engage in substantive scrutiny, his substantive agreement is the only sufficient criterion of the adequacy of the logos to the facts of the matter and is not the prejudice of a dominant opinion. But this means at the same time that in each case this one person who answers for his response in this way is decisively important, because arriving at an understanding with him authenticates the "truth": that the reason whose discovery one shares with him really is the reason that enables one to exhibit and explain the matter of fact in its necessary existence and character. Thus the other person with whom one seeks to reach agreement is *in no way different from any other person*, or better, he is needed only in the ways in which he is precisely not different from others. That is why his agreement testifies to the truth of what he agrees with. Like him, anyone else who participated in the same conversation would have to agree to the result of the conversation. If the first person refuses to agree and gives reasons for his disagreement, there is no point in involving someone else in the conversation in his place. For if he can disagree, with reasons, so can others, with the same reasons, and in that case what they are disagreeing with is refuted. So the inherent tendency of the intention of coming to an understanding is to want to do this precisely with the person whose prior opinion contradicts one's thesis most sharply. The more radical the contradiction is, the more secure the thesis that is confirmed by an ultimate agreement. If one has this idea of substantive conversation in view, it becomes clear that such conversation is not a form of talk that is essentially alien to the logos by which science discloses the facts of the matter but that, on the contrary, it makes it possible for that logos to develop into a process of cognitive disclosing and appropriating.

So it is the structure of this idea of coming to an understanding which explains why I am able, even without speaking to another person, to press forward, in a process of scientific, reason-giving disclosing and appropriating, and to arrive at the real logos. For thought that is not expressed is also speech, except that the other person with whom I speak is in this case myself. But the only reason why this is possible is that even in a real conversation, the other person is not needed for anything other than what I can do for myself: to return to an explication that has been given and to test it against my understanding of the facts of the matter. This depends on the fact that the understanding that is articulated in what we call "thought" is held fast, exactly as an enunciated explication is held fast, and is thus repeatable and capable of being returned to. Of course the possibility of confronting oneself freely with contradiction has a peculiar difficulty: it requires that one know how to get free of oneself and of the tendencies of one's comprehension as the latter grow fixed and to listen to what the facts of the matter have to say to one in response to a new interrogation. But a real conversation itself already requires one to attend only to the substantive intention of what is said and not to what the speech expresses, along with that, about Dasein. Of course, "unsubstantive" motives do contribute, in fact, to the discovery and the enunciation of opposing arguments. Even in substantive conversations, competition, which is a fundamental motive in situations where we are together with other people, sharpens our perception of what can be said against the other person's thesis. But the conversation's claim to be substantive is satisfied as long as the substantive reasons, and not these contingent motives, are the object of the argument. The other person, whom one contradicts with these reasons, takes them purely in their substantive content. Thought that confers with itself faces the same requirement. It must exclude all motives of that kind in order to make substantive headway. To confront one's own logos in a testing way, oriented toward free agreement or free opposition, requires that, initially, one disregard the fact that it is one's *own* logos. In actual fact, of course, this disregarding can be accomplished by keeping in view the possibility of contradiction by others. But this thoughtful anticipation of others sees them not as specific others, over whom one would like to win ascendancy, but as the anonymous bearers of a possible substantive contradiction—which, however, means that in this way one sees one's own thesis, too, only in its substantive content. This concern for the facts of the matter presents itself as a willingness to question and to doubt.[8] It is also a precondition of the possibility

8. Against Löwith's one-sided analysis (*Das Individuum in der Rolle des Mitmenschen* [Munich, 1928]), it was necessary to emphasize the fact that, and why, it is the case that "thought" is more than the mere elaboration of fixed cognitive assumptions and is not completely accounted for by a

of making genuine objections to one's own theses; objections, that is, that do not remain, on principle, below the level of what one's thesis asserts—so that they are not oriented from the start toward securing this thesis, and the considerations they raise are not only considerations that are seen in advance to be refutable and empty.

The concern for the facts of the matter which characterizes the claim that the scientific logos makes on the other person is also the reason for the fact that it is only such a logos that can really be taught. Teaching is a derivative mode of the kind of speaking with one another that proceeds by expounding the subject matter with substantive reasons. In teaching, the speaker is, specifically, a teacher, and the other person is a learner. But the claim to comprehension which the teacher makes in relation to the learner is in principle the same claim that is made in the reciprocal process of coming to an understanding about the facts of the matter. It is true that insofar as the teacher already has disposition over what he teaches, on the basis of real knowledge, it is not the question of his own substantive comprehension that causes him to be concerned about the student's understanding and agreement. But here the learner, too, is supposed to agree as a result of a free insight into the reason-giving exposition and the reasons given for it; that is, he is not supposed to accept anything so as to be able to repeat it but is supposed, instead, to be brought by the substantive exposition to the point of having his own knowing disposition over the facts of the matter. It is, after all, essential to something's being teachable that it is not something that only this person—and not that one—can learn; which, however, means that the other person who is the learner is not called upon in his otherness but rather in the sameness that teachers and learners have in common. Thus the teachability of knowledge follows from the sci-

logic of inference (even when it is monological thought). It could be shown that, conversely, the development of mere inference is guided by motives that have to do with the fact that we share our world—which, incidentally, is in keeping with the deeper coherence of Löwith's analysis. See my review in *Logos* 18 (1929).

entific logos's claim to address the facts of the matter in their necessity by showing how they follow from reasons.

This function of the other person within the tendency of conversation toward coming to a substantive understanding constitutes the very essence of the dialectical. For a dialectical contradiction of a thesis is not simply a contrary thesis which someone opposes to the stated opinion as *his* (or her) opinion. A dialectical contradiction is not present when one opinion is opposed by another; instead, it is constituted precisely when one and the same faculty of reason has to grant validity to both the opinion and the counter-opinion. It is not a contradiction in the dialectical sense when another person speaks against something, but only when a *thing* speaks against it, whether it is another person or I myself who has stated this.[9]

Section 4: Degenerate Forms of Speech

The claim to knowledge is confirmed by arrival at a shared understanding. The other person's agreement is the test of whether the logos that is given is really able to expound the facts of the matter in a convincing way. But here we find a specific possibility of inauthenticity to which speech, as a possibility of human existence, is subject. Plato characterizes again and again the "substantive" spirit (the spirit that is concerned with the facts of the matter) of the dialogical pursuit of shared understanding, and the same distinctive characteristics are granted to the Socratic, the later Platonic (see the *Sophist* or the *Laws*), and the Academic (*Seventh Letter*) conduct of conversation. They can be summed up, uniformly, as the exclusion of *phthonos*. *Phthonos* (see the interpretation of *Philebus* 48ff. below) means concern

9. It is significant that one can explicitly and arbitrarily allocate the advocacy of two opposed theses, each of which has some evidence in its favor, to two different partners, as is done in the *Laws* 963d9 ff. Such allocation is, clearly, only a technical matter. The important thing, dialectically, is precisely the equal respect accorded to both theses by one and the same faculty of reason.

about being ahead of others or not being left behind by others. As such, its effect in conversation is to cause an apprehensive holding back from talk that presses toward discovering the true state of affairs. So talk that is guided by this kind of consideration for oneself is characterized by a proviso: that the talk about the facts of the matter should reflect back on the talker in a way that distinguishes him or her in a positive way. This proviso prevents the talk from adapting freely to the connections in the subject matter and thus prevents, precisely, an unreserved readiness to give an account. Someone who, on the contrary, answers *aneu phthonou, eumenēs, alupōs* (without being inhibited by the pain of an aggrieved desire to be right) is prepared to give an account "*aphthonōs*" (in a manner that is not affected by phthonos).

The contrasting degenerate forms of speech are fundamentally distinguished from the one discussed above[C] by the fact that, rather than blunting the claim to coming to an understanding in regard to the facts of the matter (blunting it with the help of self-reflection), they use the appearance of making that claim as a means of distinguishing the speaker himself from others. The Greeks were governed by confidence in the power of speech and in the possibility of agreement through speech to such an extent that it was only these latter degenerate forms that were influential among them. Speech gives itself the appearance of having knowledge to the extent that it is able, through the seduction that is inherent in it, to secure other people's agreement or to refute them. Thus it is characteristic of the way in which this apparent claim is carried out that the goal of one's logos, rather than being to be confirmed or aided in its function of providing access to the facts of the matter by allowing a free reception in the form of agreement or opposition in regard to those facts, is instead to cut off the possibility of a free response by the other person. Thus such pretended knowledge takes the form of something that aims either at getting someone's agreement or at refuting them.[10] In both forms of

C. That is, in the previous section.

10. This *agonistic* sense of the logos cannot be derived from a *theory* of

such speech its function is not primarily to make the facts of the matter visible in their being and to confirm this through the other person but rather to develop in speech, independently of the access that it creates to the facts of the matter, the possibility precisely of excluding the other person in the function (which belongs to him in the process of coming to an agreement) of fellow speaker and fellow knower.

1. The claim to knowledge establishes itself through having disposition over the *strongest* logos. This "strength" is due to the impossibility of the logos's coming to grief, the impossibility of contradicting it. In this sense every logos that wants to be knowledge has to be strong, and to the extent that it is irrefutable, it is strong. "Strength," looked at in this way, is simply an expression of the adequacy to the facts of the matter of what is said. In this way, strength is not something that is striven for for its own sake; rather, it is a side effect of the striving to make what one says adequate to the facts of the matter. But it can also be separated from the idea of adequacy to the facts of the matter, and its being stronger can be striven for in the interests of ascendancy over other people. *This* way of aiming at the

---

the logos which puts in fundamental question the possibility of speech that gives access to the facts of the matter (as in E. Hoffmann's attempt, in *Die Sprache und die archaische Logik* [Tübingen, 1925], to derive Sophist eristics from a theory of language as *nomō* [by convention]). Instead, the agonistic use of the logos is itself based on the assumption that the logos exhibits the facts of the matter. This is the only way to understand the Sophists' claim to *knowledge*, which is founded on their ability to speak about everything. The only way the logos can "affect its hearer" (Hoffmann, pp. 28–29) is by the hearer's taking what is said in its substantive claim, as knowledge. Thus the motives for the agonistic use of speech lie not in a position in the theory of language and the theory of knowledge but in an inclination of actual Dasein in a public, shared world: an inclination to distinguish oneself over others, as a knower, through speech. The skeptical turning in the *theory* of the logos is itself based, first of all, on these possibilities of degeneration ("falling": *Verfall*) in factical speech.

stronger logos is characterized by the fact that its goal is, by using possibilities that are inherent in discourse itself, to make any randomly chosen logos (even a logos that is substantively weaker, that is, one that is not adequate to the facts of the matter) into the stronger one and thus to fulfil the (otherwise unfulfillable) claim always to have the stronger logos. That this claim can represent only a pretended claim to knowledge is clear from the fact that in this kind of command of speech one claims knowledge of *everything*. One is ready to answer *any* question, and one believes in advance, before one knows what question one will be asked, that one commands the power of speech in such a way that one will be able to cut short any contradiction, regardless of its substantive justification. This (in itself) impossible claim to know everything creates an appearance of validity only by virtue of the fact that its talk conceals the facts of the matter themselves to such an extent that one's opponent can no longer hit upon them. That such discourse aims to conceal the facts of the matter is betrayed by the fact that to the talker, what he says is not really important. (Even concealing talk has a substantive content, inasmuch as concealment, too, is a way of exhibiting the facts of the matter—though by exhibiting them as what they are not.) What is important to the talker is only his ascendancy over contradiction. The claim that his talk makes to knowledge always presents itself as already having been satisfied, and not as yet to be satisfied by coming to a shared understanding. If, contrary to expectation, the logos that was put forward turns out—in conversation with a really inquiring person (the kind of person, of course, that one avoids as much as possible, as will be seen shortly)—not to be irrefutable and is refuted, then what happens is not that a more correct explication of the facts of the matter is developed from the substantive content of the refutation and from the logos that was initially put forward. Instead, the place of the refuted logos is filled with a new one that is oriented toward the refuting argument, and only toward it. Thus each logos, when it is refuted, is entirely dropped and replaced with a new one that seems to be strong enough to stand up against this refutation in particular. Thus each logos is chosen only for the sake of its being stronger. It is meant to be definitive and not to open up a substantive discussion. So if it is refuted, it is not retained, but disappears entirely, without regard to whether what it said exhibited something of the facts of the matter in question or not. Thus concern about the ascendancy of one's logos obstructs one's view of the facts of the matter, which point precisely through the refutation to an explication that *makes progress*, by taking with it and retaining what is revealed in the pros and cons. Thus the unsubstantiveness of this kind of talk is manifested precisely in its evasion of possible contradiction. Part of the essence of such talk, therefore, is to avoid dialogue. It tends toward making speeches, toward *makrologia* (speaking at length), which of course makes it difficult to go back to something that was said—if only for the external reason of the length of the speech, but especially if this length lacks internal order, that is, if it drags on through manifold variations of the same thing, without making progress in substantive argument.

In making speeches, one addresses oneself, from the beginning, not to an individual, with whom one might seek to arrive at a substantive shared understanding, but to a crowd, with which a substantive shared understanding is impossible, if for no other reason than because the crowd cannot answer. Consequently, rather than being a purely substantive exhibition of something, a speech is a process of persuasion. The intention of the speech is to make the subject it deals with credible by means of the impression that the speech makes. To make such an impression, the means that is inherent in the speech, independently of its substantive content, is its pleasingness precisely as a speech. In the kind of speaking that I am trying to characterize here, this pleasingness is the real object of the speaker's efforts. Beyond its function as a means, it is meant to be appreciated in itself. Someone who is pressing for clarification of the facts of the matter and who is not interested in the art exhibited by the speech, as such, sees in the latter only the fact that its advance does not accomplish any advance in opening up the facts of the matter—that instead the same things are said in it over and over again in different ways (*Phaedrus* 235a). And when the speech is over, he hardly notices that it is over: a speech in which no path opening up the facts of the matter is taken cannot lead to an end that is inherent in the facts of the matter themselves, either. It ceases, but the enchantment lasts, until one awakens from it (*Protagoras* 328d). The most extreme form of this process by which oratory becomes increasingly autonomous, a form in which no specific other people are visible, to whom the speech is addressed, is the writing of speeches (Lysias, in the *Phaedrus*). This kind of rhetoric shows in an extreme fashion that the speaker is concerned not with the subject matter of which he speaks but only with the possibility of demonstrating his art, in connection with any subject matter. Genuine rhetoric, on the other hand, while resembling this in that it likewise does not exhibit the facts of the matter as the speaker sees them but instead presents them to the listeners as something that they are not, is governed by a substantive intention: to convince the others of something by means of this deception and to talk them into something that concerns the speaker. That is, he does not speak in order to exhibit himself or his art but in order to move his listeners to something that he would be in a position to argue for but which, in front of many people, he cannot simply exhibit as it is, because the many are not the one whom alone one can force into a process aimed at a shared substantive understanding.

2. This unsubstantive type of speech, which is aimed at showing oneself to be the knower who cannot be refuted, has a counterpart, which is the refutation of others for the sake of refutation. Here, too, one's speaking serves the purpose—through one's ability to refute—of giving oneself the appearance of knowledge. It is just that it achieves this purpose not by immediately laying claim to superiority for oneself but rather, conversely, by demonstrating to the others their inferiority. Here, too, one misuses the original intention of opening up the facts of the matter—the intention that consists in using the raising of objections to move the other person and oneself forward into a more correct explication of the facts of the matter. Here,

too, a genuine co-relationship with the other person, in being toward the facts of the matter, is missing. One's purpose is not, by refuting the other person, to bring him to the point of making another statement as part of his own developing train of thought; rather, one's purpose is precisely to silence him. Part of the essence of this refutation for the sake of refutation is a tendency to refute, as untenable, any and every thesis—which is a claim that corresponds exactly to the claim to be able to talk about everything. Here, too, this claim already shows that it cannot be a question of genuine refutation on the basis of the facts of the matter. For this claim assumes that one commands the possibility of refutation in advance, without regard to the substantive content of what is to be refuted in a particular case. Here too, then, one avails oneself of a possibility of appearing which is inherent in speaking itself: the possibility of appearing to refute any assertion by establishing its opposite. This is possible insofar as every explication is guided by an antecedent adoption of a perspective toward the thing that is to be explicated—without its being necessary for this perspective to be articulated explicitly in the explication itself, however much it determines the substantive sense of the explication. Every meaning is part of a whole connected system of meaning and is determined by this whole. Taken in itself, then, it is fundamentally ambiguous, insofar as it becomes definite only in its systematic context. Now the refutation, in its unsubstantive independence of context, proceeds in a way that leaves this ambiguity concealed. The explication is tacitly placed in a different perspective. This change of perspective remains tacit because the other person, whose thesis is supposed to be refuted, is not permitted to say anything more, or else is granted only the appearance of an answer, in the form of an unconnected "yes" or "no" (see the portrayal in the *Euthydemus*). Thus the difference between the perspectives in which what is said is placed in the two cases remains concealed because one focuses on the sameness of the words (*kat' onoma diōkein*) and thus arrives at the contradiction that refutes what was said. It is characteristic of this form of speech also that it is cut off from speech's substantive intention, from letting what it refers to be seen, in such a way that it sticks to the ambiguous possibilities of what is said, possibilities that (precisely) conceal the facts of the matter and thus frustrate the genuine pursuit of a substantive shared understanding. Here again, the motive of this tendency to conceal is to present oneself, the one who refutes, as the one who knows. This is eristic.

Section 5: The Socratic Dialogue

This general characterization of the structure of scientific speech and the forms of its degeneration indicates, at the same time, the historical horizon within which the Socratic dialogue, and thus the origins of Plato's dialectic, must be placed. The power of speech in the inauthentic forms that were just characterized is embodied in the historical fact of Sophism. The fathers of Sophism in history are at the same time the creators of rhetoric. The structural kinship between the arts of rhetoric and eristic, which was set forth in a purely substantive way above, is confirmed by the fact that they have the same historical roots. And in the opposite direction, the motives (which I exhibited) of falling into the power of speech, as such, in a shared world make the actual historical power of Sophism (in the broadest sense) understandable. Even in these un-genuine forms of speech one perceives the peculiar character of the scientific claim to be able to answer for what one thinks one knows. Insofar as someone who enters into conversation with Socrates thinks he has knowledge of what he is asked about, then, he cannot refuse the demand that he answer for it. The genuineness of his claim to knowledge is put to the test by this demand for accountability. If Plato's Socrates increasingly gives up the attitude of the questioner and tester, and if the discussion leader in the later dialogues himself becomes the person who claims knowledge, still it is not without reason that the dialogue continues to be the form in which this knowledge is effected. For there it is the leader himself who continually subjects what he says to this testing and proves the claim to knowledge (which his speech contains) by coming to an understanding with the others. The dialogue form allows him continually to make sure that the other person is with him in the process of opening up the facts of the matter and thus protects his own speech from falling (in a way that all talk in a rhetorically knowledgeable age is prone to do) into an empty speech that loses the seen object from view. Thus, in Plato's historical situation there is a reason for the fact that knowledge is no longer possible as the wise proclamation of the truth but has to prove itself in dialogical coming to an understanding—that is, in an unlimited willingness to justify and supply reasons for everything that is said.

The aim, then, of the analysis of the Socratic dialogue which I attempt in the following sketch, is to exhibit, in the structure of coming to an understanding which follows from the dialogues' character as conversation, the elements of substantive, scientific speech. The highlighting of these structural elements is meant to provide the key for the subsequent interpretation of the *theory* of dialectic. In following out this connection between dialogue and dialectic, the interpretation claims only to detect the theme of coming to a shared substantive understanding as a leading one in the various forms taken by the problem of dialectic. The hope is, by this means, to provide a framework for the interpretation of the excursus on dialectic in the *Philebus* and thus to make the function of the excursus in the context of the conversation intelligible. Thus the context that is developed here substantively is meant to become fruitful, in the second chapter, for the interpretation of the *Philebus*. For it will become evident that the *dialektikē dunamis* (dialectical power) that is discussed there represents, in the realm of dialogue, precisely the dialectic that is put up for methodological discussion at the beginning of the *Philebus* on account of needs arising within the discussion situation.

To begin with, it is necessary to indicate which preconditions of the possibility of coming to a shared understanding are given along with the objective topics of the Socratic dialogues. For the claim to knowledge which Socrates tests is a distinctive claim. What is in question is not a knowledge that one person has and another does not have, that one person claims and another does not claim; that is, it is not a knowledge by which only the "wise" are distinguished but a knowledge that everyone must claim to have and must therefore seek continually insofar as he does not have it. For the claim to this knowledge constitutes the manner of being of human existence itself; it is the knowledge of the good, of aretē. Part of being human is the fact that one understands oneself in one's aretē; that is, that one understands oneself in terms of what one can be. So the Socratic question of what aretē (or a specific aretē) is, is guided by a preliminary concept of aretē which is shared by the questioner and the one who is questioned. All Dasein lives continually in an understanding of aretē. What the good citizen must be and how he must act are prescribed for everyone in an explication that dominates the entire public understanding of Dasein: in what is called "morals." So the concept of aretē is a "public" concept. In it, the being of man is understood as a being with others in a community (the *polis*). Aretē is what makes each person a citizen, which means, however, that the understanding of aretē is not simply common and public in the sense that every person shares the prevalent opinion about it, that he knows something that everyone knows; rather, the claim to be a citizen necessarily involves the further claim that one in fact possesses this aretē that makes one a citizen (which is to say, a human being). This theme comes explicitly into play in the Socratic dialogues. Thus Protagoras describes it as sheer madness for someone to assert that he is not just (*Protagoras* 323b; compare *Charmides* 158d and *Gorgias* 461c). Everyone must be just insofar as he or she is a human being at all. This, then, is the guiding assumption from the beginning of the inquiry as to what this aretē really is: that everyone claims to have it, which (however) means to understand himself in terms of it. But in that case everyone must also be willing and able to give an accounting as to why he acts and conducts himself as he does; he must be able to *say* what he understands himself to be, with his claim to aretē, at least insofar as he is able, through the *logos*, to understand himself in terms of something—that is, to be toward something that is not present at the moment.

The Socratic discovery is that this claim, which seems to be such a matter of course, is not fulfilled as a matter of course: that Dasein's average self-understanding contents itself with the mere appearance of knowledge and cannot give an accounting of itself. So the Socratic question as to what aretē is, is a demand that an accounting be given. It asks, for example, why those whom we all take to be just are just: what justice itself is, whose presence in someone makes him just. Everyone must be able to answer this question, because it asks him about himself. Every Socratic conversation leads to this sort of examination of what a person himself is (*Laches* 187e). Even when the initial topic of the conversation is not knowledge about one's own being but a claim to knowledge in a specific area, the Socratic testing of this claim leads back to oneself. In such knowledge, after all, one thinks that one possesses something that is good. But whether it is good is decided not by whether one really has this knowledge— whether one is well versed in a field or knows how to perform a task— but by whether the use of this knowledge is guided by insight into the one thing that makes oneself and everything that one does good. No individual knowledge or ability is good in itself; rather, it needs to be justified in terms of an understanding of what one's own existence is for the sake of. One must be able to say why one behaves in a certain manner—that is, what the good is that one understands oneself as aiming at in one's behavior.

When an accounting is demanded, the prevalent understanding of Dasein proves to be inadequate. The knowledge about justice to which one lays claim in possessing it is a natural understanding of what is regularly shared by the modes of behavior that are *accepted* by the public as just. But each of these modes of behavior can nevertheless be bad, or the opposite mode of behavior can also be good. To stand firm in the front line in battle is generally regarded as bravery; but a possible tactic is to break up the enemy's front line by appearing to run away and then to destroy it. So standing firm, as such, is not the essence of bravery, because running away, in the latter case, is also brave (*Laches* 190e ff.). Thus such a natural understanding of aretē on the basis of what is common to behavior does not represent a real grasp of what aretē is, insofar as one generally contents oneself with the appearance of what is *accepted* as just, brave, and so forth.

It could be objected that, after all, one obeys the practice that is obligatory in society. Is that not an understanding of oneself? Yet a real grasp of what aretē is, is present only insofar as one is able to give an accounting of what makes what is accepted as aretē good. But this means that if the claim to be able to give an accounting of what is good becomes subject to doubt, this doubt leads to doubt about the rightness of what is accepted. The ultimate consequence of such doubt, then, is hedonism (*Republic* 538d). For if one is no longer really able to understand oneself in terms of aretē, then the idea of the good, as the formal idea of all understanding of oneself, falls back upon the immediate and simply certain experience of "feeling good." Thus the Socratic examination finds alongside the claim to understand aretē a doubt about the rightness of this ideal of aretē, a doubt that is associated with hedonism, which seems to be (as it were) the extreme case of a self-justifying understanding of Dasein.

The good of which knowledge is claimed and about which an accounting is demanded is understood, in its content, in two ways: as aretē—that is, in an orientation toward a public, moral understanding of Dasein—or as *hēdonē* (pleasure)—that is (breaking with the dominant view of morals), in an orientation toward the most direct, experiential certainty of the good. But even this experiential certainty has to constitute itself as an *understanding* of Dasein: that is, hēdonē, as what being is for the sake of, has to represent what a coherent understanding of Dasein aims at. Even then, the claim to such self-understanding as an antecedently certain disposition over oneself in all one's behavior continues to be presupposed. The critique of these claims, in the Socratic conversation, has a peculiarly ambiguous character. On the one hand, Socrates conducts the conversation as a process of refutation; but, at the same time, through this refutation, that which is sought is laid bare. It becomes possible to see what that to which the refuted accounts laid claim must be. Both functions of the

Socratic conversation have the single goal of achieving an authentic shared process of search.

As *refutation,* Socrates' questioning is aimed at showing that the claim (which, in itself, one cannot help making) to know what the good is, is unfulfilled. This demonstration takes the form of irony; that is, Socrates approaches the other person not in the manner of one who knows and who wants, through his superior knowledge, to refute the other person's claim, but rather in apparent inferiority, as someone who does not himself know. The irony appears first of all in the fact that he takes the other person's claim to knowledge as one that is fulfilled. A typical form of this irony is when Socrates declares himself to be satisfied with the other person's answer "except for a minor detail" (for example, *Protagoras* 329b: *smikrou tinos endeēs*). Thus Socrates starts his refutation not as a refutation but as a request for further information; that is, he takes the answer seriously as an explication that really is derived from an understanding of the subject that he is asking about and that implicitly addresses what he still does not understand, as well, and only needs to have spelled out in more detail in that respect. The request for supplementary information or explanation depends, after all, on this assumption: that the answer that was given already tacitly deals as well with what has not yet been explained explicitly. Now if this supplementary explanation does not materialize in a satisfactory form, the thesis itself is not unaffected by this; instead, its claim to be adequate to the facts of the matter is refuted. Part of the meaning of genuine substantive explication is that it can continually justify and clarify itself by drawing on the understanding of the facts of the matter from which it is derived—that is, that it unfolds from the thesis what is included in and consequently follows from it. A sophistic logos fails to meet this requirement because one did not acquire it with a view to the facts of the matter but rather with a view to its effectiveness in impressing the people around one.

This is evident, for one thing, in the fact that the sophist tries to make things appear to follow from his thesis that do not follow from it at all. The result is that the Socratic refutation itself has an eristic character. This should not be explained away by imagining that this process of entangling the opponent in contradictions by means of logical traps is aimed at exposing him in his inability to detect logical errors. The goal of refutation is absolutely the sole motive in the process: the goal, that is, of bringing the opponent to grant the validity of a thesis the consequences of which prove to be incompatible with his own thesis. But the fact that Socrates tries to defeat his opponent not only by means of genuine logical consistency but also by means of his own sophistical weapons does not cast doubt on the substantiveness of his intentions. For the fact that the master of logical traps can himself be caught in this way is due to the fact that his use of these weapons is based not on a superior application of language's potential for concealment (which would presuppose a genuine understanding on his part of the facts of the matter[11]), but on his allowing himself to be carried along by language and the ambiguities that it contains and exploiting it, following an instinct for what will defeat the other person, without himself understanding the facts of the matter. Precisely because the sophist's logos, with its agonistic goals, does not make explicit or stick to the sense in which it is intended in each case, it falls prey itself to these ambiguities when someone else uses them against it. Socrates, on the other hand, keeps his eye on the subject matter even in these circumstances. Just because what is important to him is not refutation, as such, but liberating his opponent for a shared substantive inquiry, he can dispute with such an opponent—for whom neither the logical consistency of a train of thought nor the adequacy of what is asserted to the facts of the matter is a subject of concern as such, but only in respect to their effect [on an audience], and for whom, therefore, the appearance of consistency and the appearance of truth are no less important—on his own level. Socrates' logical traps are merely attempts to shorten the path of refutation, which could also be carried out in a rigorous manner. Con-

11. Plato makes this clear in his critique of rhetoric in the *Phaedrus*; see p. 84, below.

sequently, Socrates is unconcerned when a logical trap that he tries out fails to work (compare *Protagoras* 350c6): he did not simply fall into it; and when it fails, his process of refutation does not become disoriented, because its goal continues to be prescribed by a positive understanding of the facts of the matter. This is, incidentally, the way to assess Plato's logical errors in general: Socrates' logical traps are not meant to be the manipulations of a virtuoso technician which are simply applied where they promise success; instead, they are living forms of a process of seeking shared understanding which always has the facts of the matter themselves before it and which finds its criterion solely in its success in developing its capacity to see these facts. This has nothing to do, either positively or negatively, with the state of the science of logic. Today as well, every living substantive conversation is full of the impatience of illogic.

But in general Socrates conducts the refutation by developing his opponent's thesis logically until he arrives at consequences in connection with which a regard for generally accepted opinions, especially ethical ones, makes it impossible for the opponent to hold to the consequences of his thesis. This is the most radical form of refutation of all: to refute the opponent on the basis of substantive assumptions that are well established for him as well and that are incompatible with his own thesis. As an example, think of the threefold process of the refutation of sophistic hedonism in the *Gorgias*. From each of the theses that have been advanced (by Gorgias, Polus, and Callicles), consequences are deduced that are contrary to the substantive opinions of the advocates of these theses. Even the most radical defense of hedonism, by Callicles, is defeated by its own consequences. Callicles' hedonistic thesis involves ideas which, despite the thesis's own content, necessarily contradict hedonism. In order to safeguard what he really thinks, Callicles too has to distinguish between types of pleasure according to a standard that is not itself pleasure. The positive ideal of strength and aristocratic self-command which is Callicles' actual, tacit standard refutes the theoretical content of his hedonistic thesis.

The refuting conversation ends with a proof of ignorance. By doing so, it maintains until the end, in every one of its steps, the ironic premise that the one who is questioned is the knower, and the questioner is the ignorant one. The proof of the ignorance of the one who was presumed to know reveals the emptiness of the claim to knowledge which the questioned person makes. Thus the end of the conversation is characterized by ironic perplexity. This is apparently the sole outcome of the attempt to read a shared understanding, and it is in fact the first point of agreement. But this agreement regarding ignorance is the first precondition for gaining genuine knowledge. For this precondition implies two things: a shared ignorance and a shared need to know—that is, an understanding of the necessity of being able to make a genuine, rationally defensible claim to knowledge. To that extent already, then, refutation in the Socratic style is positive: not a process of reducing the other person to silence so as, tacitly, to mark oneself out as the knower, in contrast to him, but a process of arriving at a shared inquiry. But there are other ways as well in which the Socratic refutation is positive: first in that, through the refutation, what the thing that is sought after is sought *as* is laid bare; and second in that from this understanding a methodical conduct of research and questioning emerges, and with it the steadiness of progress toward a shared understanding, which distinguishes the Socratic conversational procedure from the eristic technique of refutation.

In refuting the answers that he receives to his question about the essence of aretē, Socrates makes visible what it is that this aretē is sought as, namely, knowledge about the good. The good, then, is knowledge's object; that is, it is the unitary focal point to which everything must be related and in relation to which human existence in particular understands itself in a unified way. The general character of the good is that it is that for the sake of which something is and thus, in particular, that for the sake of which man himself is. It is in the light of it that human beings understand themselves in their action and being at any given moment, in terms of what they have to do and to be. In this self-understanding, Dasein finds its footing, its stance

(*Stand*)—insofar as, knowing the good, it does everything that it does for the sake of this, its ownmost will to be able to be, and does not let itself be carried along by what it encounters in the world simply as it encounters it (as favorable [pleasant] or impeding [painful]) but, instead, wants to understand it in its usefulness for or harmfulness to a "for the sake of which" that goes back ultimately to its own "for the sake of which." Knowledge of the "for the sake of which" of its own being is thus what brings Dasein out of the confusion into which it is drawn by the disparateness and unfathomableness of what impinges on it from the world into a stance toward that, and thus into the constancy (*Ständigkeit*) of its own potentiality for being.

This general sense of the good is already clear in the *Protagoras*. There, what Socrates makes use of in his refutation is the claim to knowledge which the Sophists, as teachers of wisdom, and Protagoras above all (see *Protagoras* 318d, e), necessarily make. He forces his opponent to set up a conception of a uniform goal of Dasein, a concept of the good, and makes clear by the example of what is thus asserted to be good what is necessarily involved in the concept of the good.

For what this "for the sake of which" of one's own being has to be understood *as* is not settled by the fact that it must be an object of knowledge. As was shown above, the prevalent explication of ethics in terms of aretē, which Protagoras also advocates, is not able to give an accounting of what constitutes the goodness of aretē. If that is the case, and if what is understood as the good of Dasein must, nevertheless, be capable of an accounting, then it is not clear why one should understand oneself on the basis of aretē, and not, rather, on the basis of the most immediate experience of the good, one's own feeling of well-being, which, after all, seems to be incomprehensibly restricted by the requirements of ethics. For only this well-being seems to be exempted from all demands for an accounting by the fact that it thrusts itself forward of its own accord as what Dasein is willy-nilly "out for." But if Dasein's ultimate "for the sake of which" is its own well-being, then the fact that it wants to *understand* itself in terms of its well-being means that it must have disposition over that well-being through knowledge. But in that case it must be able to have disposition in advance over that which presses itself upon it from the world, as (pleasantly or unpleasantly) producing or destroying well-being. However unambiguously good one's own well-being may seem to be when one experiences it—as the "for the sake of which"—immediately, this does not provide a unified point of view for human Dasein as it wants to *understand* itself. For if Dasein wants to understand itself as good, the "for the sake of which" of its own being is not the way it feels at the moment but its well-being as a *constant* potential that it possesses. But as a constant potential it presents itself, by its own nature, not in a permanent duration but relative to a maximum amount of it over the whole duration of a life. But this requirement—that Dasein should have disposition, through knowledge, over a maximum amount of well-being—forces it not to let something's immediate attractiveness count as establishing its goodness (even though it was precisely that attractiveness that recommended it as good in the first place), inasmuch as what is pleasant now may lead to correspondingly greater pain later on. If well-being is the uniform goal of human existence's self-understanding, then everything that Dasein meets with in the world (and not only what it is currently meeting with but also what is to be expected) must be known in advance by it, in the measure of its attractiveness. Just that, then, which presents itself unambiguously as good, in its immediate presentness, should and must be "measured," if it is supposed to be "the good," in relation to something that is not contained in its immediate attractiveness itself. So it certainly cannot be the immediate attractiveness that constitutes the goodness. Something that is pleasant in itself—the sort of thing that is constituted by measurement in relation to a maximum amount of attractiveness—no longer has the character of present attractiveness at all. Thus it is no more the case that the immediate experience of well-being is an indubitable testimonial of its goodness than that any behavior that is regarded as virtuous is so automatically, without being justified by reference to the good itself. Thus the demand for an art of measuring pleasures—which alone could justify the claim of pleasure to be the good—succeeds, despite the impossibility of such an art, in making it clear what the good is sought as. Dasein understands itself in relation to what it is "for the sake of," not on the basis of how it feels at any present moment but on the basis of its highest and constant potential.

If we hold fast to the methodological point of this argumentation, we can also see why *huph' hēdonōn hēttasthai* (subjection to pleasures) is an *amathia* (ignorance). This *pathos* (passive condition) occurs as part of Dasein's aiming at a unified self-understanding and is itself a mode of understanding. It does not occur simply as the presence of a way in which one feels; instead, even as such, it is still a way of projecting oneself in relation to things to come—that is, it is a choice. It is just that the projection does not reach beyond the most immediate things to come, and thus it is thwarted in its intention. This self-understanding is a self-misunderstanding, insofar as Dasein cannot hold fast to itself in this projection in relation to what is pleasant. It is a choice that goes wrong in its choosing (*Protagoras* 355e), so that *metameleia* (regret) continually follows it, and the result is *planē* (wandering).

The question of whether Socrates is serious in his hedonistic equation of "pleasant" with "good" is one that arises only when the discussion of hedonism is detached from the context of the whole dialogue. The function of the hedonistic thesis here is only to help demonstrate that bravery is a kind of knowledge. In this proof, the emptiness of the Sophists' claim to knowledge about aretē is fully revealed. Protagoras had explicitly asserted that bravery could be detached from the other parts of aretē. In fact, of all the virtues, bravery seems to be most of all a matter of the character one is endowed with by nature, and in any case in no sense a form of knowledge. The proof that bravery, too, is a form of knowledge is, as it were, the most paradoxical possible version of Socrates' thesis. (The brave person would be the one who knows that what the coward flees from is not something to be feared at all. Taken literally, this would seem to be entirely beyond the realm of bravery.) If the equation of pleasant and good is meant to serve this paradoxical thesis, it is no more a serious solution of the problem of the good than what is proved from it is already a solution of the problem of aretē (where one should compare the explicit refutation, in the *Laches* 196d ff., of the definition of bravery that is given in the *Protagoras*). Rather, this equation has an exactly parallel paradoxical quality in itself. For, according to it, what is truly pleasant would not be pleasant things in their present attractiveness, but both pleasant and unpleasant things insofar as they contribute to the completed whole of how Dasein fares. The methodological point of the imagined art of measurement, then, is to show that an understanding of Dasein must understand present things in terms of non-present ones and can grant them goodness only in such a relation. Thus this Socratic course of argumentation allows us to see what the good must (in any case) be sought as: namely, the central thing on the basis of which human being can understand itself. So the positive point of Socratic refutation consists not only in achieving a positive perplexity but also—by the same token—in explaining what knowledge really is and what alone should be recognized as knowledge. It is only in the concept of the good that all knowledge is grounded; and it is only on the basis of the concept of the good that knowledge can be justified.

The ultimate possibility of arriving at a shared understanding depends upon having in common a pre-understanding of the good. By going back to this ultimate reason-giver, the thing for the sake of which something exists, the latter becomes understandable in its being, and thus agreement about it becomes attainable. All further agreement is to be developed on the basis of this one.

This pre-understanding of what is sought, as that on the basis of which things are understandable and thus as that on the basis of which justification is possible, determines the character of the search itself.

Dasein must be able to justify itself in each case of its being towards something, insofar as it makes a claim to knowledge. But this means that Dasein must understand itself in each case on the basis of that in terms of which—as its proper potential—it constantly understands itself. Also, insofar as Dasein wants to have a secure disposition over the entity which it is toward in each case (whether in practical dealings with the entity or merely in knowing it), it must understand that entity in its being—in its own proper potential.

Thus the requirement of accountability that Dasein imposes on itself in this way and that is continually imposed on it by others requires it to have disposition over itself, with respect to what its being is for the sake of, and (by the same token) over the entity which it is toward in each case, in respect to what the being of this entity is for the sake of. But knowing disposition over something is given only in the logos, in the appropriation of what underlies the entity as *whatever it is*. Only in the logos is Dasein itself, as well as the entity that it is toward in each case, understood in such a way that Dasein, in its being toward the entity, lives in the security of having disposition over itself and the entity. What is required, then, is coming to an understanding about the being of oneself and the entity. Now all coming to an understanding about something presupposes, of course, that the thing about which one is supposed to come to an understanding is understood by both parties as one and the same thing. Before one can come to an understanding or give an accounting of how one ought to think about or deal with something in a particular respect, there needs to be assurance that it is understood in whatever it is by virtue of its being. Thus the first concern of all dialogical and dialectical inquiry is a *care for the unity and sameness* of the thing that is under discussion.

Inasmuch as Dasein always already allows itself to conduct its life on the basis of an explicated understanding of itself and of the world, however, the requirement of an accounting has the character, initially, of a testing of these always pre-existing explications against the idea of a rational grounding—on the basis of what one's own being and the being of the entity are for the sake of—of each instance of being toward something. Insofar as the search for the grounding that gives an accounting is a shared search and has the character of a testing, it operates, fundamentally, not by one person's making an assertion and awaiting confirmation or contradiction by the other person, but by both of them testing the logos to see whether it is refutable and by both of them agreeing in regard to its eventual refutation or confirmation. All testing sets up the proposition to be tested not as something for one person to defend, as belonging to him or her, and for the other person to attack, as belonging to the other, but as something "in the middle." And the understanding that emerges is not primarily an understanding resulting from agreement with others but an understanding with oneself. Only people who have reached an understanding with themselves can be in agreement with others.

Part II: Plato's Dialectic and the Motive of Coming to an Understanding

Section 6: The Dialectic of the *Phaedo* and the *Republic*

The accounting that is called for is an accounting *for* something; that is, it is meant to be an adequate definition of the thing for which an accounting is required. Thus the testing of the logos which is characteristic of Socratic thought is a testing that asks whether the logos provides for the thing in its manifoldness the unitary reason on the basis of which it is to be understood as always the same (in its being). In the Socratic conversation, then, every logos necessarily begins with the character of a hypothesis only. Its "strength" lies not in an irrefutability that is secure in advance of any measurement against the facts of the matter and that forestalls possible contradiction in advance but only in its substantive accomplishment of grasping a manifold reality in its unitary selfsame being. Thus Socrates calls the hypothesis of the *eidos* (form) the strongest one: the hypothesis, that is, that something that is greater than something else is greater not by virtue of the amount by which, in an individual case, one person seems to be greater than another person; for the same person can after all be smaller in relation to another person by just the same amount. Instead, everything that is greater is so only by virtue of greatness itself. Only this logos seems safe to Socrates and never comes to a fall (*Phaedo* 100a ff.). This hypothesis of the eidos exhibits the *general* principle of the logos we are looking for: that it is the reason or cause (*aitia*)—which is to say that for all possible cases of the eidos in question, it is the thing in which they are uniformly comprehended as what they are. What follows from this aitia is revealed as belonging to the being of this eidos. An accounting can be required for this logos in its turn, but not before the claim of the logos itself to provide the grounds for what was to be grounded has been tested—that is, not before one is sure that it does comprehend the entities in question, in their manifoldness, uniformly. Part of the point of giving an accounting for something is that one does not give an accounting, in turn, of what it appears that one should understand it as until one has shown that the thing is comprehended therein as what it always is. For only then is one sure that in giving the accounting for this logos, one will also compel the other person to agree about the facts of the matter in the case in question. Only when the hypothesis has proved to be adequate, as aitia, to what it has been assigned to as its aitia will one be prepared to give an accounting for it oneself, if arriving at a shared understanding requires this. And thus, in principle, every logos must be tested in this way, to see whether it really uniformly grounds what it is supposed to give an accounting for, until one arrives at a final sufficient reason, which itself is evident (*einsichtig*) and requires no further accounting. The *Republic* designates as this reason the idea of the good, and in the *Phaedo*, as well, Socrates' critique of Anaxagoras's "nous" shows that his hypothesis of *eidē* (pl. of *eidos*) can be grounded ultimately only by the idea of the good—that is, that the claim made by this hypothesis is fulfilled only if what it posits as the being of a thing is grasped in terms of what this thing itself is "for the sake of." In this context the essential thing in this well-known description of the procedure of hypothesis is that the procedure has the character of a methodical advance, which continually confirms the substantive claim of the logos (in each case) to be the uniform ground (the reason or cause) by testing it against the thing that is to be grounded. If one finally arrives by this route at a sufficient reason—

that is, at a logos in which the being of the thing is immediately evident in its goodness (that is, in what it always is and must be)—then in the unity of this reason, the organized manifold of what follows from it is appropriated as well, and thus the reason's claim to appropriate the entity in what it always is (must be) in accordance with its being is fulfilled. In this testing of the logos against what it claims to ground, it distinguishes itself fundamentally from the way in which "antilogicians" (*antilogikoi*, persons skilled in disputation) discuss reasons or causes and consequences, when they mix both things together, appealing to the unity of the reason or cause when the multiplicity of the consequences is in question, and vice versa, simply in order to flatter themselves with the appearance of superiority. The fact that the same thing, seen in its reason or cause, is one, while everything that is one in itself is, taken together, many things, seems to them to be a contradiction, by which they make any real logos impossible. On the other hand, an effort that is really aimed at obtaining access to the facts of the matter cannot be confused by this "contradiction." Precisely by exhibiting the many as one, this effort has grasped it in the aspect as which it is conceivable at all in the logos. In this way the effort succeeds in exhibiting, from the thing's ultimate grounding (that which it is for the sake of), what always constitutes its unitary being, and thus in arriving, by way of a being *toward* the thing, at a shared understanding.

Thus what is accomplished by this hypothesis of the eidos—a hypothesis that is explicitly described as "simple" (*amathēs*, 105e1; *euēthōs*, 100d4)—is that by uncovering what always makes up the being of an entity, one arrives for the first time at the possibility of recognizing entities in their capacity as grounds for this entity. For something that is necessarily given together with what constitutes the being of entities also necessarily belongs to the individual entity. So, for example, the hypothesis that everything warm is made warm by warmth can be replaced by the "more precise" hypothesis that it is made warm by fire, insofar as wherever there is warmth there must always be fire. (In the *Phaedo*, this necessary linkage of something with something, a linkage whose necessity is guaranteed only by the hypothesis of the eidos, underlies the real proof of the immortality of the soul. So it is for the purpose of proving this kind of necessary linkage of something with something that Socrates introduces the procedure of hypothesis.) So the "simplicity" of this hypothesis is due to the fact that it is one that posits as the ground of something not another entity but the being of the entity itself. But it is only by grasping what the entity, in accordance with its being, necessarily is that one can discern what necessarily belongs to it. Thus the procedure of hypothesis, and of dialectic in general, has the goal of comprehending entities, through the logos, in their being, so as to be able to have disposition over them in their ability to be together with other things. Only on the basis of this grasp of its being can one give an accounting with regard to one's own being toward it, which is what is involved, in general, in reaching an understanding *about* it.

Thus the testing of the hypothesis is a twofold process. In the first place, its adequacy to the facts of the matter, whose uniform ground it is supposed to be, is tested against those facts, which are of course always already in view. Only then is one free to give a further accounting in regard to this hypothesis: to ask about *its* ground. For only then can a grounding of the ground achieve a more precise grounding of the facts of the matter in question and promote an understanding about it.

The point of the dialectic is to arrive at a positive relation to the problem of the ground (the reason or cause), the problem that is posed by the idea of knowledge. This is made clear by the context in which Socrates presents the hypothesis of the eidos here. He tells of his anticipation and his disappointment in regard to Anaxagoras's "nous."

What he had anticipated was that here the claim that is contained in true knowledge would find fulfillment: the claim to knowledge of the reason or cause. Nothing that other speculators in natural philosophy tended to call "aitia" satisfies the claim that is implied by the meaning of "aitia": the claim that the thing of which it is the reason or cause is always determined by and must always be grounded in this unchanging ground, so that in assigning this ground, this reason or cause, one would arrive at a secure disposition over the entity in advance. Thus Socrates is *porrō tou oiesthai tēn aitian eidenai* (far from thinking that he knows the cause) (96e6). When Anaxagoras now teaches that the nous is the cause, this arouses anticipation in Socrates. For if something spiritual, if reason, determines things in their being, then this means that the consequence of the reason that determines them is the reasonableness, the goodness of what is (and also the being of what is good). In this case the nous, as what determines entities with a view to their being good, would be the unchanging reason or cause on the basis of which entities would be at our disposition as what they must be. In the nous, the search for the reason or cause would come to rest (98a).

But Socrates learns, to his disappointment, that Anaxagoras's nous does not at all accomplish what he has expected of it. Rather than *its* determining entities as what they have to be, every other possible entity is cited as the reason or cause. But what is supposed to be the beginning of a thing's coming into being in this way is not what fundamentally underlies the thing that comes into being, insofar as such a beginning is not already referred to this thing as *its* beginning—does not constitute it, as something that determined it through an anticipatory view of its being would do. This means that assigning this supposed reason or cause does not result in gaining a secure disposition over the thing in advance. For this beginning is gained by going back to another thing and yet another thing, things which themselves have such and such qualities, but without its being the case that the being of the thing that was to be grounded is determined by these qualities. And thus the beginning, the supposed reason or cause of the thing, is itself another entity and cannot be the thing's reason or cause because it is not inherent in the beginning that its outcome is this thing and nothing else. What underlies the thing in this mechanical chain of causes is, after all, defined precisely by the fact that it can also have different consequences: the same bones and sinews that allow Socrates to sit in prison could equally well have been a reason or cause of his going—and were equally ready to carry him—to Megara or Thebes. The supposed reason or cause (which does in fact underlie the thing as something that is always there: the fact that my body consists of bones and sinews) with which the determination of the thing starts (and which would thus be an *archē* [beginning, principle]) is precisely of the least consequence to the thing itself. The real reason or cause, on the other hand (Socrates explains, using the example of his own behavior), the reason or cause that is posited when he claims to act on the basis of reason, would be that it is good this way—better than if he had escaped from prison. And thus, in general, one demands of a reason or cause that when it is assigned, the way the thing is, is understood—that is, the thing is comprehended as being good as it is or as being best as it is, as what it must be always would imply. To understand the nature of the things in *this* way—which is the only thing that Socrates would call "understanding"—is something that Anaxagoras does not teach him.

Because no one teaches him that, he turns, in his "second voyage," to the *logoi* (pl. of logos). This does not mean that he reduces or abandons the demanding sense of reason or cause which is involved in understanding; on the contrary, now he seeks the reason or cause, the *alētheia tōn ontōn* (truth of things), where this demanding claim itself originates, which is in language and in the understanding that is already invested in it. What one is looking for is, after all, a reason or cause that *stays the same*: for each entity, that which it at bottom (*im Grunde*: in its reason or cause) always is. Now, this claim is fulfilled, in a certain way, in *language*. Language already contains an understanding of the world in those respects in which it remains the same. For the words by which we designate things already have the character of a universality that remains the same. Every word has its meaning, which is one, by comparison with the manifoldness of what can be designated by means of it. What we intend by the word—the meaning, with the help of which we are able to address entities—is something universal that remains the same. It provides more than a mere indication of something that is given in intuition at the moment. As something designated by the word, the given is already at the same time understood as something universal, so that I intend it in this way and can give it to myself through speech, without such a thing being given to my senses. Thus language makes the identical universality of a nature stand out from the manifold of what is given in changing perception and designates each entity by means of what it always is. And in this way, as the giving of names, it is a first appropriation (through understanding) of the world. This is also true in the case of proper names, inasmuch as an entity that is named such and such is one that I can call in that way henceforth, that I can intend as the same thing despite its absence at the moment, and that I can even present to others, so that, knowing its name, they can henceforth have it at their disposition in the same way. Thus God introduced the first human being to the enjoyment and possession of the creation by bringing the created things to him "to see what he would call them." In principle, every individual entity can have its proper name in this way; as something known to man in its individuality, it is named by him. Thus the proper name is universal insofar as it names something individual as it is known in its identity with itself and, being the same thing, is intended *as* the same thing. So this construction of proper names becomes possible for man only when he becomes able to differentiate and recognize the individuality of what is named. Originally he understands every name as a general term, for in establishing himself in the world, man takes an interest in what a number of individuals have in common. In the process of providing for himself in his existence, the one thing and the other *mean the same thing* to him. A lack of interest in the individuality of single things—or, positively, an interest only in what they identically share—is the origin of the general name. What man thinks of in the entities as significant for him and for his Dasein-like dealings with the world is something general. And to the extent that the individual does not acquire familiarity with his world by his individual efforts but does so in a shared life with others (family, neighbors, and so forth), he has the world presented to him by others in terms of what it means to man. And so he learns language by at the same time learning the world. The sharedness of vital interests unfolds into a sharedness of understanding of the world in the development of language, in which those who have already come to an understanding in this way understand one another and can come to ever new understandings. So the intersubjectivity of language is based on an intersubjectivity of understanding of the world, and the general meaning of names is based on the structure of this understanding as one that is guided by practical interests.

Thus language is by no means a mere *image* of entities. And if this second voyage seeks the reason or cause of entities in the logoi, rather than in looking directly at the world, this does not mean merely contenting oneself with an image. One misunderstands this Socratic turning to the logoi, with its absolute bindingness for classical Greek philosophy, if one misses the irony with which it is introduced as a second voyage.[12] So that we should not miss it, but understand that this way is superior to immediate sense experience, in particular, Plato has Socrates say this explicitly, albeit with the irony of a "perhaps" (99e6). In fact, the immediate sense experience of entities apprehends them precisely not in their reality—in what they always and truly are—but as mere eikōnes, images. To the senses they show themselves ficklely, now this way and now that. This is what would much more properly be called a "mere" image. For an image is, after all, precisely what is variable, in contrast to the original, which remains. An entity can be reflected in one kind of image or another, while itself remaining the same. Logos, on the other hand—language and the understanding of language—is not an image of this kind. For meaning is precisely what is identical. What is meant by a word is something that remains while points of view fluctuate. The thing that remains in this way and is posited as the cause or reason is the lasting aspect of appearance

12. For this reason Stenzel's use of this passage in support of his attempted demonstration of an effort by Plato to mark himself off from Socrates seems to me to be mistaken.

(eidos): that which always makes up the thing—its essence. Thus one can in fact find in language what Socrates seeks: a reason or cause that remains the same, and, by assigning which, one comprehends the entity in what it always is. The identity of what one intends is presupposed as the sameness of the eidos, and thus one comprehends, in the unity of the cause or reason, the manifoldness—previously beyond the reach of comprehension—of the changing entity that presents itself differently to the senses from one time to the next.

So what is gained by this hypothesis of the eidos? Its trustworthiness is undeniable. This logos does indeed exclude the opposite one. And that is just what the hypothesis accomplishes: that the reason or cause, the ground, holds only for what presupposes it, so that it has its own ground in the thing that it grounds, and it sets out beforehand just this ground, on the basis of the thing that it grounds, for it. What is gained, then, is an unambiguous identity, which is a positive solution to the fundamental problem of dialectic, that the one is many and the many are one.

On the other hand, the "simplicity" of this hypothesis is clear enough, and we have seen that in fact, as Plato sees it, it is not an end but a first beginning. What it does, to use Hegel's words, is only "to convert the immediate phenomenon into the form of reflected being."[13]

But it is only when the logos of the eidos is opened up for repeated testing and giving of accountings that dialectic is really distinguished as the resolve to give a final accounting for entities by understanding them on the basis of their being. To set up assumptions from whose unity the multiplicity of what they ground necessarily follows is, after all, already the business of the mathematician, and just this capacity—by which mathematicians are distinguished—of

13. *Hegel's Science of Logic* (cited in n. 2 above), p. 459; *Wissenschaft der Logik*, 2:80. It would be a separate task, and (as the result would show) a fruitful one, to interpret Hegel's dialectic of the ground (both in the Jena Logic and in the Great Logic) on the basis of its relation, which history also suggests, to the problem of Plato's dialectic.

seeing isolated facts of knowledge together, in the unity of a coherent system of grounding, already makes mathematicians, in this respect, dialecticians.[14] But mathematicians themselves give no accounting for

14. In connection with the description of the education of the later guardians, in the *Republic* 537c, the capacity to bring the *mathēmata* together "synoptically," according to their affinities, is explicitly described as a dialectical capacity, though in such a way that the actual exercise of dialectic as such belongs to a later stage in the guardians' education (537d6 f.; see also 531d67). The *oikeiotēs tōn mathematōn* here is not to be understood exclusively or in the first place as the kinship between the scientific disciplines (as Schleiermacher, Natorp, and Stenzel assume on the basis of the doctrine of science at 521–534) but rather, as one can see from 531c and d, as the substantive belonging together of things that are developed out of the same premises. The passage at 537c relates to 536d and e—the "playful" teaching—as the serious scientific appropriation of the facts of the matter (*monē . . . hē toiautē mathēsis bebaios* [c4]). "Understanding" substantive systems of grounding is dialectic *within* the positive sciences as well. Common to these two stages of learning (the playful and the serious), then, is the realm of the propaedeutic sciences. (Thus *paidia*, at 537c1, would be more in keeping with the meaning than *paideia*; at least in *paideia* one should not miss the echo of the *paizontas* at 537a1, which should usually be heard as part of the message elsewhere in Plato as well, and which often makes it almost impossible to decide between the readings *paideia* and *paidia*.) On a related subject, Stenzel's "refutation" (*Plato's Method of Dialectic*, trans. D. J. Allen [New York, 1964], pp. 79ff. [= *Studien zur Entwicklung der platonischen Dialektik von Sokrates zu Aristoteles* (Leipzig and Berlin, 1917 and 1931), pp. 49ff.]) of the relation of the *koinōnia* (fellowship) (531d1) that is referred to here to the later form of the dialectic is outwardly justified but fails to appreciate the substantive connection. For the *mathēmata* that are under discussion here are "the sciences" only in the sense of the word that refers to *objects*. So their "fellowship" and "kinship" are on the same level as the kinship of numbers (531c–d). The search for the *koina* of the mathematical sciences (F. Solmsen, *Die Entwicklung der aristotelischen Logik und Rhetorik* [Berlin, 1929], p. 117) is of the same kind as the search for the *dia ti* of

their ultimate assumptions but concentrate solely on making sure that the entities that are their objects are deducible from those assumptions. That is, they do not take these assumptions as assumptions, but rather as though they were really the archai of entities. The dialectician, on the other hand, sees that assumptions as such do not yet present a final grounding of what is deducible from them. He regards them as only the threshold to an ascent to higher assumptions, by which to push on to the ultimate source of grounding which alone no longer has the character of an assumption but is the real archē of the whole—that is, that on the basis of which the whole is determined and understandable in its being. But this primary thing, which has no assumptions prior to it, is also seen as the ground of everything that is included under it. Just because it is gained, as the ultimate source of grounding, by an ascent from one assumption to another, each of which is seen in terms of what is deducible from it, it makes it possible to carry out the descent (to the things that are grounded) in such a way that the necessary being of entities is deduced from it. This well-known train of thought in the *Republic* (511b) goes beyond the description in the *Phaedo* in one decisive respect: by adding an absolute beginning that has no prior assumptions. In the *Phaedo* we hear only of "something sufficient"—that is, the dialogue describes the procedure of dialectical progress from one prior assumption to the one preceding it, with a view solely to the always relatively limited

---

the *sumphonia* of the numbers. Accordingly, *ta chudēn mathēmata*, which are learned effortlessly, are not the isolated scientific disciplines with the internal rigor of their connectedness; rather, this *chudēn* characterizes the kind of effortless learning that precedes all "science" and is unconcerned about the connections between the things and about their reasons. This is not to deny that the requirement of *sunagōgē* necessarily extends, in the end, to the connections between all the realms of things that are the subjects of the component mathematical disciplines; but it does so precisely as a mere continuation of the tendency toward systematic grounding which inquires, *within* the individual realms, about the grounds of their connections.

horizons of concrete processes of coming to an understanding, which are processes in which the giving of accountings reaches its goal when one's partner's demands for an accounting cease and agreement is reached. In the *Republic*, on the other hand, it seems that what needs no further accounting is determined not in terms of the relative situation of coming to an understanding, but absolutely, as a beginning that is free, in itself, of prior assumptions: that is, as the idea of the good. But the question arises as to whether the relation between the two lines of thought is, unambiguously, that in the *Republic* this absolute beginning, the idea of the good, takes the place of relative beginnings of shared understanding. Is the unity of this idea absolute generality, in which, in mutually understood logical sequence, the differentiation of things by their particular contents is based? Or do this beginning and this unity express an inquiry that is aimed in a different direction?

Plato says that the idea of the good goes beyond all entities because it is an *aitia* (cause, reason). It is the ground of the being of everything and thus at the same time the ground of cognition of everything (508ff.). It is this idea that makes all the many just and beautiful things "good" and thus enables us to understand them in their being. Thus the ascent to the presuppositionless archē is for the sake of the descent. It provides the ultimate guarantee of the knowledge claim which cognition of being as the ground of entities makes in each case (*Republic* 533d). But this evidently does not mean that the idea of the good is something that is one in its *content* and to which one could recur in reason-giving accountings because agreement is the rule in this most general, presuppositionless certainty. The idea of the good is not an entity any longer, at all, but an ultimate ontological principle. It is not a substantive determination of entities but the thing that makes everything that exists understandable in its being (517c). It is only in this universal ontological function that the idea of the good is in fact the ultimate basis of *all* processes of coming to an understanding—not as a highest-level, universal eidos but as the formal character of everything that can really be called "understood," which means, however, as the angle of vision to which the claim to understanding itself submits itself. In this respect, the idea of the good is nothing but the ideal of complete cognizability and cognition.

But what all this articulates is nothing but what Socrates had already called for continually in the *Phaedo*: the ground of all moral action, in terms of which man understands himself when coming to a moral decision, but also the ground, the reason or cause, in terms of which all entities in the world can be understood in the way that they are. In our context, in which the importance of this approach for the problem of ontology is left to one side,[15] the question is how these positions taken in the *Republic* can be understood as a positive solution to the dialectical problem of the one and the many. For the connection between these positions and those of the *Phaedo* is sufficient to justify us in assuming that the upshot will be such a positive solution to the problem, rather than a concealment of it. The universal claim made by the solution in the *Republic* must also be demonstrable in the case of the Socratic problem of the unity and multiplicity of the virtues, which is the key concern for Plato's Socrates both as a question and as a clear requirement of moral consciousness.

Now Stenzel has interpreted *diairesis* (division), which is developed in detail and practiced with methodical consciousness in the later dialogues but which actually plays no role, as such, in the methodological discussions of the *Phaedo* and the *Republic*, as a consequence of Plato's grappling with the problem of the one and the many. This, he says, first became a pressing task for Plato when the Ideas began to free themselves from their origin in Socrates' problematic of aretē. In the *Phaedo* and the *Republic*, we are told, dialectics, which is bound to the circle of Socratic problems (which admittedly did

15. Since this was written, Martin Heidegger has indicated, in his "Vom Wesen des Grundes," in the *Festschrift Edmund Husserl* (Halle, 1929), pp. 98ff. (= *The Essence of Reasons*, trans. T. Malick [Evanston, Ill., 1969], pp. 90ff.), the ontological problem that is involved here.

include the being of things in the world, in the concept of aretē), is still only *synopsis* (seeing all together). At this stage of Plato's dialectic, the problem of the one and the many is still latent.

But the question arises as to whether it is not, from the very beginning, only in its unity that the double direction of a synoptic and a diaeretic motion constitutes the essence of a grounding that gives an accounting. After all, the teleological unity of the idea of the good springs precisely from the dialectical problem of the unity and multiplicity of aretē. And this problem is so far from being latent in the early dialogues that, beginning with the *Protagoras*, it represents the guiding theme of Socratic elenctics. Both things are given in the facts of moral experience: the way in which customary morals are composed of a multiplicity of individual virtues[16] and the unity of the person who conscientiously adheres to them. When the taken-for-granted binding force of a public morality loosens, so that the individual begins to feel a need for an accounting for what he or she does and omits doing, this means that the dominant moral explication of Dasein becomes questionable both in regard to what is to be understood by each of the individual virtues and in regard to the way they combine to form the unity of the person who practices them. Thus the dialectical demand for an accounting finds both things present: the demand for a unified moral understanding of Dasein and the demand for a grounding of the differential multiplicity of the aspects of such understanding which the public morality conceives as virtues; and it has to deal dialectically precisely with the explanation of this puzzling coincidence of the one and the many in moral consciousness.

The aporetic dialogues about virtue teach this clearly. It is only an apparent matter of course (to which Socrates appeals ironically)—and in reality the ultimate root of all confusion—that people

16. That the unity of the aretē ideal produces the individual virtues only through progressive differentiation, as Stenzel says in his *Realencyclopädie* article on "Sokrates" (cited in n. 3 above), col. 834, contradicts both the historical facts and the essence of the ethos.

regard it as easier to define a part of virtue than virtue as a whole. For when this is assumed, the individual virtue is, from the start, external, understood as the mere common acceptance of the appearance of a kind of behavior, an acceptance that cannot fulfil the claim to knowledge of aretē. For an understanding that aims at aretē must be a unified understanding of Dasein in all its possible forms of being and behavior—in other words, a unified understanding based on what Dasein itself is for the sake of. There is no way for behavior to justify itself except on the basis of this looking toward the good itself. A preexisting agreement, for example, about what bravery requires of the individual—the agreement that constitutes the accepted, customary norm—does not give an accounting in the required sense. All agreements on the basis of customary norms are questionable from the point of view of the moral conscience. For the latter wants to understand itself in its behavior, and the kind of agreement with others that one has in view in obeying customary norms is not sufficient for this purpose. For what is "good" cannot just appear and be accepted as such; it must be good in reality. Because man is concerned about his being, everything that he encounters is good or bad for him, as he understands himself. What is supposed to benefit him must benefit him in reality, not only in appearance and in the opinion of other people. For he himself experiences it as what it is. Thus the "good" is the point of view from which an unconditional understanding of one's own action and being, not dependent on or formed by the acceptance and opinion of others, is required, just because the good means the beneficial, in the unconditional sense of something to which everything else, in turn, proves to be either beneficial or harmful. The good, then, is the beneficial without qualification—a possession whose enjoyment is not only salutary for one's being but itself makes up one's authentic potential for being. Thus the "good" for an entity is not only a good that is good for something. It is not something that it has but something that it itself is: understanding of itself in its highest possibility of being. Everything beneficial that occurs is an act of an understanding. When something is experienced as good, then it is understood in relation to what it is good for and, just by that fact, is understood in its being. Thus the ultimate basis of this understanding, the good itself, is at the same time the understood possibility of Dasein itself—what it can be. And that is: something that understands itself in a unified way. It is no accident that it is precisely in the *Republic* that a positive understanding of what an individual aretē is, is achieved for the first time. For in the larger image of the state, the connection of the individual virtues with the idea of the good is presented in the unity of an order whose uppermost element is the *phronēsis* (intelligence) that sees the idea of the good itself and precisely by so doing understands the being of all the members that comply with this order (the other parts of the soul), on the basis of the idea of the good, as the manifold unity of the aretē that makes up man. Just as it is part of the essence of the ordered constitution that the individual orders himself in relation to this order, so the order of the individual's own self (the *psychē*) is not something commanded by others, in the form of a customary ethic; rather, it produces itself through the unity of Dasein's self-understanding.

Thus the need to bring together synoptically the many into the unity of the ultimate ground does indeed occupy the foreground of the theory of dialectic in the *Phaedo* and the *Republic*. But as a unified understanding of oneself, being dialectical means precisely to use this understanding in the multiplicity of situations so as to keep oneself in the organized unity of an order. Insofar as this ultimate unity is a cause or reason (a ground), this idea of a ground is accompanied by the *idea* of grounding as well, and thus necessarily by the whole structure of dialectic. After all, the only reason why the synopsis that leads to the highest unity of the good is "dialectic" is because one can deduce from this unity of the ground the multiplicity of what is grounded in its necessary being. Of course this unfolding process does not have to have the explicitly conceptual character of the "division" of a genus into species. But insofar as this giving of an accounting is supposed to ground entities as they are concretely experienced in each case, it is necessary to show them—precisely in the particularity in which they are experienced—as something that they always are. It will become evident that the idea of an ultimate indivisible unity (*atomon eidos*) is only the conceptual formulation of what the thing that is to be grounded, in every grounding, is understood as. But as a deduction of what follows from the highest universal ground, grounding is, after all, separation. And the fact that this demonstration based on the ultimate intelligible ground represents a cogent appropriation of the (already familiar) thing in its necessary being is due precisely to the relation of ground and consequence which is unfolded in the ascent to the ultimate ground. The whole emphasis of the presentation of dialectic in the *Phaedo* and the *Republic* is, after all, on the fact that the logos's ability to appropriate the thing in its being depends upon protecting the relation between the unity of the ground and the multiplicity of what is grounded from being confused by the sophistic art of refutation. Thus a positive relation to the problem of the one and the many is required here too, already (and cannot be assigned only to a later development of the problem of dialectic), if the dialectician is to be positively distinguished from the "antilogician."

So Sophistic antilogic has to do with the problem of the one and the many exactly as Socratic dialectic does, but with an eristic intention, not one directed at the facts of the matter. Its point of departure, just like that of dialectic, is the claim to grounding which is made in knowledge itself, and it likewise employs language for its technique of refutation. Plato says of it that it confuses grounds with consequences (*Phaedo* 101e). This must mean that in setting up an *antilogos*, it takes (precisely) the consequence as the cause or reason (the ground), and the ground as the consequence. This is possible, however, only because language always understands and addresses a thing as something concrete with manifold characteristics, which thus show themselves in the thing as equally constant and lasting. Each of these characteristics, then, can be defined as a ground insofar as one takes it as the *essential* one. In linguistic understanding itself there is no indication as to what is essential and what is inessential in a thing, insofar as in assigning all the characteristics that it assigns, language proceeds in the same way, with understandable and identical meanings. If one regards one of them as a ground, the others are understood as merely being added to it. But insofar as this is not unambiguous, no such ground—which is a ground only in view of other things, which are merely added to it—exhausts the thing itself. Every such ground is a one-sided ground. What it fails to deliver—which consequently cancels the certainty of understanding to which it lays claim—is the grounding or linking together of all these facets, which alone constitutes the unchanging unity of the thing. If someone is a head taller (*Phaedo* 101a), this means: than this particular other person. For he or she is also shorter by the very same head—shorter, that is, than that third person. So the head—this particular entity—is not *in itself* the reason or cause of someone's being taller but only in regard to this other person. When the points of view are changed, something else can become the reason or cause, or (as the case may be) the head can become the reason or cause for something else: for being shorter. Both characteristics are true characterizations of the entity: namely, of this person in respect to his or her size; but the connection between them and a unit of magnitude is not grounded in the supposed ground (the head), which is not at all a ground extracted from the thing itself but rather is taken as a ground by going beyond the thing to other things that it is not.

But such "grounds," which fall prey to antilogical quibbling, are precisely the grounds to which the traditional explanation of nature was accustomed to tracing entities back. So it is the manner of explanation employed by the traditional philosophy of nature that makes this antilogical confusion of ground and consequence possible. Now this dialectic of the ground, which abrogates talk of grounds and understanding, is overcome in a positive manner by Socrates' hypothesis of the eidos. For what is assigned here as the ground is precisely the intended unity of the thing as the unchanging ground. The hypothesis of the eidos is a logos that cannot be brought to a fall, insofar as it understands the thing not on the basis of something else, which it is not, but on the basis of what it itself is intended as, at that very moment. Because it is *only* a hypothesis, it is impossible to refute it on the basis of a characterization of the thing which is gained from some other point of view. It is the common character as which it is intended in advance of any determination by reference to other things.

So in testing each hypothesis against the multiplicity of what it is supposed to ground as a unity, a further accounting becomes possible in the positive form of a progressive grounding, which protects the hypothesis from the eristic leap back into the multiplicity of the phenomena that are comprehended under the unity that is to be grounded. If in this way an agreement about the thing is finally reached—that is, an understanding of what it remains unchanged as—this needs no further accounting. Whether this is the idea of the good itself (in the realm of the moral conscience's unconditional demand, which transcends every specific content, for an accounting) or a characterization of the thing which is substantive but sufficiently general that there is no dispute about it, in any case the thing itself can be grounded, on this basis, in its necessary being, by a methodical advance from ground to consequence. Nor is a grounding of the thing which is other than the grounding in the eidos achieved in Plato's developed theory of diaeresis—not, indeed, that he hoped for any such grounding, as further reflection, and reflection with a view to the *Philebus* in particular, will show.

Section 7: The Theory of Dialectic in the *Phaedrus*

The motive of coming to an understanding becomes most clearly apparent as the root of the theory of dialectic in Plato's critique of rhetoric in the *Phaedrus*. Here we also find the plainest presentation of dialectic. For both its structure and its function are expounded here by reference to the examples of speech that are presented. In this concrete application, dialectic is observed at work, as it were, and not only illustrated by examples, which could, after all, be arranged by the theory in advance. The *Phaedrus*'s doctrine of the soul, which is contained in the myth in the third speech, will be left aside here.

The important thing here is only the method of speech that is actually employed and its conceptual explication in the second part of the dialogue.

It is certainly no accident that the theory of dialectic, in its original motive of coming to an understanding, should be presented specifically in the context of the critique of rhetoric. In the situation of giving a speech, the original mode by which people can come to an understanding—namely, by questioning and answering—is impossible. For just that reason, the situation of giving a speech acquires exemplary importance in relation to the possibility of *developing language in itself into a sufficient means of coming to an understanding*. For a speaker who wants to talk other people into an opinion about something without being able to assure himself through questioning that his listeners are with him must exhibit the facts of the matter as what he wants them to be understood as. By an apparently cogent progress, starting from something in regard to the subject in question on which the speaker knows in advance that his listeners are in agreement with him, he must characterize the subject in its being in such a way that what he wants to demonstrate about it follows necessarily from this characterization. In the same way, the goal of dialectic is to comprehend the facts of the matter, in their being, on the basis of premises that are accepted as such by everyone. Thus, although it strives for persuasion rather than for true shared understanding, the art of rhetoric, as a semblance of such understanding, reflects its structures.

In fact, Plato shows that the skilful mastery of this semblance itself requires dialectical understanding. It is true that the speaker cannot set forth how the facts of the matter really stand but must present them in such a way that they will be evident to his listeners in the light in which he wants them to be regarded—that is, he must consider what the listeners themselves are and what their opinion is. But insofar as his goal is, nevertheless, to bring it about, by working through prior opinions like these, that the subject matter is understood in the way that he himself regards it, this process of a supposedly cogent unveiling of the matter (an unveiling that actually depends on tricks) must be guided by an insight into the matter's true being and its true grounds. Deception is successful only when one gives out in place of the facts of the matter something that *looks like* them. So in order to be able to deceive, one must know what the facts themselves really are, so as always to be able to give out as the facts themselves what looks most similar to them and thus, step by step, to lead one's audience to the intended result (262a–b). When the facts are already recognized in what they are by all, such preparation will not be needed; instead, the speaker will be able to develop directly, on the basis of the shared understanding of them, what is to be done in regard to them. But when the facts are in dispute, he will have to take this path of exhibiting them to the hearer, through speech, in the way he himself sees them, in order to infer from their shared understanding the need for what he wants to happen in connection with these facts (263a ff.). But if this is really supposed to be achieved through a mastery of the art of speech and not through a blind routine (which as such could never be sure of success), it requires dialectical insight into what the facts of the matter really are and on what basis this being of theirs can be demonstrated.

That, then, is the first requirement: to make sure that what one is talking about is necessarily understood by the others as the same thing that one understands it as oneself. In the example used in the *Phaedrus* (237ff.), if one wants to convince someone that it is better to give oneself to a person who does not love one, then one must persuade him that love is something bad. But one can be sure of achieving this only if one is certain that the other person understands love as the same thing as one does oneself when one declares it to be bad. However, this agreement about what it is can be reached only (since love itself is a controversial subject) by first of all characterizing it as something that the other person already understands it as. The fact that it is an appetite is clear to everyone, though of course it is also clear that this characterization does not apply only to love. So it is necessary to determine what kind of appetite it is. Only if one has ensured in this way that the other person understands the same thing by love as one does oneself can one develop, from this understanding of its being, what kind of benefit or harm it represents for the person who is loved. Now in his first speech Socrates characterizes love more precisely as an *irrational* appetite—that is, as a kind of madness. In contrast to reasonable appetite (*sōphrosunē*), then, it is bad. The harm with which it threatens the boy is inferred from this characterization. Nevertheless, Socrates later describes this speech as a spurious logos, because it conflicts with the established fact that Eros is a god. Reflection on this fact makes clear the deception in the proof given in Socrates' first speech: it assumed that all madness is similar as far as badness is concerned (244a). But there is also the madness that is god-sent—this madness of love. If the speech had been intended to arrive at the proposed result by genuinely unfolding the facts, it would have had to show that this madness is sent to man to harm him (245b). Only then would the proof of its being bad be not only rhetorically compelling but also substantively valid—that is, valid for everything that we call *eros*. In his palinode Socrates shows that, on the contrary, this divine love-madness is given to human beings as a blessing.

In these two speeches Socrates makes visible the structural elements of dialectic, which alone, when skilfully manipulated, could make rhetoric into a real science (265c). The first of these elements is the synopsis of the manifold in experience into the unity of a view. The first requirement for speech is agreement about what that which the speech is about should be understood as. Only in this way will the speech achieve concord; that is, someone who wants to impart advice or a lesson must first secure a uniform understanding of what the speech is about, which everything subsequent must be understood in relation to (263e). If one omits this characterization of what the entity is in its being, one cannot be sure of remaining in harmony either with oneself or with one's listeners, insofar as one will say things that seem correct in view of something else which one happens (or the others happen) to understand the subject matter as but which are incompatible with what one previously understood it as (265d3–7, interpreted in the light of 237c1–5). Only by considering the uniform being of what is experienced in each case as eros—the eidos of love itself—does it become possible to make declarations about "love" which are not determined by accidental experiences and so refutable by the same, but instead necessarily apply to it in accordance with its own essence. Accordingly, bringing out and appropriating this unifying point of view in the logos is a condition of the possibility of coming to an understanding.

But Socrates' two speeches, and especially the substantive contrast between them (the transition from censure to praise, 265c5), show that a general agreement about the unitary essence of love does not necessarily fulfil adequately the requirement of unity which is entailed by the intention of coming to an understanding. "Irrational appetite" does not yet sufficiently grasp the specific being of love. There are other irrational appetites that are not love. So this characterization has to be divided into kinds, in order to grasp the specific essence of love.

The division is guided by having an eye to the thing that is to be characterized. It divides the proposed eidos not blindly or arbitrarily, but at its joints (265e1); that is, it divides it into the parts that are inherent in it. Every part must itself have an eidos, we read in the *Statesman* (262b). That is, it must not be solely a piece of something (a piece which is a unity only when it is together with other pieces); instead, as a part, it must itself be positively one thing in itself. Apart from being (along with all the other parts) common to the thing, it must be different from them all, and in this difference must itself be, in its turn, a unity and a whole for a manifold that is comprehended under it and only under it, not under any of the other parts. Thus, within irrational appetite, Socrates' first speech distinguished between gluttony, drunkenness, and, in the third place, love; and likewise, in the second speech, between the four kinds of divine madness. Only by such division of a unity into unities does one arrive at the adequate characterization of the thing—at the *oikeios logos* (fitting account) of its being, in which only the thing itself, which stays constantly in view, is addressed, and nothing that is intended along with it. This is the indivisible eidos of the thing, which alone secures the unified understanding of it which a shared understanding requires: a logos that characterizes in such a way that it prevents one person from conceiving what is being addressed in one way and another person in another way.

Now, in this process of division, Socrates' first speech made an error the conscious use of which would be important for a speaker who (in the example that is discussed) intends to win a boy for his erotic enjoyment without presenting himself as being in love and who must therefore—for a pre-existing purpose—persuade the boy that love is something bad. The speech pretended that every kind of ir-rational appetite (which Socrates only later calls "madness": 244a; see also 265a) is opposed to prudence, because it is bad. The speech passed over in silence the fact that madness is not absolutely bad, and, by thus passing over god-sent madness (that is, by concealing substantive differences), the speech succeeded in its purpose of dis-paraging love.

Thus dialectic proves to be a prerequisite for the artful mas-tery of speech. It is the ability to draw together the manifold of what is experienced into a selfsame single thing and to make the specific eidos of the intended thing available with the aid of this universal unity of the *horos* (limit, definition). But it is only on the basis of such knowledge of the true being of the thing that rhetoric is able to sub-stitute for the true logos one which, while false, resembles the true one. For of course it is only from the undisguised thing itself that one can learn what looks so similar to it, without being it, that one can pass it off as the thing itself.

But dialectic has a special function *within* the specific activity of rhetoric, as well (266c ff.). Dialectic proves to be indispensable not only as a necessary precondition of finding the right content but also within what the doctrine of the art of rhetoric itself portrays. For it is involved in the structure of technē as such. Every technē requires an insight into the nature of what it deals with. So the art of speaking requires, besides the knowledge of the usual means of rhetorical art, an insight into the nature of what this skilful speech is supposed to be applied to, namely, the human psyche; and in fact the purpose of this cognizance is to see what the soul's nature can be influenced by or (as the case may be) what influences it is itself capable of exercising. But in order to be able to see clearly this capacity for action or passion which is in the nature of something, one must first know whether this thing is in fact uniform in itself or whether it consists of heterogeneous things. For in the latter case one must examine separately, for each individual kind within it, what it can be affected by and what, by its nature, it can itself affect. Thus the claim made by every techne to an antecedent assured disposition over the thing that is to be produced requires that what the techne deals with—both what it intends to have an effect on (producing it) and the means by which it intends to have the effect—should be known not just in its generic character but also in its specific differences.

So, on the one hand, rhetoric has to know the various kinds of techniques of speech in their nature—that is, in what they can accomplish (this is what is taught in the usual art of rhetoric). But it must also know the individual forms of the soul, on which it intends to operate, in their different capacities for being affected and for having an effect. For when the soul is affected by speech, it not only gets, as a result, into a *pathos* (a state of being affected), but it can also itself be moved on account of this pathos to an action (270d). It is only from a mastery of both these elements of the process of speech that a real mastery of speech as the power of persuasion comes about: the ability to adapt the form of one's speech to the particular nature of the soul in each case. It is only on the basis of insight into the various forms of speech and of the soul, and their nature, that one can know why the one should always be adapted to the other in a particular way (271b). Arriving at ultimate unities, ultimate differences in kind, is a condition for the possibility of a kind of dealing and performance, in *any* techne, that is truly certain, characterized by understanding and not blind. Of course, the practical exercise of the technē—for example, persuasion—also requires an ability to recognize, in the case at hand, which general nature of the soul, and thus an opportunity for which type of speech, is *present*. This ability is a matter of perception (271c ff.)—that is, of praxis itself (compare the relation between *technikos* and *praktikos* in Aristotle, *Metaphysics* A 1, discussed on p. 23 above).

What can be learned from the *Phaedrus* in general is what dialectic accomplishes for the possibility of science and technē: in the manifoldness of perception, it is only through dialectic that one can see at all (and have any disposition over) selfsame things as the unitary essences of what changes. Only the logos makes it possible (in the context of practical dealings) for what is comprehended, in its being, in it, to be visible in advance in its potential compatibility with other things (its potentiality for being with other things). This compatibility can be compatibility between species of the same genus or between species of different genuses that come into relation with one another only in the carrying out of a task, and it can be a compatibility that is *produced* (<u>hergestellt</u>) (in the case of technē) or one that is only put at our disposition (<u>beigestellt</u>) (in the logos).

So this makes dialectic the core of all true technē. For it is only as something comprehended in ultimate unities of manifold materials that entities become accessible to us in their ability to stand in relations of being together or of mutual exclusion with other things that have different ultimate unities. But that is what knowledge claims: to show that the factual, observed presence of something with something is necessary—which, however, means to exhibit it as a result of the joint existence of the *being* of one and the *being* of the other.

Section 8: Dialectic's Ontological Presuppositions (the *Sophist* and the *Parmenides*)

Thus the dialectician's task, in general, is to set forth in its limits this capacity of the *eidē* or *genē* (pl. of *eidos* and of *genos*, kind) to combine with one another. The natural key to such an investigation is the logos. For the fact that genē can be combined with one another is already evident from the fact that one *says* of all of them that they *are,* which means that they can be combined with being. It also seems clear that not all of them can be combined, indiscriminately, with all of them. What we are left with, then, is that some of them can be combined with one another and others cannot. And just as among the sounds in language there are some that run through all like a band— the vowels—so perhaps there are also, among the genē, some that are always present with all the others and that hold them together like a band and perhaps also others that (correspondingly) bring about their separateness from one another (*Sophist* 253c).

Such an investigation (which is described here, in the *Sophist*, as the dialectician's task) evidently refers to something more than the special dialectic whose meaning, in terms of the theory of science, we have already laid out in connection with the *Phaedrus*. Here the question seems, rather, to extend beyond that, to the *possibility of the very procedure of dialectic*—to its ontological preconditions. Just take a look at the subsequent discussion in the *Sophist* of the five genē. Their combined presence is not, after all, comprehensible through the schema of diaeresis—of the unfolding of differences of kind that are posited within a highest generic unity. If one looks closely, one finds that this possibility is explicitly refuted (250b, c). Motion and rest *are*; must one not, then, gather up this common thing (the fact that they both are) and, ignoring what they both are in themselves and attending only to what they have in common, to being, regard this as a third thing, which is neither in motion nor at rest but shows itself "over and above these two"? But this seems impossible, for if something is not in motion, it must be at rest, and vice versa; that is, if one disregards the fact that something is in motion, then in this disregarding, what one sees is not being, which is neither at rest nor in motion, but something that is necessarily at rest. The embarrassment in which (in this way) the investigation becomes entangled leads, in what follows, to the demonstration of the *reciprocal koinōnia* (fellowship, kinship) of the highest genuses. They are the ones of which it would be said that they are given, together, in everything that exists, and that they represent the cause of the separation or combination of the genuses. They themselves, then, are not (in the same sense) genuses of what exists but ontological concepts that are given, together, with every entity as such. These genuses do not, of course, stand in a fixed relation of mutual superordination and subordination. This becomes evident from the demonstration of the fact that they are given, reciprocally, with one another. (It makes no difference, here, that this is true of rest and motion only because the koinōnia of knowledge is equally understood as koinōnia. Koinōnia designates, in general, only the co-presence of something with something, and not the particular manner of this co-presence.)

Nevertheless, they are called genē on account of their conceptual generality. Plato pays no regard to the fact that their generality is specific in character: that not everything that is different falls into kinds of differentness under the genus of difference (in fact, he elucidates the relationship of the *heteron* [other] to the *hetera* [others, pl.] by comparing it to the relation between science and the individual sciences: *Sophist* 257c). But the reciprocal relatedness of the highest genuses, which was emphasized above, and still more the way in which they function as the aitia of special, substantive koinōniai, certainly allow us to see their purely formal and ontological character.[17] If an entity is understood as a *dunamis tou poiein kai paschein* (power of acting and being acted upon), then in fact these most general characteristics of being, of sameness, difference, but also rest (as a condition of the knowability of entities) and motion (as a condition of their possessing knowledge), are also the ontological conditions of the possibility of substantive koinōnia.

This is the context of the much discussed definition of the

17. On the difference between "generalization" and "formalization," see Husserl, *Ideen zu einer reinen Phänomenologie und phänomenologischen Philosophie* (Halle, 1913) (= *Ideas. General Introduction to Pure Phenomenology*, trans. W. R. Boyce Gibson [New York, 1931]), sec. 13.

dialectician (*Sophist* 253d). Stenzel has shown that in the twice two terms of this definition the structure of dialectic is formulated in its two aspects of *sunagōgē* and *diairesis*—that is, just as dialectic was presented in the *Phaedrus*. Apart from matters of detail, this interpretation is certainly correct.[18] From it we can learn, not least of all,

18. The definition of the dialectician, *Sophist* 253d, is still extremely obscure. Stenzel's careful analysis (*Plato's Method of Dialectic*, pp. 96ff.; *Studien*, pp. 62ff.) has definitively clarified its formal construction: that it is not a matter of three terms (as Natorp interpreted it) or of an ascending sequence of four terms (as Schleiermacher assumed) but rather of twice two terms. But Stenzel's interpretation of the content is unsatisfactory in the case of the first one. The separateness of the eidē is not present in advance as a condition of their unification, but rather the reverse. So what is meant here (and this leads to Natorp's interpretation of the first term) is that in gathering together many things into one selfsame thing, one needs to ignore the specific concreteness (*phusis*) of each of the many, in order to get in view what they have in common, and to do so in such a way that other perspectives in which these many things could also be placed do not emerge at all. This is why we are told that the unifying perspective embraces it only superficially. It is only in the diaeretic descent from this posited unity that the other perspectives explicitly come out, some of them as going together with and some of them as divorced from the thing to be defined.

Both actions, *sunagōgē* and *diaeresis*, contain the *hen/polla* (one/many); but only *diaeresis* unfolds it in its positive sense, as a thing that is one in many ways and is separated from many other things. [In the text, this difference between sunagōgē and diaeresis is brought out by the counterposition of *exōthen periechomenos* and *di holōn pollōn*.]

So it is not a matter of an ascent and a descent within a "pyramid of Ideas" which is pre-given in its articulation; instead, sunagōgē presents, in an undivided form, the realm (the *genos*) that diaeresis articulates, by demarcating, in its diverse contents.

Schleiermacher's interpretation of the passage is untenable. Of course the interpretation of dialectical procedure also includes the *aitia* of mixture and separation, but these are distinguished precisely by their

that in this synoptic unification and taking apart into (indivisible) unities in which something manifold is summed up in such a way that it is seen in its difference from other things that belong to the same generic unity, one in fact succeeds (as we showed in the case of the *Phaedrus* both by the conceptual formulation and by practical example) in understanding—in its *dunamis tou poiein kai paschein*, which in this case means its possible coexistence with other things, a priori— what is grasped in the *atomon eidos* (indivisible form) as something specified from the genos.

The koinōnia that is under discussion here in the *Sophist* is, of course, primarily a koinōnia with the generic characteristics that are combined (*sumplokē*) in the atomon eidos—that is, with the mul- tiplicity of characteristics that make up the latter's being—and which at the same time covers what in each case, as its heteron, does *not* belong to this eidos but to a different eidos of the same genos. But when it is addressed in this way in its specific being, the entity is at the same time made accessible for dealings with it; that is, one sees how it can be together with other things, affecting them or being affected by them, and how (as something seen in this way) its being together with other things can be produced, as the example of the koinōnia of the sounds in speech shows. (Compare the *Phaedrus*: from the being of eros, one realizes its beneficial or harmful character; and from the being of the soul, one realizes its potential for being affected by words.)

If dialectics, in this way, is the knowledge of the koinōnia of genera, insofar as diaeresis (as something based on the unity of the characteristics that are unfolded in it) is koinōnia, then dialectic at the same time represents the koinōnia of the genera on which its own ontological possibility depends. Thus in dialectic's general structure, not only the summing up of genera and species in the *horismos* (process

---

absolute combinability with everything: *dia pantōn* (253c1) as opposed to *dia pollōn* (d5). [A different account has been given more recently by A. Gomez-Lobo, "Plato's Description of Dialectic in the *Sophist* 253d1–e7," *Phronesis* 22 (1977): 29–47.]

of definition) is understood as koinōnia, but also the reciprocal relatedness of the genera which makes this summing up ontologically possible—especially the relatedness of sameness and difference or (as the case may be) of being and non-being. For the possibility of dialectical synopsis and taking apart in fact depends on these two. The fact that one sees in many things something that is the same—the unity of the kind, of the eidos—and (likewise) that it becomes evident that various eidē are comprehended in one genos depends upon the sameness of a "regard" or "point of view" (*Hinsicht*). Thus in all such gathering together into a unity, sameness is co-present. Only this co-presence of sameness makes it possible to get into view, in various things, something that is substantively one because it is the same.

Conversely, diaeresis, the unfolding of unity into ultimate units, requires one to pay regard to difference. The division of something that is generically the same is guided by a view of the thing that is to be specified on the basis of this unity. By keeping a continuous hold on this thing as what it already was[19]—which is to say, by gathering together all the generic characteristics that belong to it—we see it continuously as different from other things with which it is generically the same; it is just this that constitutes its specificity. And by seeing, in this way, the difference between the thing (as one retains it) and all the things with which it was hitherto the same, one also sees everything else, which each thing is not, as different from what it is. Thus it is, in the first place, on difference (which of course itself presupposes sameness) that the possibility depends of moving from generic unity to the ultimate indivisible specificity which a thing possesses. So difference is in fact the *aition* (cause, reason) of diaeresis. But the ability of these two "regards" to exist together is, as a whole, the condition of the possibility of dialectic.

This distinctive importance of the koinōnia of the highest genera as the ontological precondition of concrete koinōnia—that is, of the characterization of an entity on the basis of its generic and

19. *Exomenoi tēs tou sophistou koinōnias, Sophist* 264e2.

specific characteristics—also seems to be the key to understanding the second part of Plato's *Parmenides*. There, the dialectical mixture of the eidē is presented—that is, it is shown that the one is necessarily many, and the many, one. Just like the proof of the koinōnia of the five genē in the *Sophist*, this dialectic in the *Parmenides* cannot be grasped within the schema of diaeresis as it is developed in the *Phaedrus* and the *Philebus*. If one takes one's orientation from this as the positive idea of dialectic, one can easily have doubts about the serious, substantive importance of this dialectic in the *Parmenides*. It is certainly not a mere "exercise"; but one exaggerates its intention if one sees in it a "solution" to the problem of *methexis* (participation) which was opened up at the beginning. Plato did not intend this as a proof that the Idea as a unity is and can be the plurality of what comes to be. (Aristotle, too, after all, regarded the methexis problem as unsolved and insoluble.[20]) What is proved dialectically in the *Parmenides*

20. An actual interpretation of the fundamental intention of the *Parmenides* would have to realize the suggestions given in the text. Such an interpretation cannot be given here. Nevertheless, it would not have been possible to bring out correctly the "positive" dialectic of diaeresis which the *Philebus* formulates without glancing at the *Parmenides* and its "negative" dialectic. The usual approach to the problem of individuation misses, from the start, the way the problems that Greek ontology addressed stood. In spite of his critique of the concept of methexis and of the Platonic *chōrismos* (separation) of the Ideas, even Aristotle, for his part, simply left standing the relationship of the particular thing to the eidos exactly as Plato had done, without seeing it as a *problem* of individuation. If Plato makes the particular thing's methexis with the Idea into a problem, he is not thereby formulating an unsolved problem of his ontology: he is not posing the problem of individuation; instead, the aporia of this "problem" is itself meant, indirectly, to make the assumptions of the ontology visible: the fact that in the logos the individual entity is encountered only as an ahyletic eidos. The fact that the eidos is always the eidos of an individual thing does not require, for Plato or for Aristotle, an explanation of how the thing becomes individual, but always only—conversely—an interpre-

is not that the one is the many of the things that come into being—which would mean that the undefinable manifold of what comes to be had been comprehended and "pinned down" *as such*. The *Parmenides* proof takes place entirely *within* the eidē. It shows that the idea of unity does not exclude, but posits together with itself, the idea of multiplicity. So this is the positive intention of this dialectic, which seemed so lacking in direction: to show that the Ideas, as things in regard to which there is unity, do not need to be absolutely one but can embrace a multiplicity of things in regard to which there is unity. This possibility is the positive expression of the impossibility, which is demonstrated in the *Parmenides*, of being able to think multiplicity without unity or unity without multiplicity. But this shows that the task of comprehending in unity concepts the manifold of what comes into being is not already performed when unities, as such, are posited, because one must arrive at unities of a kind that do not themselves, in turn, contain differing comprehensible things, or unities of comprehension, but are "indivisibly" one, so that they comprehend the thing in the character that it has in its ultimate comprehensible unity. This is why Parmenides calls for his dialectical exercise *before* the Socratic business of *horizesthai* (division, definition) (*Parmenides* 135c). This "before" allows us to see what makes diaeresis possible in reality. The dialectic of the *Parmenides* does not itself provide positive defining characterizations of things but provides a grounding (in the same way that the five genera in the *Sophist* do) for the possibility of the substantive defining characterization of entities by dialectical diaeresis. So the problem of methexis, as it was formulated at the beginning, is not solved but transformed into another problem and is solved in that form: it is shown—by pure concepts and with the smooth sophistry of language in the *Parmenides*—that the unity of an Idea can include

---

tation of the claim to being of the eidos. It is very significant that the relation between "first" and "second" substance in Aristotle (not only in the perhaps not authentic treatise on categories, but also precisely in the seventh book of the *Metaphysics*) is not formulated as a *problem* needing solution at all.

a multiplicity of Ideas under it. Just this is the basis of the "solution" to the problem of the one and the many which takes the place in the *Philebus* of a solution to the insoluble problem (which is formulated there, too) of methexis. The one is shown to be many, but not as the undefined manifold of things that are coming to be but as a definite—which means a comprehensible—multiplicity of unities.

The crucial point in showing the possibility of substantively illuminating speech, by demonstrating the koinōnia of the highest genera, especially those of being and non-being, is to arrive at the positive meaning of the contradiction. That something is identically the same thing and yet different is not a contradiction if it is each of these things in a different respect. Precisely as something that is identical with itself, it is in fact different from other things. Insofar as it is, at the same time it is not—that is, not everything else. So the non-being that is given together with being itself does not mean the latter's contradictory opposite, which is indeed not compatible with being, because in its own intended meaning it does not mean something perceptible but the sheer denial of being. But Plato identifies non-being as a distinct, positive, perceptible characteristic of entities (it is an eidos: *Sophist* 258c7), which, while it stands opposed to a regard for being, is also found, like being itself, in entities. So it is in distinguishing the different regards in which being and non-being are simultaneously given in entities that we find the solution to the contradiction (a contradiction that could be used as a means of sophistic refutation only by concealing this difference in regards). Non-being as a positive characteristic of entities means being different from other things; not being other things.

This resolves the difficulty, which arises in dialectic, that the one turns out to be many and the same turns out to be different. As the uniform common element in things that are different (in species), a substantive genus does not cease to be one; and insofar as the manifold that is comprehended in it as one has no other common elements in its manifoldness except this one, in which they are all the same, they are in fact ontologically (that is, in regard to their possible knowability and characterizability) only one. But if, within the one commonality of the genus, there are still other commonalities to be found, in which one part of the manifold differs from another, then the manifold is not, ontologically, only the one commonality of the genus; it can also be comprehended under a plurality of special points in regard to which there is unity, which are all included under the same genus. Bringing out in this way the substantive differences of species which are given along with the identical genus is the business of diaeresis. It does in fact turn the one into many; but it does so in such a way that the one is many precisely not in the respect in which it was one—in that respect, rather, it remains one—but instead it is many insofar as each of the many is itself (apart from what it has in common with others), in its turn, one, and thus different from the others.

But part of the meaning of scientific comprehension of the manifold through the logos is to define and characterize the manifold as one that is itself no longer many or different in kind but that comprehends a manifold in an ultimate unity, by addressing which, one comprehends the manifold in what is comprehensible in it as one and always the same. Thus part of the tendency of the logos's positive opening up of reality is that it conceives the unity that it posits in each case as many, not so as to expose the meaning of its positing, and thus itself, as impossible, but so as, by positing a more specific unity of the manifold, to arrive at its true potential for appropriating the thing in its being. For it is only when one arrives at an indivisible unity that one comprehends the thing, in the logos, in what it always is *and what only it is*. Only then is the claim to coming to an understanding fulfilled and does it become possible to give an accounting for something. As something understood in this way, the thing is made available: that is, one knows and can give an accounting for how one must deal with it.

So the definition, the oikeios logos ousias, is not an end in itself but, rather, makes possible a scientific manner of dealing with (or, as the case may be, thinking about) a thing. The true objects of dialectical investigation are the most important and most esteemed things, which are not accessible through any perception, but only through proper search in the logos (*Statesman* 285e–286a). The examples that Plato uses, such as fishing and weaving, are not investigated for their own sake, since one can easily become informed about them (what they are and how one must behave in them) through perception. They serve only as exercises. Serious topics, on the other hand, are those that are not sufficiently evident from intuition in experience, such as what the real statesman, the real philosopher, the real orator, is: possibilities of human existence whose being and nature is in dispute.[21] So the dialectical clarification of these existential possibilities, the gaining of their oikeios logos, means giving an accounting in regard to what man claims to be. This general sense of dialectic as man's giving an accounting regarding the existential possibilities to which he lays claim and regarding his claim to knowledge of entities in general makes dialectic important, at the same time, in a way that reaches beyond each particular object of investigation and accounting: it makes us, in general, "more dialectical," by grasping the possibility (which is inherent in human existence) of understanding ourselves and of justifying the claim to knowledge wherever it is made.[22]

21. It is a misunderstanding that misses the essential motives of Platonic philosophizing when Stenzel (*Plato's Method of Dialectic*, p. 34; *Studien*, p. 94), on the basis of *Statesman* 285d–286a, regards the search for what the statesman is as not an ultimate concern of the investigation and claims to see, in the *megista* and *timiōtata* (greatest and most esteemed things), the highest genera (see, e.g., *Statesman* 302b9!). The indications above may be sufficient to set this matter straight.
On the *amphisbētēsimon* (debatable matter) as the object of dialectic, see *Phaedrus* 263a.
22. Compare *Statesman* 286d and, e.g., the beginning of the *Sophist* (218b).

2

Interpretation of the *Philebus*

The following outline is meant to clarify the composition of the dialogue, as it is brought out by the interpretation. Its validity, of course, depends on that of the interpretation.

The Structure of the *Philebus*

Division I: Developing the problem and making sure
of the method of the investigation

Part I: Interpretation of *Philebus* 11a–19b

Section 1: The Topic of the Conversation (11a–12b)

The topic of the *Philebus*, we are told at the very beginning, is the concept of the good, and specifically that of the good in *human* life. There are two different and opposing interpretations of human life. The first sees the good, for human beings as well as for all other living creatures, in pleasure, enjoyment, gratification; the other, which Socrates advocates, believes that man's being has a distinctive potential. Human Dasein has the potential of thought, understanding, and memory, and therefore the potential of having disposition over the world, in thinking reflection, and of bringing the world into its presence through calculation. This human potential, Socrates thinks, is the most beneficial or advantageous of all, so it is the good.

Several things should be noted in this formulation of the topic:

1. Note that "the good" is characterized as a highest intensification of beneficiality (advantageousness), which is in keeping with the connection between beneficiality and understanding; see p. 00 above.

2. Note that, rather than in the presence, at any given time, of how one is faring (*des sich-Befindens*), Socrates sees humanity precisely in the possibility of being toward things that are not present, by being cognitively at home in them (*sich daraufhin verstehen*). In this opposition to the mere presence of affect and to how one is doing in terms of it, one hears a suggestion of the connection between memory (*mnēmē*) and desire (*hormē*) which is uncovered later on; and insofar as this connection aids precisely in interpreting affect, Socrates' formulation of the topic already contains the seed of the elevation of the *hēdonē* (pleasure) problem into the specifically human mode of existence that is characterized by self-understanding.

3. Note that being toward non-present things also, through understanding, is described here as a potential of being in which man only participates. This points ahead to the constitutional deficiency of the human *nous* (mind) vis-à-vis the divine one—that is, vis-à-vis the *pure* potential of itself.

These two explications of human existence are introduced as the outcome of a previous conversation, which itself is not given. Thus the present conversation enters the context of a more extensive, perhaps necessarily endless argument (compare 50d). The advocate of the first position, Philebus "the fair," has withdrawn from the conversation but remains present. The advocacy of his thesis has been taken over by another, Protarchus. This withdrawal by Philebus makes clear, by contrast, a first prerequisite for the possibility of a genuine conversation.[1] Philebus, who listens while reclining comfortably, is charac-

1. This introductory scene is, by the way, highly significant for the de-

terized as the dogmatist of hēdonē, with whom no discussion is possible. The first thing that Socrates extracts from Philebus's representative, as a concession, is that he is prepared "to attain the truth by every possible means." This concession means that Socrates' partner is willing to answer for his statements and to listen to reasons. It is only with such a partner that Socrates can conduct a fruitful conversation: the opposition between their theses becomes the object of real inquiry. "To attain the truth by every possible means" is the mark of dialectic, which develops comprehensively, in its substantive consequences, what speaks for and against something. The comprehensiveness of the dialectical discussion means that there should be no dogmatic, undiscussed clinging to a logos, but always a testing that is prepared for discussion.

The next requirement, then, is for the question to be posed. This means more than mere asking; because asking is always already at the answer that it asks for. It is only indistinctly that this expectation of the answer contains an understanding of what the answer is already understood as in the question. Even a so-called open question is open only insofar as it has not yet decided between the answers that it expects. *Posing* the question, on the other hand, means openness in

---

velopment of Plato's dialogue style. The conversation that is conducted with Protarchus differs from that of the *Gorgias*—with which it is connected, thematically—by the fact that it does not involve the refutation (in the manner of a contest dialogue) of a *dogmatic* hedonist but, instead, a positive conversation is prepared from the very beginning by the steps explicitly taken to ensure the partner's suitability for substantive argument. Accordingly, the refutation of hedonism is accomplished not by an elenctic demonstration that it is unable and unwilling to give an accounting, but positively, by drawing distinctions that show its relative legitimacy and by limiting its pretensions by means of definition. The fiction of a conversation, preceding the *Philebus*, between Socrates and Philebus, refers back to an elenctic dialogue in the manner of the Callicles conversation in the *Gorgias*. The *Philebus* itself is thus elevated into the same sphere of substantive discussion as, e.g., the *Sophist* is by the scene at *Soph.* 217c.

a different sense: in it, the asking is explicitly pulled back from the expected answers to what every answer is already understood as in the question. To pose a question means to bring out what that which is asked for is already understood as in the asking and to what, as asking, it must address its inquiry. This dwelling on the question, before asking, is called posing the question: it is a dwelling on what already precedes every answer.

In the question about the good in human life, a guiding role is always already played by a pre-understanding of the thing that is asked about. The good that we are looking for is supposed to be a state in which the soul finds itself (*diathesis*), or a manner in which it behaves (*hexis*), which is capable of making the lives of all human beings "fortunate." Thus the good is understood in advance as a condition of the human soul. So it is not something that man has (as *agathon* = "good" commonly means, to begin with) but a manner of his very being. For man *is* his soul. The question is: What is the condition of the soul that makes the lives of human beings "fortunate"? "Fortunate" (*eudaimōn*), here, is not a material characterization of what man aims at as the good (say, in the choice between happiness and virtue) but refers to the highest degree of desirability, in which there is nothing left to desire. The question of whether this is a state in which one finds oneself or a way in which one understands oneself is left completely open. The answers that are given will have to refer back to this natural pre-understanding of the "fortunate life." But we can see from this pre-understanding what the asking must address its inquiry to—what the object is that the asking interrogates. It is human Dasein as something that desires and chooses and that reveals in its desires and its choices what is the good that it seeks. Whether the condition of the soul which is specific in them is "the good" is determined by whether a person would want to lead his life entirely in this condition (compare the discussion at 20b ff., esp. 21d3–e3).

So bringing out the way in which what is asked for is understood in advance secures the antithetical character of the two answers that are given: both of them do in fact answer the same question understood in the same way. It is just for this reason that it is possible to decide between them. Furthermore, the characterization of the thing to be interrogated (that is, human life) makes clear the path which will be taken by the investigation: that of seeing how each of the answers deals with life. But at the same time this observation suggests the possibility that neither of the two answers may fully satisfy the demand posed by the question. In that case the decision between them would be arrived at by awarding the victory to the one that grasps the aspect of Dasein which is most closely akin (*suggenēs*) to the condition of the soul which is really best. The substantive importance of this restriction is this: that which is the good can and must be only *one* thing. But this means, on the level of these two theses, that it can be only the one *or* the other. But perhaps it will turn out to be necessary to go beyond the discussion of these two theses. There would be no sense in assuming a third one *alongside* them; but it does make sense to ask whether the desirability in both of them might have one and the same basis. In that case hēdonē and epistēmē would be good insofar as they belonged to the genos of this single good. The controversy would then have to do with the question of their inherent proximity to or distance from this good. To put it materially: which of the two ways of living is more akin to—that is, more turned toward—the good itself?

Section 2: Making Sure of the Method (12b–14b)

At the beginning of the actual investigation, then, stands the question of whether the phenomena that are registered in the two theses are unified in themselves and, indeed, first of all, whether *pleasure* indicates a uniform condition of the soul. Once it is clear that the claim made by the two theses is one and the same, they themselves must be questioned in regard to what is meant by them. But this means, from the start, that it is necessary to bring out what *manifold* of phenomena is embraced in a unified way in the one thesis and the other. For it is implausible, at first glance, that pleasure signifies a uniform condition of the soul, which as such constitutes the good: the one name evidently comprehends very different—indeed antithetical—forms of enjoyment. What does the pleasure of the "bon viveur" have in common with the satisfaction that the "well-bred" person takes precisely in his sober self-command—that is, in denying himself gratification? Surely the condition of the soul (which is what is at issue here) is fundamentally different in the two cases.[2] This reference to the generally known and acknowledged differences in ethics should be enough, Socrates suggests, to make clear to his partner the necessity of distinguishing specific kinds within the single genus of pleasure and of marking out among them the only ones that could be intended when pleasure is identified with the good. For in the natural way of understanding these matters, these forms are understood as different precisely in regard to their being (or not being) good. Pleasure itself is met with as something different in each case.

Socrates' opponent's answer shows, however, that he intends to sacrifice the natural understanding of the phenomena to the defense of his thesis. The examples by which Socrates explains the differentness of the forms of pleasure warn Protarchus that an admission that pleasure has substantively different forms would be fatal to his thesis. (The fact that this recognition is the motivation for the expedient he adopts is clear from his second answer, 13a6: if you regard the differentness of the forms of pleasure as comparable to the differentness of colors within the genus color, what bad consequences does this differentness have for my thesis?) Now, his expedient is to say that it is not the pleasures themselves that are opposed to one another but

2. Regarding *Philebus* 12c1: The call to philosophical inquiry about the unity of what is referred to as "hēdonē" is contrasted with concern about the correct name for the "goddess." Regarding the nature of pleasure, Socrates *knows* that it is something that is manifold in itself. Regarding the names of gods, on the other hand, he does not dare to know anything. This is irony directed at Philebus, who evidently thought that he was promoting his cause when he declared hēdonē to be a goddess, and who is thus forced to claim to know, for the goddess who is known as Aphrodite, a more correct name than the one under which she is worshiped.

only the objects in regard to which one feels pleasure and from which the emotion of pleasure arises. For insofar as all these pleasures are, after all, pleasures, they are as similar as anything can be. That is, he seeks to escape the logic of Socrates' distinctions by not admitting that the demonstrated differences are inherent in the condition of the soul itself. But he carries out this defensive move by falling back on the shared character of the generic name, in regard to which all the different desires are indeed the same as each other—in comparison, that is, to everything else. But Socrates had intended precisely a differentness *within* this generic sameness and identity of name.

Socrates demonstrates the theoretical inappropriateness of his opponent's expedient by means of a random example of a genus and the different species that are comprehended within it. The generic unity is so far from excluding substantive differences that, on the contrary, consideration of these specific differences necessarily presupposes unity on the generic level. It is only within the radius of the field that is limited by the unity of the genus that there are differences. All differentness presupposes a regard for something that is the same, against which the differences become apparent. Objects that cannot be regarded in terms of some shared dimension are not different, either. The "warmth" or "glaringness" of a particular color, for example—that is, what distinguishes it from other colors—is not at the same time something by which it is distinguished from a particular *number*. For these characterizations (warm, glaring) are distinctive only on the basis of the fact that they, together with their opposites, are characterizations of *color*. A particular number and a particular color are not different; at most, color in general and number in general are different in their shared character of being something, as different ways of being something.

Socrates' opponent is willing, on this level of theoretical generality, to grant that this is the case, because he sees no danger for his thesis—specifically, no difference of value—in this general sense of difference in kind. But what Socrates does in applying this agreed-upon principle is to find the mutually different parts different precisely in their empirically evident differentness in respect of "goodness and badness," thereby making doubtful the asserted identification of pleasure and the good. This would leave his opponent with the impossible—or at least paradoxical—task of pointing out the shared element in the so-called good and bad pleasures (that is, above the empirically evident differences), in view of which they should all, contrary to the *doxa* (opinion), be described as good.[3] So Protarchus retracts his partial admission that there are different kinds of pleasure: they cannot be different from one another *as pleasure*. Or better, he does not explicitly retract but, rather, sinks back in that direction, without noticing it, at the same time that the differentness, which he has admitted was neutral, wants to present itself as a difference in *value*. Thus, because for the natural understanding, distinct forms of pleasure always show themselves as differing in their "goodness and badness," he begins to defend himself again against the assumption of any differences in pleasure at all.

But this recoiling from differences that are confirmed by natural experience to the selfsameness of the genus makes it impossible to come to any substantive understanding. For the point of unification in the genus is not to bring things to a halt at what is comprehended as being shared (and which the generic name designates) but, rather, to present a first comprehensible aspect of the manifold of what shows

3. The sentence at 13b3–5 offers textual difficulties. If, in view of the grammatical construction, one regards the received text as untenable (which, however, does not seem to me to be beyond doubt—see Stallbaum's attempted grammatical explanation of the passage, p. 105 of his edition), then the proposals to replace *enon* with *enorōn* (which Wilamowitz also supports) or *ennoōn* are, nevertheless, unsatisfactory, because they give up the parallel, which is essential to the structure of the sentence as a whole, with the previous *kaka d'onta* (b1). If one prefers not to think in this case that the daring of the living language extends beyond what grammar permits it, it would still be better to prefer as an emendation *<kata>ti* . . . . (d2), which at least does not detract from the symmetrical function of the clause. Compare *Phil.* 34e3 and *Laws* 963e1.

itself to sense experience, as the delineation of a region to be investigated. The process of comprehension could cease, on arriving at the genus, only if there were nothing further that is comprehensible within the manifold that is brought together in this way—which, however, means that there would be no features shared by narrower parts of it, which would be the case only if the thing itself (insofar as it has comprehensible—that is, invariable—features) could be encountered in the comprehension of this shared thing. But the presence of distinctions does not in itself by any means signify that something is indefinable and changing; on the contrary, it signifies comprehensible, differentiated unitary kinds. But to restrict one's view here to this first shared nature means to conceal the things themselves as they show themselves (and as they show themselves within the unity of what is generically the same to be dissimilar to each other). The purpose of establishing such dissimilarity is not, of course, to show that the unity which the things are comprehended as is invalid but rather, while holding firmly to this shared thing, to explicate what is comprehended in this way by differentiating it and thus to make it evident that something can be agreed upon in a uniform way *about* it and about what belongs to it. So turning the attention back to selfsameness does not open the way to an appropriation of the things in the differing substantiveness in which they are encountered and intended and does not secure for the process of coming to an understanding a common understanding of what is intended, insofar as it is not selfsameness but different things, in their specific difference, that we encounter as selfsame (13d8 ff.). This turning back the attention has the formal correctness of reflection on the logos, a reflection that sacrifices the thing in favor of the mere thought of it. The substantive meaning of establishing dissimilarity is not that the two dissimilar things, as dissimilar, are as similar to each other as anything could be. For that would be correct only if they were only dissimilar and nothing else. This example makes clear how Protarchus has fallen into Sophism— that is, into the givenness of *logos* and *onoma* (word and name), divorced from the facts and from vision. Nor does the appeal to hēdonē as such give access to the reality, any more than the name does, which merely tells us what the reality is called. When Socrates refuses to argue about the name of the gods, this is in keeping with the familiar Socratic effort to get beyond the onoma to the eidos. In the same way, the Socratic thesis that understanding is the good would be masked, in its substantive content, and all further progress toward shared substantive understanding would become impossible if Socrates refused to unfold the substantive distinctions in what is meant by knowledge and understanding and relied on its selfsameness as knowledge and understanding. Knowledge, too, must be unfolded in the variousness of what is comprehended in it, even if mutually opposed modes of knowledge and understanding should emerge in the process. It is only Socrates' acknowledgment that, in spite of the conceptual unity of knowledge, there are different kinds of knowledge and understanding that obtains his opponent's agreement (although here [13e10] the existence of *opposed* kinds is not suggested as positively as it is at 13a4). Protarchus is reassured by the fact that both theses are alike in this respect. So he agrees that further investigation of the two theses must consider this differentness that they embrace.[4]

4. 14b1: *Tēn toinun diaphorotēta* . . . refers to the just demonstrated substantive differentiation within the two kinds hēdonē and phronēsis. For the point is not that the two theses should not be concealed in their differentness *from one another*. Protarchus's reassured response that the parity of the two theses pleases him could suggest such a reading. But since the difference between the two theses constitutes the topic of the discussion, which has always been in view, Protarchus, when he speaks of the parity between them, thinks only that up to this point neither has any advantage over the other in regard to the final outcome. So the correct interpretation of the passage is that, for the subsequent discussion, the admitted *internal* differentiation of the two kinds should be followed up. (See also the *toinun*, pointing back to the *content* of the foregoing summing up, which ends with *kai diaphoroi*.) Stallbaum's view is similar (p. 109 of his edition).

The construction of b1–3 is obscure. In any case, the subject

Section 3: The Excursus on Dialectic (14c–19b)

This concession is of the utmost importance. It is only this which secures for the investigation the possibility of speech that gains access to the facts and of shared substantive understanding. In what follows, Socrates explains this in detail to his partner (who had previously accepted guidance without having a proper methodological understanding: compare his motive for agreement at 14a7), so as to make sure of his real agreement. The content of the explanation is a radical foundation of the theory of dialectic. It is motivated, then, by the intention of elevating Socrates' partner in the dialogue beyond an agreement that has been arrived at purely agonistically to a recognition, independent of any *agon* (contest), of the substantive import of the Socratic demand. As a methodological excursus, the passage requires an interpretation that both considers its function within the present conversation and clarifies the connections that one is reminded of to presentations of the dialectical method which Plato has given elsewhere. The essential point in this task is to hold fast to this double concern as a unified one. For there is a double danger in wanting to separate Plato's methodological expositions from their context in the interest of a systematic interpretation of dialectic: first, there is the danger of taking the extent to which Plato expresses himself on methodological issues to be the measure of his actual consciousness of method in his work; and then there is the danger of seeing the method that he actually employs only in the light of his conceptual theory of method rather than, in reverse, illuminating the characteristic features and the limits of his self-comprehension from the primordial motives of his philosophical "procedure." But his procedure is reaching shared understanding through conversation, through the Socratic dialogue. The special importance of the *Philebus* lies precisely in the fact that the dialectic that is discussed in it becomes aware of itself in the

---

(from what went before it) of *mēnusōsin* is *logoi*, which should probably also be read into the *tou te emou kai tou sou*—from what went before it—instead of the text's *tou agathou*.

actual conduct of Socratic dialogue. The theory of dialectic must be grasped on the basis of the concrete situation of coming to a shared understanding. By comparison with this, all inquiry regarding a change and development in Plato's dialectic is secondary and must itself get its orientation from the genesis of dialectic from dialogue. The structure of speech as a process of coming to a shared understanding about the facts of the matter makes it possible to elucidate primordially the connection between the elements of dialectic (sunagōgē and diaeresis). The fact that the explicit development of the second of these elements, diaeresis, into a "method" belongs only to a later phase in Plato's works, as Stenzel has plausibly argued (*Studien*, 1917 [= *Plato's Method of Dialectic*, 1940]), should not be interpreted as meaning that Plato did not already practise this method from the beginning. This is not to say that the important thing is to show that Plato provided "classifications" all along; rather, the important thing is to show that the significance of these classifications— their characteristic accomplishment—corresponds exactly to what he later formulates explicitly as the diaeretic method leading to the atomon eidos (indivisible form). The element of diaeresis is rooted just as primordially as the element of synopsis (seeing all together) is rooted in the structure of coming to a shared understanding, the *dialektos* (conversation) (understood in its literal sense). Here the goal of coming to a shared understanding and of knowledge, which guides Socrates in the *Philebus* just as it has guided him all along (albeit mostly with a premature, negative termination), formulates its own conditions as a theory of dialectic.

The *Philebus*'s discussion of the problem of dialectic arises from the need for Socrates to make clear to his partner in the conversation, by means of fundamental reflections on the nature of the logos, that an appeal to the generic selfsameness of pleasure does not achieve a sufficient appropriation in understanding of the experienceable manifold of pleasures, and thus does not make possible a real test of pleasure's claim to be the good. Thus the theory of dialectic is brought in explicitly as giving grounds for the possibility of true dialogical progress toward a shared understanding. After all, all knowledge of something claims an understanding of the facts of the matter which is such that, when it is articulated conceptually in the logos, every other person can also be brought into the same being toward the facts that the knower himself has. Knowledge and coming to a shared understanding demand an appropriation of the reality in what it always is, so that Dasein is brought into the possibility of having disposition over it through knowledge. Now, indubitable though it is, the thesis that all pleasure, however it may present itself, is nevertheless pleasure does not make possible this kind of disposition over pleasure through knowledge—that is, it cannot justify pleasure's claim to be good. For this appeal to its selfsameness as pleasure leaves us without any comprehension of why the usual moral understanding of Dasein distinguishes between good and bad kinds of pleasure. It is a mistake to think that an undefined manifold of entities is already entirely appropriated in what constitutes its specific being, and thus that a uniform disposition over it is permitted, when it has been summed up in one uniform respect or perspective and comprehended as the same in relation to that. For one will remain in uncertainty as to how each individual thing that is included in this unity is to be regarded in a particular connection (for example, whether it is to be regarded as good or bad) as long as there is no assurance that what is brought together in this way into a unity is homogeneous in itself, so that the individual thing, in the understanding of what it has in common with others, is comprehended in its specific being. For without this assurance it could be the case that while some members of this commonality are indeed always good or bad, not all are, so that such goodness or badness is precisely not on account of what is common to the whole manifold and which it is understood as in the logos. Thus if such consideration of the unitary selfsameness of something manifold is to give sufficient disposition over the manifold in its being, the manifold must not be comprehensible in other unifying perspectives which would be included in this unity.

Someone who, nevertheless, wants to show that pleasure is

the good, although there are different kinds of pleasure, some of which are generally regarded as bad, must demonstrate for every existing kind of pleasure that it is good; that is, he or she must identify in each of them a sameness in view of which they are all good. Protarchus's vision has moved too quickly from the differentness (multiplicity) of pleasures to their sameness (unity) (13a3). In doing this, he has availed himself of a capacity for turning many into one (or one into many) which speech has, one which causes it to lose its power of giving access to the reality. When it is made one in this way, the reality is not comprehended in the characteristic that, after all, it was first seen as having: heterogeneity. Making many one in this way, and one many, is not a comprehension of the reality but a means of creating confusion: of leading away from what is seen in each case by asserting its opposite, which seems to be incompatible with it. More precisely, it is not a means of confusing other people which leaves its user in a secure position in relation to the reality; rather, it is a process of being affected (*pathos*), oneself, by the potential for concealment that lies in the logos as such—a being affected that does not preclude agonistic application of that potential, but in which it is not applied with the freedom of being *able* to confuse: *eis aporian hauton men prōton kai malista kataballōn* (15e) (getting himself into a muddle first and foremost). But the problem of the one and the many must be appreciated in its positive function in the logos. For the fact that something that is one is at the same time also comprehensible as many seems to nullify the claim of comprehension. So there is a need for a fundamental clarity in regard to the sense in which something that is one may nevertheless be many.

Of course, that the same thing can be one and many is not a serious problem in connection with the things in the visible world, which come into being and cease to be. The problem is not that *one* thing shows itself to be many through the multiplicity of the characterizations that apply to it, which, depending on the respect in which they are asserted, can even make contradictory assertions about the same thing (remember that Zeno, in the *Parmenides*, thought that he could prove from this the impossibility of the many). Nor is it even that a whole is one and at the same time, seen in regard to its parts, many (on this problem, see Plato's aporetic aretē dialogues and, especially, Aristotle, *Physics* A 2 185b12–16, and the commentaries on this passage). The intensification (*mēde* [not even], 14d9) is due to the fact that in the first case what leads to the pluralization of the one lies not in the one itself but in its relations to other things. Here, on the contrary, it is the one itself that is, in itself, many, and in such a way that each of its members is nevertheless the one itself. My hand, which strikes, is I, myself. Nevertheless, this way in which one thing is many is not the problem that Socrates has in mind here, either. For in both cases the unity that is spoken of is not "pure" unity; that is, it is not thought of as the one as which a manifold of entities is addressed in its being; rather, the one entity can be addressed and specified as one in multiple respects, insofar as, as an entity, it possesses multiple characteristics, such as being larger than this and smaller than that and having various members that are parts of itself. It is one in the sense of the whole of its parts and in the sense of the substratum of its specific characteristics.

The *real* problem of the one and the many, on the other hand, first arises in the case of the pure unities, which are not individual entities but unity as the selfsameness of the being of many entities. These unities, like "man as such" and "the good as such," are respects in which a multiplicity of things is "synoptically" seen together and comprehended. Precisely as unities, they are the condition of the possibility of *dialegesthai* (conversation, argument) in general (compare *Parmenides* 132a, 135c). Only insofar as such a "respect" is a unity can one reach a shared understanding of entities that are seen in this way. It is only insofar as things that come into being and cease to be are understood in a unitary way as always the same, despite all the change that is their coming into being and ceasing to be, that they can be known and determined in a way that gives us access to the facts of the matter. But it is nevertheless a problem how there can be such unities and how, in the realm of what comes to be, they can be many.[5] They themselves, as pure unities, can surely not be divisible—

5. The sentence in which the problem is formulated in the *Philebus*, 15b, is obscure and perhaps corrupt. The formulae *prōton* (b1), *eita* (b2), *meta de tout'* . . . (b4) suggest, initially, *three* different questions. The first is whether such pure unities are to be taken as really *existing*, and the third is how these unities are supposed to be found in the realm of becoming— whether divided up and having become many or entirely contained in each of the many and thus detached from themselves (*Philebus* 15b6 = *Parmenides* 131b). But what the second question is supposed to be is unclear, not only textually but also, above all, substantively. Stallbaum's interpretation, how these unities could remain free from generation and destruction, hardly hits upon an independent issue. The same is true of Wilamowitz's exemplary supplementary emendation before *homos: en de tois pollois phainomenēn*; this question is, precisely, the third one. Other attempts to discern an independent issue here destroy the unified context of the first and third questions. I heard an orally transmitted version of the interpretation by Friedländer which he presents in his *Platon*, vol. 2 (Berlin and Leipzig, 1930), p. 566, n. 2 (= *Plato*, trans. H. Meyerhoff [Princeton, 1958], vol. 3, p. 534, n. 27). For reasons whose presentation here would take me too far afield, I cannot regard it as practicable. The first point against it is that it is not intelligible to the reader of the *Philebus* without having explicit recourse to the *Parmenides*. But this would contravene the highest maxim of all Plato interpretation: that every dialogue is intelligible—if not necessarily *adequately* interpretable—in terms of its own premises. So one will have to unite this supposed second question very closely with the third one (as Schleiermacher and—with the help of a transposition—Natorp, too, already did): "Furthermore, how should these unities—each of which is always the same and untouched by generation and destruction—nevertheless each be steadfastly one, and yet later be in the things that come into being, whether . . ." etc.

[Cherniss, appealing to *Metaphysics* 14, 13, and M 9, 1085a3–31, related *Philebus* 15a–b to Speusippus (H. Cherniss, *Die ältere Akademie* [Heidelberg, 1966], pp. 55, 89–90) [= *The Riddle of the Early Academy* (Berkeley, 1945), pp. 43, 82].)

that is, cannot include different things in themselves—since, if that were so, considering them would not enable us to comprehend the many in a unified way. On the other hand, the many things that are supposed to be comprehended in their being in such a unity are after all supposed in each case to be this one, itself; for example, each beautiful thing is beautiful by virtue of the presence of the beautiful itself in it. But then how can the beautiful itself still be one, if it is supposed to be present in many things?

This problem was gone into in detail in the first part of the *Parmenides* and was answered, to a certain extent, in the second part, insofar as there precisely the "mixture" of the unities themselves—

Krämer goes further. In his view, the issue, in relation to Speusippus, is not only *genos* and *eidos* but also the *atomon* or the individual.

He appeals to *Metaphysics* B 3, which must indeed reflect a discussion in the Academy.

The usage of *ta atoma* seems to be very vague; *sometimes* it can mean the *atmēton eidos*, though certainly not always. In any case, as *Theaetetus* 202ff. shows, it is not only in connection with a *hadroisma*, etc., that one must assume the presence of the atomic theory (*stoicheion*, *atomon*).

This does not exclude the possibility that Speusippus and Xenocrates and Aristotle, too, for a while, may have pursued paths of this sort. Aristotle's inclusion of Democritus among those who prepared the way for *horismos* (*Meta.* M 4, 1078b20) would suggest this.

But in *Meta.* B 3 one should, after all, expect the procedure to resemble that in the late aporetics in B 2 (996b). So it is intentionally left unclear whether *eidē atoma* are intended, in each case, as *kath hekasta atoma*.

However, the Cherniss–Krämer interpretation of the *Philebus* does not stand to reason: *amphisbētēsis*, certainly, but only when it can lead to *euporia*. And on the linguistic side, the substitution of *homōs* is hopeless. The supposed second case passes by the plural *tautas* without *de! men de* argues for *two* cases. On the reference to the *Parmenides*, compare D. Perce, *Idea, Numero e Anima* (Padua, 1961), and H. J. Krämer, "Aristoteles und die akademische Eidoslehre," *Archiv für Geschichte der Philosophie* 55 (1973): 119–190.]

which Socrates has doubts about and which must be the basis for positive prospects for the Socratic launching of the eidē and their justification against the Eleatic critique—is presented. But that justification is given not in the *Parmenides*, where the problem is dealt with only as an *aporia* (difficulty), but here in the *Philebus*. I have already emphasized, above, that the *euporia* (solution) that is prepared here does not really represent a "solution" to the methexis problem. The *chōrismos* (separation) of the world of the Ideas from the world of what comes to be is never "overcome" in Plato (compare *Philebus* 59a). Only the essences *are*; that is, they are the unities that alone make the manifold of what comes to be comprehensible. But that these unities do not need to be indivisible and that the indefinite manifold of what comes to be is not comprehended, with each positing of such a unity, in the way in which it can be defined and comprehended only as something that comes to be, but rather only in *indivisible* unities (the ultimate species determinations)—this is the only positive attitude to the problem of the one and the many that is meaningful on the basis of the Platonic idea of *being*.

As he does so often, Socrates introduces this positive attitude to the problem of the one and the many indirectly, in mythical garb. It is, as it were, a second gift of the gods, a second Promethean fire, one that makes *vision* possible.[6] Like the fire that Prometheus stole, this gift is another endowment by which man is distinguished as its only possessor. It is described here explicitly as the foundation of all technē (16c2), just as the gift of fire brought man technē (*entechnos sophia sun puri*; *Protagoras* 321d1). In fact all technē is based on the fact that the individual item that is dealt with in it is understood in advance as the kind of thing as which it is producible, again and again, as the same. If it is understood only as something that it shares with other things (which, perhaps, have to be dealt with completely

6. This inversion of the Prometheus myth plays with the name. *Prometheia* means an *advance* knowledge about something, which is in fact the distinguishing feature of *technē*, as already at *Gorgias* 501b4.

differently), it is not producible as what it must be for purposes of dealing with it. But, on the other hand, it is comprehensible as different, in its *specific* being, from other things, only insofar as it is the same with them in some other respect. It is determined, itself, only in a unified context of technē, which, however, means: in connection with other things that are different from it.

Everything that is, is composed of one and many and contains defining and indefinable elements in an immediate unity (*sumphuton*). Now the real dialectical procedure consists in methodically explicating, in the logos, the unity of many which thus is inherent, and therefore always to be found, in the thing: first, to seek out a comprehensive "respect" or perspective (*Hinsicht*) in regard to all of it, and then to see, within this, whether what it comprehends can be summed up in two (or, as the case may be, several) further unifying respects, each of which in turn is itself to be analyzed—like the first one and keeping the thing in view—into the respects that are included in it.

In this way one shows not only *that* the one is many but also—and this is the sole purpose—*how many* it is, which is to say, how many ones it is. Only at the end of this path of explication—only when the ultimate "respect" under which the entity is seen is indissolubly unified in itself (that is, the things included under it are not conceptually graspable in any other respects whatever)—does definability come to an end and the respect of the *apeiron* (boundless, undefined) come into its own, which of course in itself means the impossibility of all definition and comprehensibility but also, positively, that this indefinably manifold thing *means the same thing* for Dasein, that it is indifferent to the manifold of the particular things that belong to it. On the other hand, to leap over the intervening terms—to assert, immediately, the oneness of the indefinite multiplicity of the things that come to be and the indefinite multiplicity of the one—is not a genuine dialectical inquiry, not a progressive opening (which achieves shared understanding and appropriation) of access to the thing, but a confusion about substantive matters which disguises itself with a pretense of superior knowledge.[7] The mere smashing of the one into an undefinable multiplicity without gaining new unities is, after all, a dissolution of the very possibility of comprehension. For addressing entities and reaching understanding about them requires that the manifold entity be grasped in a unified way, in that which, as this entity, it always is. So true dialectical division must always arrive at unities again, and necessarily comes to an end (with the atomon eidos) at the point at which a cutting up of the unity (into individual cases) would cease to produce unities—that is, concepts in which the entity is grasped and at one's disposition as what it always is. It is true that in the process of particularization, in each case a one is shown to be a not-one; but in the demonstration itself, the unitariness of what was comprehended in this unity continues to be contained in each of the new unities into which it is analyzed. So when a final, indivisible eidos is arrived at, part of what is arrived at is that, in it, the thing that it sums up in a unified way is comprehended in a logos that fixes the thing, and only it, in what makes up its selfsame being. It is only by unfolding posited unities (the genera) into a definite multiplicity of species in this way that the addressing of entities maintains its scientific certainty and the guarantee of coming to an understanding: that the entity, in its specific definition, is understood as what always constitutes its being.

A basic form of this classifying process of definition is definition in accordance with numbers, as the examples from the theory of music, in particular, show. A true musician is one who knows and commands all the numerically defined note relations (and not one who merely knows the general difference between higher and lower notes). Here the leading role does indeed fall to the number relations. But

7. At 17a1, I would like to read *ta polla* instead of *kai polla*, understanding this, however, not (like Dindorf) in the sense of "mostly" but rather as the (surely, after all, indispensable) grammatical object: they make the many into one and then immediately into the indeterminable manifold. *Kai braduteron* can be elucidated with the help of *Statesman* 277a7–8 and 264a–b: the "faster" way is in fact "slower."

here, too, what number provides is not only the definition of the individual notes and relations of notes, as such; rather, its essential function here as well is to embrace the totality of possible notes in the determined multiplicity of the notes that result in this way from numerical relations. In general, in the description of the dialectical process of diaeresis, number is not itself the actual defining quality of the species but represents their definiteness in general. The number that belongs to a particular species within the unity of the genus is not the characteristic that constitutes its substantive definition; it only guarantees that the differentiating comprehension of the thing will be a continuous methodical progress that does not make leaps. So Natorp's view that the role that number plays here expresses an awareness of the mathematical form of all knowledge of law (*Platos Ideenlehre*, 2d ed., p. 319) is mistaken. Number, here, stands for counting that has taken place, which ensures the continuity of the process of specification (*arithmos* = arranged in rows). Stenzel recognizes this general methodological importance of countability (*Zahl und Gestalt*, p. 14), though he does so in order to find in it the beginning of the general sense of the doctrine of ideal numbers. Nor do I want to deny that, besides the methodical meaning, to which I have drawn attention, of the emphasis on numbers here, there are also suggestions of motives that point beyond the proper concept of number (which in Plato, too, presupposes the sameness in kind of the units), whether it is toward a mathematical logic of qualities, as Natorp thinks, or toward a fundamentally intuitive-perceptual (*anschaulich*) characterization of number as a unity determined by a Gestalt, as in Stenzel's attempted interpretation. Everything we know about the doctrine of ideal numbers does indeed point back importantly to beginnings in the *Philebus*. But the methodical meaning of the relations that this doctrine postulated between numbers and characteristics of things remains extremely obscure. The only thing that is certain is that what really connected numerical definition and ideal definition was the derivation of the manifold of the Ideas from a unity. Knowledge of how many is knowledge of how many kinds and is thus characteristic of technē (compare, for example, *Gorgias* 501a8; *Phaedrus* 270d6, 273e1).[7a]

Definitions of things that can be expressed in purely numerical relations, like musical intervals, are only an extreme, limiting case of definition. This is also shown by the example of linguistic sounds, especially when it is used to illustrate the fact that when one is faced with an undefinable manifold, one should not immediately look for a comprehensive unity that is shared by all the manifold but rather should proceed by way of a numerically definite manifold of kinds, each of which is a unity of an indefinite manifold of entities, to the unity of the genus in general. That the sounds within a class of sounds are counted—which is called for, here—evidently does not constitute their definition as things in the way that the numerical definition of note relations constitutes theirs. Thus in every case the essential thing accomplished by number is that the domain of things is grasped, through it, as a *definite multiplicity of unities*, a multiplicity whose completeness is discovered by counting it. The presence, in full strength, of something that has been counted is something of which one can always convince oneself by counting it again. When it is finally elevated into the general concept of a linguistic sound (a letter), the unitary connectedness of all linguistic sounds is also seen as the common object of a technē, insofar as the sounds are derivable, in their particularity, from this highest unity. The individual sound itself still has a unitary and definite character insofar as it is not this unique acoustic pattern but a sound of language, which can be reproduced, always as the same sound, in indefinitely many individual acoustic events. Only as a sound of language is it a unit—that is, it is defined in its systematic connectedness with other sounds of language (that is, with other possible units). And it is only insofar as it is defined by its membership in a definite class of sounds—for example, the

7a. [On the doctrine of ideal numbers, see my later "Plato's Unwritten Dialectic," in *Dialogue and Dialectic* (New Haven, 1980), pp. 124–155.]

vowels—that it is really available for use in language; that is, it is known in advance in its *combinability or non-combinability with other sounds to form the unity of a word*. So what dialectic accomplishes—which is evident, above all, in the technai—is not only that the sense-perceptible manifold of entities is defined in terms of genus and species (that is, in what it always is and what constitutes the being of each entity) but also that this definition gives us a disposition over it. Insofar as it is known in what it always is, the individual and the particular is seen, just as certainly, *in its potentiality for being with other things*.

This is what the dialectical comprehension of entities in their being accomplishes which makes that comprehension the precondition of all concrete coming to an understanding about something. So it is only the dialectical distinguishing of the kinds of hēdonē and epistēmē that makes it possible for both of them to be known in their potentiality for being good (their potentiality for being together with the good). And insofar as the good in human life will turn out to be a mixture of hēdonē and epistēmē, the question of the good will have to be decided, through the knowledge of their compatibility with one another, precisely by testing both of them *in their individual kinds* for their potentiality for being with one another—which means, ontologically, that their compatibility with each other is based on their potentiality for being (or their non-potentiality for being) with the ontological features of the good itself; that is, it is based on their acceptance or non-acceptance of *measure*. So the demand, which results from this general theory of dialectic, for a dialectical distinguishing of kinds of pleasure and knowledge is based on the fact that the being of pleasure should be examined *in its relation to other things*, that is, to the good (*Philebus* 13a7!), and *therefore* must be comprehended in the actual heterogeneity in which we encounter it, if agreement about its claim to be good is to result.

That the method of investigation which is sketched out in this way is not bound to a rigid dichotomous process of deduction is made clear by the use of the example of language as an illustration of dialectic: inventing "grammar," language takes as its point of departure not the unity of the sound but the indefinite manifold of sounds, which is elaborated into a definite, organized manifold of letters. But the system that is arrived at in this way could just as well be derived and taught on the basis of the highest generic unity. This is how the example of "grammar" functions (17b).

One can observe this double direction of the dialectical method in its application to pleasure and to knowledge. Where there is real *investigation*, namely, in the analysis of pleasures, the point of departure is the manifold as it is experienced; whereas when there is only *presentation*, as in the case of the doctrine of knowledge, Socrates deduces from the unity. But the goal in both cases is the same: to comprehend the heterogeneity of what is grasped (or to be grasped) in a unity, keeping in view the thing (in each case) that is seen, and on the basis of a comprehensive unity. All unification of the many aims at multiplying the one, but in such a way that it recovers, as a *multiplicity of unities*, what it originally was as an indefinable multiplicity.

Part II: The New Posing of the Question (19c–31a)

Section 4: The More Precise Formulation of the Topic (19c–23b)

It is remarkable that the fundamental discussion of dialectic as diaeresis is not applied right away. Socrates makes a new start, while seeming to forgo the rigorous path of dialectic. We find this kind of forgoing of the rigorous mode of presentation frequently elsewhere in Plato as well, and it is always motivated by a concern for the partner in the conversation and for the concrete requirements of the situation (compare *Alcibiades* I. 130c, *Meno* 100b, *Republic* 435d). Here, admittedly, the peculiar circumstance is that this divergence does not mean a definitive abandonment of the path in this dialogue; it will be taken up again later (31ff.). Instead, it has the character of both a substantive and a didactic preparation. For Socrates' partner, Protarchus, shrinks from Socrates' demand, which Protarchus correctly gathers from the theory of dialectic (at 19a5 he says that he would prefer to give the task back to Philebus), and suggests that Socrates look for a more direct, less detailed and rigorous response to the so immediate, practical concern that the question of man's highest possession represents (19c: *deuteros . . . plous*; 20a6: *ei pēi kath' heteron tina tropon hoios t'ei . . .*).[8] Socrates appears to comply with this request. He "remembers" a logos that can serve to spare the conversation the painstaking process of classification (20c4). Of course, in reality, it will turn out that he uses this logos (though without explicit methodological notice) precisely to lead into the dialectical examination of the phenomena.

So he remembers a logos according to which neither hēdonē nor phronēsis, in itself, constitutes the good for human life. We need not take this "recollection," as Natorp does, as a reference back to the corresponding discussions in the *Republic*. Rather, Socrates is said to remember because what he refers to is not something that would first have become evident through an explicit discovery, but something that one has always already known—namely, the characteristics (already marked out in all inquiry about *the good* of life) of the object of one's search as a reality. The sought-for condition of the soul is always already tacitly understood as something complete in itself, finished, self-sufficient; negatively, as something that for its part has no need of anything else in order to be what it is (*dei gar . . . mēden mēdenos eti prosdeisthai*, 20e5). Measured against this formal preunderstanding of the object of the search, both the life that consists only of "pleasure" and one that consists only of "thought" prove inadequate.

The first case is refuted in greater detail. At first it seems as

8. This scene, too, is undoubtedly a conscious development and modification of the discussion process in the "Socratic" dialogues. Protarchus tries to head off the familiar aporetic outcome of Socratic elenctic argument (and with the help of Socratic wisdom, at that! [19c2]—one is reminded of Clitophon's critique of Socrates)—and Socrates responds to the invitation in his most Socratic oracular tone.

though a life that consisted in continual enjoyment would leave nothing to be desired and as though such a life would have no need of knowledge. But if one takes this seriously, such a life immediately turns out to be impossible. If there were no knowledge in it, neither would there be any knowledge in it about itself. But in that case the enjoyment itself would remain unenjoyed. Such a life would not be the life of a human being (*ouk anthropou,* 21c7); that is, a happy life for a human being necessarily means self-knowledge in the possession of gratification. "Happiness," "the good" as the highest potential of human life can be understood only on the basis of and by means of the knowledge by Dasein of itself which is posited in human Dasein.

It is noteworthy that enjoying oneself is seen here as totally dissociated from "possessing" this enjoyment—from *knowing* that one is enjoying. This approach continues, in a certain way, to be characteristic of the whole subsequent analysis of pleasure, as the resumption of this theme at 63c shows. Thus the fact that a human being "has" enjoyment is understood as a presence-at-hand of enjoyment in being affected by the presence of the enjoyable thing, just as everything that is, is present at hand. So it is not, in itself, already "had" in a specifically human way but is initially only present-at-hand in the way that *everything* living is characterized by its present state and is then "had" through an explicit grasping of its presence-at-hand, a being cognitively at home in this potential that one has. This is all the more remarkable since enjoyment, as the further progress of the analysis quickly recognizes, is not a state of the body but is "in the soul." How can one describe such a life, which is continually filled with the pure presence of enjoyment, as desirable and yet regard *phronein* (thought) and so forth as superfluous (unneeded)? The phenomenological root of this approach is the fact that pleasure signifies an absolute self-forgetfulness of Dasein in devotion to the object of enjoyment. It is this self-forgetfulness, as being carried along by the object of the gratification, that initially makes the advocate of the life of gratification [that is, Protarchus] happily renounce all knowledge. It is, after all, precisely as forgetfulness that this life presents itself to him as the highest thing. But in truth, as Socrates immediately makes him realize (21b6), this forgetfulness, too, is still a mode of Dasein's primary knowledge of itself. For one thing, Dasein after all enjoys itself precisely in this forgetfulness. If it perceives this forgetfulness as desirable, it is just because it still *has* itself in this forgetfulness—because it knows (doxa, c4) that it is anaesthetized in this way by gratification, which means that the attractiveness of this kind of forgetfulness is due precisely to the fact that Dasein for the most part cannot forget itself in this way, which is evident from the fact that it strives to forget itself even in the memory (*mnēmē*, c1) of gratification and the expectation (*logismos*, c5) of gratification. If self-forgetfulness in gratification were a kind of abandonment to the object that is not appreciable as such by Dasein itself and is not something that Dasein is cognitively at home in as a potential that it has—if, that is, gratification were really not inwardly manifest to man—then a life of gratification would cancel all real life, that is, all self-understanding on the part of Dasein. Such a life would not indeed be the life of a human being, but at the most that of an animal of the lowest level of organization (21c7). So an interpretation of the real fundamental motives of the hedonistic theory shows that it is specifically *human* motives that lead to seeing the highest potential of human Dasein precisely in something that is characteristic of *animal* existence. It is the reference to this human quality of its motives that invalidates Socrates' opponents' thesis. This thesis misunderstands itself if it dismisses the human potential of phronein and so on, for it is only on the basis of the latter that the thesis's hedonism has meaning at all.

The reverse proposition, that a life in pure knowledge without any pleasure would not be the sought-for "happy" life either is not demonstrated explicitly. It is clear from 23a1 that what is said on this subject at 21d9 ff. is not meant to be taken as such a proof. Instead, it seems to be taken for granted from the outset that the question is not aimed at such a life—that is, that the thesis that knowledge has precedence over pleasure does not (analogously to its opposite thesis) tacitly have in view freedom from all pleasure. But this means that this thesis was arrived at in direct cognizance of the reality of human beings and that it seeks its possibility not *against*, but *in*, that reality. A life in pure knowledge without any pleasure would not in fact be in accordance with the natural self-understanding that human Dasein has of itself. So we necessarily come down to a life that is a mixture of both. Only such a life satisfies the condition of being desirable. But this statement already points to the further question of how this mixture is put together: what share hēdonē and phronēsis have in this mixed life and how this share is determined. So Socrates lays out the new question in terms of which the dispute between the two must be posed: which of the two is more decisive (*aition*) for the shared, mixed life? His thesis is that whatever it is that makes this life desirable and good, it is not hēdonē but phronēsis that is more akin to this decisive thing (*aition*). This new posing of the question of the closeness of their "kinship" (a question that was already anticipated in the consideration of a third possibility, at the beginning, and that now becomes tangible and pressing—see p. 106) marks the *ontological* turning: that the cause is not an entity (pleasure or knowledge) as such, but an onto-logically structural role that can fall to such entities. The third, "mixed" thing can have one of its constituent pieces as the cause of its being good only if this piece is already, in its *own* being, what it must be in the mixture; that is, if it already of its own accord places itself under the norm to which it is subordinated in the mixture.

Section 5: The Doctrine of the Four Kinds (23b–27b)

Since Socrates' opponent does not grant this more precise thesis, it must be examined. And indeed, for this purpose a new contrivance (*allēs mēchanēs*, 23b7) is needed. To be sure, some of what has gone before is also used; for Socrates links up with the first, fundamental discussion of the dialectic, in which the divinity had revealed two kinds of all entities: *apeiron* and *peras* (boundless and bound). These are joined by a third, which is a mixture of both; and this, too, links up with Pythagorean tradition (Philolaus, fragments 1 and 2). But a fourth item still remains to be added; Socrates soon strikes himself as ridiculous, with his division and counting up of kinds (which is what he had shown above to be the scientific form of dialectic!). The fourth item is the aitia (cause) of the mixture. (The mention of a possible fifth kind, the cause of separation, is brought about only by a malicious question from his opponent, at 23d9. It has no substantive basis. The cause of mixture is, after all, nous, which divides just as much as it unites. So an allusion to Empedocles' principle of strife, which some have thought they saw here, can at most be imputed to the questioner, who fails to recognize the ontological meaning of the fourth kind, the cause.)

Why does Socrates lay out this equipment here? For what does he intend it? These four kinds of being represent a fundamental preparation of the way for the new question. After all, the object of the inquiry, the "good" in human life, has turned out to be a mixed thing, and the dispute between the two opponents is supposed to be decided by an investigation of what makes this mixture good. To move in the direction of this decision, one needs to work out the general schema of mixture—that is, what ontologically defines mixture's mode of being—and in such a way that what makes mixture "good" comes to light in the analysis of its existential conditions. So the intention is an ontological one. Mixture is not one kind of entity alongside others; rather, in the schema of mixture one grasps a general character of being. *Everything* that exists (we are told explicitly, at 16c9) is a mixture of definite and indefinite. So being mixed is being definite. Being is mixture, because the latter's being is being definite.

Now, the substantive authentication of these universal structural elements of being, as definite things, proceeds (in accordance with the earlier fundamental discussion of dialectic) in such a way that the universal character of these elements is not simply asserted, but we are shown how it is that they are kinds—that is, how it is that they are split in many ways, and yet one. (*polla hekateron esxismenon kai diespasmenon idontes, eis hen palin hekateron sunagagontes*, 24e4–5.) This is done first of all for the apeiron. How is the indefinite many?

For example, as being warmer and being colder. The indefinite reference of these comparative statements contains no limit or definition; instead, they are always characterized by a more or a less. As something warmer or colder, the entity that is defined in this way is necessarily unfinished and indefinite in itself: it is always still more or (as the case may be) less than any particular how-much or how-little. Everything that is defined as "very" or "a little" also belongs to the same mode of being, of the indefinite. It too has the character of something comparative, of being much or a little only in comparison—except that in this case the comparative quality is not expressed in the linguistic form. (It is true that Socrates uses the comparative forms even of "very" and "a little," but he does so as interpretation, so as to bring out the comparative quality that is *hidden* in them.) Incidentally, there is a substantive reason for the fact that in "very" the comparative quality remains hidden. In it, the term to which the comparison refers is the average, or the middling. As "more than this," even "very" has a certain average definiteness.

The common feature showing that all these kinds of indefiniteness belong to the same genus is the fact that no definite "how great" or "how many" can appear in them. Thus wherever a definite measure takes effect in an entity, these forms of indefiniteness are excluded from it. For the still more or the still less is replaced (*prochorei gar kai ou menei* [progresses and does not remain the same]) by a definite measure, by being established as so and so much (*to de poson estē*). Thus, at the same time that it arrives at a particular limit, the indefiniteness ceases to be what it was (for example, *thermoteron* [warmer]). It becomes establishable, definite. The generic unity of the apeiron is constituted by the fact that, in this way, the peras, as the how-many (*poson*), is excluded from it.

The generic character of the peras results from this too, by virtue of its opposite role. Everything that exhibits the characteristics that are opposed to those of the more or less (the verb is *dekhetai*; that is, everything that by its nature "accepts" these characteristics) can be combined under the unity of the peras—the same, the double, and so forth; everything whatever that has a firm numerical and quantitative character.

To understand the meaning of these two genuses in their contrast to the third genus, the genus of the mixed, one must see their ontological character. What falls under the genus of the apeiron is being warmer—not an entity that has the quality of being warmer, that is, that is defined (or definable), as an entity, only as "warmer than . . . ," but rather the species of this indefiniteness itself. Similarly, what falls under the unity of the peras is not an entity that is always definite, and thus gives definiteness, as an entity; rather, it is that very quality of conferring definiteness. Indefiniteness and measure exclude one another; that is, where a definite measure is seen in an entity, it is no longer something undefined. It ceases to be defined as "warmer than . . ." when it is defined as having a definite temperature. This clearly does not mean that the entity has changed in its substantive nature. When something indefinite is made definite, by measure and number, the entity does not become different, but its existential character certainly changes. Ceasing to be something indefinite, it becomes something definite, established. So the same entity can present itself to us in the indefinite character of more or less and also as something made definite by relations of measurement and number.

Admittedly, Plato shows no conceptual awareness of the purely ontological nature of these characterizations (and we will see why: because one of these characterizations, the genus of the mixed, is not only an ontological characterization but something else as well). After all, as genuses that in their turn embrace in themselves species (eidē of being indefinite and of giving definiteness), each of them circumscribes a highest-level region of entities, which is divided substantively according to genus and species. Seen in this way, not only does the "respect" (*Hinsicht*) of indefiniteness include particular kinds of indefiniteness, but these kinds embrace a manifold of indefinite entities which possess indefiniteness in their substantive reality. Similarly, the kinds of "giving-definiteness" include a manifold of existing numbers and measures. Seen in this way, the mode of existence of the indefinite entities (and thus of indefiniteness itself) and of the entities that give definiteness (and thus of the quality of giving definiteness) would be ontologically the same: both of them are present-at-hand as belonging to different substantive realms (*genē*) in the single existing world. Only in this way can we understand the fact that Plato sees the giving of definiteness to the indefinite in terms of the schema of mixture. Noises that are high- and low-pitched become notes and musical sounds by the addition of definite numerical relations. If this is conceived in terms of the conceptual schema of mixture and mutual intercourse, it is understood as a bringing together of something indefinite, which exists, and a measure, which exists.

Nevertheless, Plato's true opinion here is an ontological one. The indefinite is not an entity that could be combined with another entity, number, so that a new entity, the definite, would result. In music, the numerical definition of note relations does not create note relations that did not exist previously; instead, note relations are established by being defined and are made producible by the art of music only by being defined in this way. Only notes that stand in such definite relations *are* the notes of music—that is, the objects of an art that has a command of notes and has disposition over them by knowing how to produce them always anew. Thus we arrive at an understanding of being only when the same entities that are first of all encountered as indefinite, and consequently are withdrawn from all determination and disposition, are defined through enumeration and measurement and thus are understood, in their being, as producible. Entities really *are* insofar as they are understood in their being, as indefinite things that are defined by something that gives definiteness.

It is characteristic of the ontological character of what is understood as a mixture that, as the togetherness and unity of two things that are present-at-hand, what is mixed in this way contains the two things in a different form from what they were in themselves before they were combined. A combination of two things that are present-at-hand in which both remain what they were is not a mixture. A mixture has to be *one* thing; that is, all its parts must be homogeneous with the whole. But on the other hand, the constituent parts of a mixture must not fully cease to be what they were, either. Otherwise the whole would not be a mixture, but a coming into being of a new thing, together with a disappearance of what had existed previously. This modification which the constituent parts of a mixture undergo as a result of their being mixed is the basis of the suitability of the image of mixture (despite its conceptual inadequacy, in itself) for what Plato means, ontologically: in a mixture the constituent parts do disappear in a new unity. This unitedness of the mixture is the ontological character that Plato wants to bring out. In the case of indefiniteness, this modification of the constituent parts of the mixture is clear: of course, the indefiniteness had to disappear in the face of the definite measure—that is, precisely when the mixture occurred. At the same time, it is continually, and necessarily, seen together with the mixture. For example, together with health, as a definite, concrete state, a penumbra of indefinite possible disorders that would not be in keeping with it is also seen. So here the image of mixture is right. The question regarding the genus of that which gives definiteness (namely, measures and numbers) is more difficult. Number and measure have the character of the peras, the limit, which defines entities in their visible being. They are thus opposed to what is distinguished by the character of indefiniteness, unlimitedness. But the real antithesis of the unlimited is not the limit but *that which is limited*. In fact, number and measure as limits of something are always limits of something limited and define something definite. As something that defines, number is the number of something—that is, it furnishes the how-many of a manifold (*plēthos*). Similarly measure, as something that defines, is what makes a magnitude (*megethos*) definite. The number of something is the manifold—defined by a number—of entities of a kind, and the measure indicates the definite magnitude of something extended. Thus number and measure are really a limit only as the number of, or the definite magnitude of, an entity; but this means that the limit, that which defines, is present only *in* the limited thing— that is, in what has the existential status of a mixed thing. We can go even further. Must not the limiting thing, in order to be able to limit something, itself be limited? The number of something provides definition because it is in itself a definite number—that is, the how-many of a unit. Similarly, measure defines an extent because it is itself a definite measure—that is, the so-many-times of a unit of measure. Further, that which defines the number—namely, the one— is itself the ultimate defined thing, something absolutely indivisible. The situation is even clearer in the case of measures of magnitude. A unit of measure, too, is a measure precisely by virtue of its definiteness—by virtue of the fact that it is definitely one and indivisible, not indeed in the strict sense of indivisibility, like the one, but as far as appearance is concerned. A unit of measure for a thing is, after all, in each case the part of itself that is sufficiently fixed in its definiteness—that is, is small enough not to be taken as smaller or larger without the mistake being noticed. The unit of measure measures insofar as it is applied as *the same* measure to the thing to be measured. Seen in this way, then, the measure is already *something definite*. What it measures must be of the same kind as it is itself. The one can only count units; the unit of length can only measure a distance. (On this subject, compare Aristotle, *Metaphysics* I 1.)

Must not that which defines necessarily belong, then, to the genus of the definite, the mixed? This difficulty becomes evident in the *Philebus*.[9] The original characterization of the generic unity of the

9. Regarding 25d–e: it is clear that the received text is not intelligible as it stands. Bury discusses the possible remedies in Appendix A of his commentary on the *Philebus*. The best seems to be the one originally proposed by Jackson, of transposing the sentence at d7: *all' isōs . . . drasasi . . .* (as Wilamowitz and, incidentally, Badham, before him, have it) to after e2: *apergazetai.* In any case, if one wants to avoid more extreme

peras as the clear opposite of the apeiron (25a) is later treated as inadequate (at 25d, flatly as *ou sunēgagomen*); and even after the third class has been illustrated by examples (25e–26c), Protarchus still does not understand what this third class is—that is, he does not understand what is new about it by comparison with the second class. So in fact, as the above discussion showed, he does not understand the second class without already taking it as the third. That this lack of comprehension on the part of Socrates' partner is not an accident is also shown by the emphasis Socrates lays precisely on this transition from the second to the third class (25b: *theos men oun* . . .). In fact, it really is as the definite number and the definite magnitude of entities that number and measure are definitive. Nevertheless, it is possible to disregard this connection of number and measure to things and to define their existential character in this detached state. In that case,

---

measures, d7–9 must immediately precede Protarchus's answer at e3. Even then the passage remains difficult to interpret. This difficulty seems to me to express the substantive difficulty presented in the text, that the thing that defines must itself already be definite in order to give definition. A textual difficulty at 26d9 is in fact disposed of by this consideration— that is, the received text seems to me to be correct there.

Another possible way of making do with the small emendation that Burnet gives in his text was laid out by Johannes Vahlen (*Gesammelte philologische Schriften* [Leipzig and Berlin, 1911–23], vol. 2, pp. 62ff.). His interpretation is attractive, but still doubtful (even disregarding the linguistic objection that Wilamowitz raised) for three reasons: (1) it seems that *geneseis* . . . *sumbainein* (e4) has to correspond to *kataphanēs* . . . *genēsetai* above, at d8; the sunagōgē of the apeiron has already been accomplished at 25a and is only repeated at 25c–d (see 25c–d10!); (3) Vahlen's reading makes it difficult to understand 26d4 properly; it makes no sense to deny that the peras is many; at least otherwise, if the peras were described as having remained unanalyzed, Protarchus's answer would be unintelligible.

In any case, Vahlen's interpretation is an attempt to extract from the text itself precisely what the above analysis has made plausible as the motive for the whole detour.

their being is still characterized by definiteness, but in a special way. The definiteness of number as number, of measure as measure, is distinguished by the fact that it constitutes the essence of number and measure themselves. There is no number that is indefinite. It defines itself, insofar as it is a member of a series that begins with one. The same holds for numerical measures, which—taking as a basis the unit of magnitude, which measures—are themselves just the result of counting these units. This definiteness of number and measure, which necessarily belongs to their being, constitutes the shared generic character of the peras. It is a definiteness that, as such, has no relation to anything indefinite.

Admittedly, it remains problematic how the genus of measure and number, seen in itself in this way, can become present-at-hand as a constituent part of a mixture. What is modified in it as a result of the mixture? After all, the number, and the defining factor in general, does not cease in the mixture to be what it was. As the number of something or the definite measure of a thing the defining factor is no less and no more definite. The indefiniteness which it defines and thus causes to disappear does not detract from its own definiteness. But the rule with constituent parts of a mixture is that they reciprocally modify each other in the mixture, and that, precisely by being suspended in their earlier separateness, they are retained as determining one another to the unity of the mixture. So they can also be separate again, if the mixture ceases to exist. For numbers and measures, this sort of being present again as separate things has no meaning. So the image of mixture is not suited to illustrating this situation. Nor can the facts of the matter be illustrated by some other relation in which things present-at-hand are gathered together. The two earlier genera are just not constituent parts of the third, but rather its existential moments (*Seinsmomente*).

This ontological character of the genera is also evident from the content of the third genus. For precisely from the way in which the actual examples of this third genus show that entities possess the character of mixtures even in the literal sense, as mixtures of things that are present-at-hand, it becomes evident that the mixture of in-definiteness and definiteness can describe only the character of the *being* of these mixed entities. The third genus embraces everything that results from the combination of the first two. Its character, as a genus, is defined by this combination as *coming into being*,[A] or, more accurately, as the being that comes or has come *to be* (27b8, because the important thing here is not the becoming, but the unified being of the indefinite and the measure—that is, the existential character of entities as *definite* and as defined for something). It is not my intention in what follows to deny that the phrase "coming into being" has a metaphysical importance that is grounded in the whole Platonic ontology but only to set that fact on one side. The basic Platonic thesis that this, our visible world, is "becoming" (and not "being") has the result that its being is called "becoming" ("*Werden*") here. But when it is called "coming into being" ("*Werden zum Sein*"), this implies that this world of becoming, as something defined by measure, in fact ceases to be mere becoming—that is, pure indefinable mutability. For understanding the being of this visible world on the basis of the definite numbers and measures that prevail in it allows one to "understand" "becoming" in view of the "true being" of measure and number, which means to establish it and make it definable and under one's disposition, so that it "becomes" "being." Thus the ontological sense of "coming into being" is that of the understandableness and definable-ness—through definition by measure and number—of the being of the world that is becoming. Plato's examples of what is definite—health, music, the seasons, and so on—all have the character of the good or the beautiful. When this analysis is applied to pleasures, which receive fixed measures and limits, what constitutes the character of the good that belongs to all these cases of definiteness becomes clear. Natorp saw what is most important here: "that the goodness of a thing, for Plato, signifies at bottom nothing but its *self-preservation* (*aposōsai*, 26c)" (Natorp, 2d ed., p. 326).

A. Compare *Philebus* 27d8.

"The teleological concept of the good" is the fundamental concept of Plato's ontology. Being good and being definite signify, at bottom, the same thing. Something that is defined as something is characterized in its being in what it is defined as and for. Only what conforms to the defining measure (*emmetron kai summetron*) *is*, insofar as, as something defined by measure, it is revealed in its being and put at our disposition to be produced. If it were not something definite, it could not really *be*—that is, it would not be determinable and producible as a unit. This general ontological perspective also determines the sense of the doctrine of the Ideas. What really *is*, is only the Idea—that is, that which makes up the unitary selfsameness of what shows itself and in view of which, alone, the change in what shows itself to the senses is understandable. Thus, that it is the "presence" of the Idea in the individual thing that makes it exist is due to the fact that the individual thing can be understood only in view of what it always is. Only when it is understood in its being, in this way, is the entity revealed and available for dealings with it: only then is it understood in its ability to be with other things—its potential for being together with others. It is seen in its *compatibility* insofar as it is known in its capacity to affect other things or to be affected by them. So the unity of this being together is based on the definiteness of its elements. But that definiteness has the ontological character— which makes up the generic unity of the third genus—of conformity to measure.

At the same time, this character makes up the essence of the good and the beautiful. For the "beautiful" and the "good" is, of course, something that is such that it lacks nothing and cannot be added to. This natural empirical concept of the beautiful as the perfect or complete also remains the leading concept in Aristotle's interpretation of human Dasein. Man's potentials, his *aretai* (virtues), have the character of the mean (*mesotēs*)—that is, man produces himself, or understands himself as one who is to be produced, in such a way that he hits the mean, the measure; that is, he "makes" himself as the artist makes a work: so complete that nothing can be taken away or added without destroying the beauty of the work (*Nic. Ethics* B 5, 1106b9). This same anticipatory concept of the complete or perfect also guides the inquiry about the good here in the *Philebus*. As sufficient and leaving nothing more to be desired, the "good" is defined in human Dasein, at any rate, as something that nothing can be taken away from or added to. Of course, when Aristotle shows that this attempt at defining "*the* good," as a universal ontological principle, in its constitution, is not in keeping with the claim to understanding which human Dasein makes in reference to itself, he parts company precisely from the fundamental Platonic position, which undertakes to define man's being privatively, on the basis of a *universal definition* of the meaning of being, rather than positively, on the basis of man's ownmost understanding of Dasein.

So the characterization of being definite as being mixed turns out, after all, in a different sense, to be an accurate characterization of being. It remains true that the ontological meaning of definiteness is inadequately expressed, conceptually, when it is described as a mixture in which indefiniteness and definition are gathered together. Indefiniteness and definition are not constituent parts of the mixed thing but the constitutive existential moments of its unity. But an entity itself, which is defined as a unity, is no doubt always a mixture of things that are present-at-hand. A healthy bodily state is a mixture of contradictory elements. (According to Plato and Aristotle, it is a good mixture of warm and cold; see, for example, Aristotle, *Physics* VIII 5, 246b5). Music consists of harmonic mixtures of notes, and similarly, as a general principle, all concrete entities are mixtures of elements.[10] But *ontologically* the good mixture of the ontic constituent

10. Regarding 25e ff.: the choice of these examples has been incorrectly described as accidental or as determined by looking ahead to the mixed character of pleasure and displeasure as harmony (see C. Baeumker, *Das Problem der Materie in der griechischen Philosophie* [Münster, 1890]). It is not the fact that pleasure has the character of mixedness and harmony but the fact that the good of life is a mixture of pleasure and knowledge

parts—that is, the being of health, of musical harmony, and so forth—
depends upon the *appropriateness* of the shares of the opposed constituent parts. That is, it depends upon the correct proportion, on the
numerical or mensurational definiteness of this proportion.[11] Only this
definiteness of proportion, which Plato characterizes ontologically as a
unity of indefiniteness and definition, makes a mixture into a unity
that can *exist*. A mixture that was not definite in this way would not
really be. For the things that were mixed in it would not be understood
and available in their capacity for unity. An indefinite mixture is a
mixture whose constituent parts do not stand in any fixed proportion
to each other. This kind of mixture can always be mixed together
differently, again (in a different proportion). So it is indefinite in relation to the production of the mixture—that is, it is not producible
again as this mixture—insofar as one does not know in what proportion
one has to mix the component parts in order to get the same mixture
again. So an indefinite mixture is a coming together of its component
parts now in one way and now in another. Only insofar as a mixture
is definite in its proportion, then, is it definite in what it is and is
supposed to be—in its being and its being good. The fact that what
is collected together in the mixture is secured, on the basis of its
definite proportions, as mutually compatible, and is thus defined as
this unity, makes the mixture available—which means producible
again and again as this definite thing. As something produced, it is

---

that is the anticipation governing not only the examples of the third kind
but the whole doctrine of the four kinds, in general. But this too is only
an external observation. The deeper reason is that everything that exists
is, when seen in an ontological perspective, something mixed. It is good
insofar as it is mixed well, that is, as its parts are in the right relation to
one another—as it is *definite*.

11. Since this was written, Otto Toeplitz (*Quellen und Studien zur Geschichte der Mathematik, Astronomie und Physik* [Berlin], vol. 1, pt. 1,
pp. 3ff.) has made the relation between the mathematical concept of proportion and Plato's doctrine of the Ideas more intelligible by approaching
it from another direction.

always an individual thing, but insofar as the production always produces it as something that is definitely thus and so, this individual
thing is understood and produced as what it always is. So *the ontological "mixture" of the indefinite and the defining*, producing definiteness, *is the condition of the possibility of the being*, and the being
unitary, *of (ontically) mixed things*.

So this unity-conferring definiteness of proportion in the
mixed things must be *seen* in the process of mixing. The fact that,
besides the three genera (the definite thing itself, as it comes into
being, and the two genera from which it comes into being), the being
of the mixed thing requires a fourth genus as well—the cause—is
immediately understandable if one notices that the third genus, that
of the definite thing, is not only the unity of indefinite and defining
but also at the same time embraces everything that, as such definiteness, is the unity of something ontically mixed. If, on the other hand,
one takes the three genera only in their ontological character, then it
is hard to see, initially, why once one arrives at the definite proportion
that makes up the goodness of the mixture, the constitutive existential
moments of the mixture should not be used up. Thus Natorp, who saw
in the third genus only the ontological idea of *law*, was in an awkward
position with the fourth genus. Insofar as, through their proper combination, indefiniteness and definition make up the character of the
third genus, the latter, it seems, is itself the principle of their combination. Definiteness, as the unity of the indefinite and the defining,
does in fact constitute the existential character—briefly, the unitariness—of health, musical harmony, and so forth.

But this togetherness of something indefinite and definition is
at the same time the definiteness of an ontic proportion. The definition
of the indefinite produces, from opposed things that are present-at-
hand, a unity. So the defined thing is not the principle but the result
of the combination. But as something that is produced in this way it
points to a producing thing that precedes it, something that is not in
the thing that is caused but that, on the contrary, must already exist,
so that the thing that is caused can exist. So this *cause* is not the

mixed thing, the produced thing, itself. Nor is it the defining thing (peras). For however correct it is that the defining measure "makes" the definite thing out of the indefinite, nevertheless, it does not have the character of a cause. After all, it only really exists, itself, in the mixed thing as that which makes it definite. Taken in itself, the defining measure is only a possibility of definition, in general. For the production of the definite thing, itself, it is only useful (*douleuon*, 27a9), which means that it is not itself the producing agent; instead, it too is something that the definite thing is produced from. So the cause of the production, to which the produced thing points, must define the indefinite into something definite by means of a definite measure, which means, ontologically, that the thing to be produced must be *seen* as something to be produced, or mixed, in a definite measured proportion. This measured proportion, after all, constitutes the being of the entity. Proportion means "logos." Something that is addressed in its proportion is addressed in its being. That which sees and produces the definiteness of proportion which makes a mixture a unity is the cause, the fourth genus. So the genus of the cause, which is arrived at within this horizon of production, is indeed at the same time an *ontological* moment of definiteness—and not a dispensable one that, say, is only added when the subject is brought into the picture, but, on the contrary, the one in which the meaning of being really presents itself for the first time. The being of an entity does not consist in a definite measure and an indefinite matter having *happened to come together*, but in the fact that the entity is *intended* through this definite measure as a unity—that it is understood, addressable, and thus producible *as* a selfsame thing. It is only the fact that a proportion can be cited in a mixture that makes it an entity that is such and such. Mixture proportions that cannot be cited do not *exist* alongside those that can be; rather, they do not have the character of definiteness and of being. Their occurrence lacks an invariable reason or cause. An essential part of definiteness is its discoveredness and addressableness.

Section 6: The Application of this Doctrine to the Question (27c–31a)

If one now applies these four genera of being to the conflict between hēdonē and phronēsis (and this is what they were set up for at 27c7!), then it is clear that the sought-for "good" of life belongs to the third class, the mixed—that it is a part of this third class. Only a part, because the mixed being that came into existence was defined, in general ontological terms, as the binding of the indefinite by measure. Here, in contrast, we are dealing only with a special mixture, the mixture of hēdonē and phronēsis. This too, as a definite mixture, must be comprehensible as an ontological combination of indefiniteness and definition. But it does not follow from this that the mixture's two ontic constituent parts correspond to the two ontological genera of the undefined and the defining. Rather, it is first necessary to investigate what in the constituent parts of this mixture that is supposed to be the good gives it the character of being good. That is, it is necessary to ask how the two constituent parts of the mixture relate, *in their being*, to these ontological moments of a good mixture, and especially which of them is akin to the cause of the mixture's being good—that is, which of them is by its nature such that it wants only to be in a mixture that is good, that is, defined by measure.

Now Philebus himself describes pleasure as boundless (apeiron). (It is important that this is the intervention of Philebus, who does *not* conform to the really dialectical steps taken in the investigation— that is, to the really substantive questions. His response, accordingly, falls short of the level of insight that the discussion has reached.) It is precisely on account of its boundlessness, he says, that pleasure is the entire good. Socrates takes up this answer with ironical willingness but suggests—from the perspective of the insight that has been arrived at into the mixed nature of the good—a different claim to goodness on the part of pleasure than the claim that is implied in its boundlessness. (He had already suggested, similarly, at 28b, that precisely the limitation of pleasure might contain the possibility of its preservation and its goodness.) There is, after all, an implication in the identification of unlimited pleasure with the good that, conversely, unlimited pain would be the absolutely bad. In which case the same unlimitedness would be the cause both for the good *and* for the bad; so it cannot be unlimitedness that constitutes the goodness of pleasure.

However, there is also a substantive background to Socrates' taking up of Philebus's answer. Taken in itself (as *amiktos bios* [an unmixed life]), hēdonē may indeed belong to the genus of the measureless. But that would mean that its share in the good, which (by assumption) it must have, would not be grounded in itself; which is to say that insofar as man premises his existence on the possibility of an enjoyment that aims to be unlimited, he does not comprehend himself meaningfully in terms of a potential that he possesses. Part of the self-understanding of a life that is directed only at enjoyment is to set itself no limits and, for just that reason, to have to accept no end of pain, as well, which results in its necessarily failing in its own intention and not being able to *be*. So "measurelessness" is not, as Philebus thinks, the character of pleasure which positively enables it to be the good but (on the contrary) a negative characteristic of it: that which makes it impossible for pleasure, on its own, to fulfil itself and to be an unvarying perspective from which to understand existence. Thus in regard to the good, pleasure and pain, since they are measureless in themselves, have the negative character of being (when taken in themselves) incomplete—that is, dependent on something else which gives them the share in the good that allows them to *be* good.[12] (This substantive significance seems to underlie the choice of the word *aperanton* (boundless)—compare 31a8–10—even if, initially, the statement has only the superficial import that Philebus's

12. At 26b8 a goddess is referred to who sets limits to the pleasures and, by that very means, allows them to *be*, so far as they can be; this goddess, as becomes evident from the subsequent discussion regarding the fourth kind, is phronēsis. This interpretation (which can be found in Bury) is the only tenable one. So at c1, *autēn* is to be understood as the subject and *hēdonai* as the object.

answer is not sufficient and that when hēdonē is introduced as limit-less, the question should be allowed to stand as "unfinished."

In accordance with this discussion, the examination of the question to which genus of being nous belongs[13] is also oriented ini-tially not toward how it helps to constitute the good *of human life* but toward what existential character it possesses when taken by itself. The first indication here is that all the wise men agree that nous, for us, is the ruler of heaven and earth (28c6); so it belongs in the genus of the cause. But this can also be proved from the facts. For the universe (*tode to kaloumenon holon*) is not governed by accident; rather, it is reason that constitutes the order of the world. Socrates' opponent shares with him this (at first purely cosmologically oriented) conviction. From it, Socrates makes the transition to man—this too, initially, in a purely cosmological perspective: the bodily nature of a living crea-ture is, like that of the universe, a combination of all four elements (*sustasis*).[14] But "in our case"—that is, in our body—each element is

13. Regarding 28d ff.: W. Theiler has recently argued, in his treatise *Zur Geschichte der teleologischen Naturbetrachtung bis auf Aristoteles* (Zurich and Leipzig, 1925), that Diogenes of Appolonia is the probable "source" of the train of thought that begins here. But the idea that one can clarify the peculiar compositional problem presented by the function of the doc-trine of the four kinds within the whole of the dialogue as resulting from the intrusion of this source into Plato's train of thought must be rejected. That nous is not peras but aitia is just as central a theme for Plato as that "our" nous points beyond itself to the divine nous. The prejudgment that one can *clarify* a completed intellectual creation like the *Philebus*, in any substantively important feature, by the knowledge of sources still seems to be at work even in Theiler.
14. Regarding 29a10: the image of the sailors in the storm, which is often applied elsewhere in Plato to confusion in speech (as it is by implication here at b1; compare *Laches* 194c, *Euthydemus* 293a, *Republic* 472a), is found here in a form that has so far, strangely enough—I do not know why—been understood unanimously in a way that would indeed make it (as Schleiermacher remarks in this connection) a very chilly joke. Should

present only to a smaller extent, in comparison with the presence of the same element in the universe, and is nourished by the latter. So just as we call the unity of the elements that are together in a living creature its body, so there will also be a "body" of the universe, from which our body nourishes itself. And just as we say that our body has a "soul," so also the so much greater and more beautiful "body" of the universe will have to have a "soul." Here the unity of the four elements, as the body of a human being, is based on its containing all four of the ontological generic characteristics of being, of which it is the fourth, above all, that constitutes *life* in the body and thus creates (in reference to the body) the ways in which it is trained and healed and, in general, all the kinds of *sophia* (wisdom) (both those that put together and those that produce and heal). Now insofar as the same four elements are present, in the larger, in the whole universe, and in a purer and more beautiful state, is it possible that the nature of what is most beautiful and best should not be produced from them? That is, must not the four genera of being also be contained therein in the proper way, under the direction of the fourth, which makes up the life of the whole and its entire reasonableness (*sophia*)?[15] Must not

_____

not the point of the allusion to what sailors say in a storm be this: that in a storm one sees all four elements confused in one single commotion? In that case the point is not that the seamen in a storm, seeing the land that promises safety, cry "Land!" That would fit the present situation in the conversation poorly. Thus I understand *kathaper . . . phasin* not as connecting with *gēn* but as referring to what follows: "*enonta en tēi sustasei.*"
15. Regarding 30a9–b7: the syntactic construction of this section is obscure. From *ta tettara ekeina* up to *tetarton enon*, the fourth kind, the nous, is brought out as the true subject by the *touto* (as Schleiermacher accurately represents it, II, 2, p. 339). Correspondingly, in the second clause, no doubt *memēchanēsthai* is to be understood as in the middle voice and to be completed with *touto* (that is, *to tēs aitias genos*). By the explicitly parallelized neuters *en men tois par hēmin* (b1) and *ton d'auton touton* (b4), which are picked up by the *en toutois* (b6), on the other hand, we are to understand the ontic elements (or their *sustasis* as a body), as

the sustasis (union) of the elements—as in us, so also in the universe—exhibit the structure of a proper, definite mixture; that is, just as much as in our case, must not the constitution of this sustasis require the presence in it of the four genera?

Here the *ontic* mixture of elements is very clearly eclipsed by the *ontological* structure of a proper mixture. The latter is a condition of the possibility of this ontic mixture's becoming *the unity of a living whole* (of the "body" that has a "soul," that *lives*). Thus the nature of the universe, more than anything else, is a proper mixture. In it, apeiron and peras are contained in the correct way, under the dominion of nous, which orders everything and produces the order of the ebb and the flow. The universe, too, has a soul, indeed, a kingly soul, and a kingly nous, which governs everything. "Life" is the being of things that are united as wholes. Its essence is soul, and soul is the *archē kinēseōs* (principle of motion). Whatever lives, moves of its own accord, and that also means: as one. It, itself, moves itself, even if it moves only a single member. It is characteristic of lifeless things that they are what they are composed of. Living things are more than a gathering together of different things. They *have* themselves as a number of things, and they are primarily this reflexive having in its unity.

This precedence, in terms of unity, over everything non-living is the advantage that living things have over non-living ones. The latter can also be the unity of a mixture, as something understandable to one who understands, but not as something that understands itself in its unity.

It is clear from this reflection that the nous, by its generic descent, belongs in the highest genus, that of the cause. With that, the question that we are concerned with seems to be decided. As Socrates had predicted, nous is kin to the cause of motion—to what

is confirmed by the reference of *ta par' hēmin* (b1) back to the corresponding 25b–c and of *kata megala merē* (b5) and *eilikrinōn* (b6) in the same direction. This *distinction between the ontic elements and the moments of the ontological structure of the mixture* is a precondition of a correct interpretation.

makes it good; it is only kin to it, though, because of course our human nous (which is at issue in the debate) is only on a small scale what the nous in the universe is. In the case of hēdonē, on the other hand, it has become apparent that in itself, of its own accord (*en hautō aph heautou*, 31a10), it has no limit at all, but is indefinite, so that its share in the proper mixture that constitutes the good life can in no way be determined and justified on the basis of itself; which means that its share in eudaimōnia—that is, its potential for *being*—cannot be understood on the basis of its self-understanding.

Part III: Investigation of the Kinds of Pleasure (31b–52d)

Section 7: Corporeal Pleasure and Psychic Pleasure (31b–35d)

The application of the investigation of the constitutive moments of a proper mixture (the investigation that the doctrine of the four genera amounts to) to the topic of the discussion as a whole is not treated as though it were sufficient to decide the issue. The reason for this remains obscure. Substantively, it seems that the conclusion that has been arrived at does not measure up to the sense of the question about the good as it was originally conceived. The issue has to do with actual human life (this is made clear by the reference to the life of the divine nous, at 22c5). For human life, however, pleasure had proved to be present necessarily when the good is present. The generic assignment of pleasure to the genus of the indefinite is not able to explain the relationship—which is assumed in the meaning of the question—between pleasure and the good of life. The problem is, rather, precisely how pleasure, however unbounded it may be in itself, enters into what is limited and measured. So the question is *which* pleasure is able to take on the character of limitedness without thereby ceasing to be itself or, in other words, which pleasure remains pleasure—that is, no less desirable and acceptable—even when limits are placed on it that stem not from itself but from something else. If the general provenance of pleasure in terms of being does not clarify its share in the good, then one no longer ought to ask about pleasure in general at all, but rather *which* pleasure it is, without which human life would not be the best that can be desired. But this question is not to be answered on the basis of pleasure's self-understanding, for in its own intention it surpasses all measure (*Gorgias* 494b2: *hōs pleiston epirrein*). Instead, actual human life itself needs to be interrogated as to how pleasure appears in it.

But the transition to this new question of how pleasure *arises* is carried out in a remarkably tacit way, as a matter-of-course continuation of the inquiry. This tacitness can hardly be a consequence of mere literary unconcern and carelessness. The transition's matter-of-course quality is manifestly incongruous in relation to its substantive importance. For what follows is an analysis of the kinds of pleasure: an analysis, that is, that satisfies the demand for *dialectical method* which Socrates set up in the beginning and which he had apparently abandoned. The fact that this discussion begins now without any announcement is extremely significant. Dialectical differentiation, such as Socrates had called for, is not a subtle and laborious method of which a layman, like Protarchus, should be afraid, but the natural way in which shared understanding comes about, one which happens entirely of its own accord when one approaches the facts of the matter with an objective intent. The tacitness of this transition represents a highly ironical situation. For if Socrates were a mere competitor in the *agon* (contest) of the logoi, as his partner initially presented himself, then he would have won his match at this very point, for the pre-eminence of nous over hēdonē is clearly evident. Precisely because the situation is so unfavorable for Protarchus, Socrates succeeds in drawing him into the exact dialectical investigation. The fact that such an investigation is indeed still needed cannot remain hidden from the attentive reader. For it is only from a concrete knowledge of the various kinds of pleasure that one can learn what its claim to goodness is based on and which of its kinds vindicate this claim. To deny the justice of this claim outright would be to set aside the assumptions on which the inquiry was based.

The analysis of the kinds of pleasure takes as its guide the question of where and through what pathos (passion, receptive state) of the soul they come about. Here one will always have to consider pain (*lupē*) alongside pleasure. This is of decisive importance. For it was in connection with the presence of pain along with pleasure that the hedonistic thesis ran aground on its own impossibility: pleasure's limitlessness linked it to pain, and this meant that it was unable to *be* as what it thought it was. This presence of pleasure and pain along with one another turns out to be substantively important in connection with the very first kind of pleasure. For both pleasure and displeasure appear, by their nature, in the genus of the mixed, in which, for example, health and harmony belong. (The latter was not specifically named previously but was certainly intended in substance: after all, all the examples of the mixed which were named had the character of harmony, insofar as harmony is the agreement of opposing components which is determined by a fixed relationship.) It is in relation to the harmony of our bodily nature that the affects of pleasure and displeasure make their appearance. Pain is a disturbance and a dissolution, and pleasure a restoration of the natural harmony. So this bodily kind of pleasure and pain, illustrated by phenomena that everyone is familiar with (for example, thirst and its quenching: satisfaction), is based on the essence of our bodily nature, which is a mixture of undefined and definite and is animated as such. Disturbance of this definiteness—discord—is bodily pain, and a return to the natural definiteness is bodily pleasure. This, of course, presupposes that the entity in question is not simply a physical thing but an animated, living body. So—as is already implicit in the approach being taken— this body must *perceive* what happens to it: the disturbance and the restoration of its natural state. But this unspoken assumption is not important initially for the analysis, insofar as this perception is stipulated as occurring with every ontic modification of the state of the living body. That is, the interpretation connects pleasure and pain so closely to processes in the body that they are not conceptually distinguished from those processes. Thirst is pain as the lack (the nonpresence) of the body's natural moistness; and the quenching of thirst, as the restoration of the natural amount of moisture, is pleasure. Understood in this way, pleasure and its opposite are bound together: pleasure cannot arise without prior displeasure. It is clear that the claim to be "the good" of human life, the claim on the strength of which human existence would understand itself as good, cannot be founded in this kind of pleasure. As something that is given immediately with the natural fluctuation of bodily states and is necessarily linked to the prior appearance of displeasure, this kind of pleasure is not at all designed in such a way that a human being could see himself as good because of the pleasantness of this state. For this state does not represent a possibility of existence that can be taken care of and developed in its own right, independently of displeasure.

Now, alongside this bodily kind of pleasure and displeasure Plato sets a second kind, associated with the soul, which consists in the expectation of pleasant and unpleasant things. These two kinds of expectation—the pleasure of hope and the displeasure of fear—are defined initially so as to correspond to the forms of bodily pleasure and displeasure discussed above. However, they represent a new, independent kind of pleasure and displeasure, because they are purely psychic states, distinct from the state of the body at the moment. They are incorporeal; that is, this pleasure of expectation is not at the same time a state of bodily pleasure. This psychic kind is also distinguished from the bodily one by the fact that, here, pleasure and displeasure are not bound to one another in a uniform experiential sequence. The pleasure of expectation is not necessarily preceded by the displeasure of fear, as being filled was necessarily preceded by being empty. For the expectation of being empty is not necessarily associated with its actually being impending, any more than is the expectation of being filled. This constitutes a special feature of the psychic kind of pleasure, by comparison with the bodily kind (at least according to the interpretation of the latter that has just been given). (It is, admittedly, questionable whether this special character of the psychic kind of pleasure and displeasure—that they can each appear on their own— is really intended, and is being cited as grounds for their being methodologically privileged, in the text beginning at 32c6.[16] This special character is, in any case, implied, as a matter of fact, in psychic pleasure.)

16. Regarding 32c6–d6: a positive interpretation of this passage is very difficult. That *en gar toutois* (c6) means only the second, psychic kind of pleasure and displeasure (as Schleiermacher and Ritter assume when they interpolate *pathēmasin*) is rendered unlikely by what follows, which begins the investigation with the first kind again. In that case, we should (with Badham) interpolate *eidesin*. The result, then, would be that in both kinds of pleasure there would be pure and unmixed pleasure, which as such cannot (of course) justify pleasure's claim to be good, but by its own legitimacy makes the illegitimacy of this generic claim evident. In fact, at 51a ff. pure pleasure is acknowledged both in *aisthēsis* and in *epistēmē*. A counter-argument could be that at 66c5 the pleasure of aisthēsis as well is explicitly described as purely psychic. But this is done on the basis of the deepened understanding of bodily pleasure, which is not yet available in this first section but is first reached at 33d3 in the analysis of aisthēsis. But just this deeper understanding of bodily pleasure makes it possible to recognize pleasure in the bodily realm, as well, which involves no parallel displeasure (51b5) and which then, of course, can just as well be called "psychic" pleasure. So the position of the passage we are examining is that this unmixedly good pleasure enables us to understand both why pleasure can make a claim to be the good in life at all and also that this justified claim is not based on its universal, generic character as pleasure. The fact that we read here (c8) of pure displeasure as well as of pure pleasure should not cause confusion. Of course, only the pleasure is at issue; but if it is pure, there must also necessarily be a corresponding pure displeasure. Bearing in mind the meaning that the terms *eilikrinesin* and *ameiktois* have in the *Philebus*, it surely will not do to understand them merely formally here, in terms of the neat separation of the two kinds, as Apelt does.

In any case, the subsequent analysis is guided by the anticipation (of which one must find an intimation in the program stated at 32c6 ff.) of discovering pure pleasure, unmixed with pain, within the described radius of the two basic kinds of corporeal and psychic pleasure, so as to gather from it when and what kind of pleasure is good. To that extent, the psychic kind of pleasure does indeed have a methodological priority—by comparison, that is, with the interpretation of bodily pleasure that has been given so far—insofar as pleasure can appear here without its opposite. But this methodological priority will lead, in what follows, precisely to the acquisition of a deeper understanding of the first, bodily type of pleasure as well. For it is clear that the interpretation of bodily pleasure which has been given so far is not suited to justifying any claim by pleasure to be the good. On the contrary, it follows with necessity from this conception that there is, beside pleasure and its opposite, a third state of the body as well: for, if neither a disturbance nor a restoration of its natural harmony is present, there must be an intermediate state in which one feels neither pleasure nor displeasure. That is, in fact, the state that corresponds to life in pure thought, in its ideal perfection (compare 21e ff.). If this state of neither-nor exists, then this life is possible *in itself*; indeed, it is certain that it is the most divine life. But of course it does not correspond to the *human* ideal of the good, because human Dasein always already understands itself as experiencing pleasure and pain. Nevertheless, a priority of nous over pleasure is evident here which must necessarily be a factor in the decision between the two. A life of enjoyment would require, for its own completion, the presence at the same time of nous; while a life in pure thought does not require the presence at the same time of pleasure, but, on the contrary, a state of being unaffected by pleasure and displeasure—a state that exists in itself, even if it is unattainable for man as a continual mode of existence and therefore does not represent what constitutes the good of human life, which is what is being sought.

The second, purely psychic kind of pleasure is rooted in the pathos of *mnēmē* (remembrance), in the "soul's" capacity to retain—

that is, to keep hold, "mentally," of—something that is no longer corporeally present. A long path must be traversed in order to make clear what this retention is and how it is that it characterizes the psychic kind of pleasure in general. Twice the analysis is, as it were, pushed back, a step further each time, to an investigation first of aisthēsis (sense perception) (33c9) and then of *epithumia* (desire) (34d1).

"Retention" (memory) points back to a previous bodily perception (aisthēsis), which is based on a corporeal pathos: a sense impression. But there are two ways in which the body is affected by the world. The first way is when things undergone by the body cause a change in it, a change that comes to a halt in it without penetrating the soul—that is, without being felt. The second way is when the change penetrates, through the body, to the soul. So the first remains hidden from the soul. It is the absence of sensation. This hiddenness can be characterized only privatively and not, for example, as forgetting, since forgetting always presupposes that something has been experienced and therefore can be retained. The second way, in which body and soul are both affected by something that presses upon them, is sensation or perception. So a constitutive requirement in this case is that the corporeal impression is also a psychic one. This distinction prepares the way for a deeper understanding of so-called corporeal pleasure. The purely physiological characterization of this kind of pleasure turns out to be insufficient, insofar as the mere modification of the body does not yet entail any pleasure or displeasure but does so only when a sensation of this modification is added. Thus it is shown that corporeal pleasure and displeasure, in the widest sense, also belong to the psychic system.

The second, purely psychic kind of pleasure, which is now investigated, is distinguished, by comparison with the (now more correctly understood) first kind, by the pathos of mnēmē or anamnēsis. Retention has the character of a keeping of the sensation, or, more correctly, of what was sensed and perceived, without the latter's remaining present so that the sensation or perception continues. So memory and recollection are a being of the soul toward something that itself is no longer corporeally present to the senses. Plato distinguishes anamnēsis more precisely from mnēmē, the retention of something perceived, as a making present of something that is no longer present, whether this proceeds directly, with something that was perceived, or whether it is the recovery of a lost (forgotten) memory of something perceived or learned. (In *On Memory* 2, 451a20, Aristotle rejects this characterization of recollection, and does so justifiably, because in recollection we do not remember something retained as something retained, but instead we remember what we perceived, itself, and only this recovery of the thing itself that we previously perceived makes it possible, again, to retain it. Thus, whether we have first retained and then forgotten what we perceived or have not retained it at all makes no structural difference between kinds of recollection.)

The distinction between mnēmē and anamnēsis (which is not held to firmly, as terminology, in what follows, for mnēmē embraces both retention and recollection and other things as well, as will become apparent) makes completely clear, for the first time, what Plato is concerned with here. He wants to show that there is a being toward perceived things which does not depend on the latter's being perceived in a bodily, sensual manner—that is, on their being corporeally *present*. It does not necessarily depend on that even in the way in which one might regard retention itself (which one can after all conceive as a being toward non-present things which begins with perception and therefore belongs together with it in a unitary way) as depending on perception. Instead, anamnēsis represents a pure possibility of the soul's being able—purely of its own accord—to be toward non-present things. It is on this capacity of the soul that purely psychic pleasure is based, and specifically in terms of desire (*epithumia*), which must be investigated first of all.

Desire is the character of hunger and thirst, for example— that is, of just those phenomena that were cited in the beginning as examples of corporeal pleasure and displeasure. The realization that these phenomena cannot be explained solely by the presence of a bodily pathos carries with it a fundamental deepening of the interpretation of pleasure and displeasure in general. As psychic *pathē* (pl. of pathos), they cannot, from the beginning, be characterized by means of the mere sensation of something present. Rather, desire is a being toward something that itself is precisely *not* present. Someone who is thirsty does not feel a mere emptiness, which is present in him; rather, he is directed, at the same time, toward the opposite of the present state of emptiness: toward being filled with something to drink. So this desire cannot be constituted solely by the feeling of emptiness. It does not at all have the character of feeling something that is present, because it is always a desire *for* something, and this something that one desires is precisely not one's present bodily state. So it is not the body that desires (*verlangt*) at all, but the soul. The soul, after all, has the capacity to reach (*langen*) for something (*ephaptesthai*, 35a7), to be toward something that is not present; it has this by virtue of its capacity for retention. All desire, which has the general character of being "out for" something, is the business of the soul.

The fact that desire is based on retention is clearly not due to an ontic-genetic relationship. Socrates asks how a person who is in a state of emptiness for the first time can be directed at being filled. Certainly not through perception, since perception is always directed at something present. How can it be possible through mnēmē, if he has never experienced a filling that he could have retained? But all desire contains this kind of reaching out for non-present things, something that is made possible only by mnēmē. The limiting case of the first experience of emptiness which is described is clearly not intended to show how, genetically, a memory of being filled is gained and added to this state of emptiness so that the desire can be constructed for the first time; rather, it is meant to show that, ontologically, desire contains the structural element of mnēmē. So in general the concept of mnēmē guarantees this capacity of the soul *to be toward something that is not present*. Memory (recollection) of something earlier that was pleasant does not just have the character of a being toward something *past*. Rather, as something pleasant, the past thing is retained as something that *would* be pleasant if it recurred. *So ontologically, being out for something is a precondition of retention.* Someone who wants not to forget something but to "keep it in mind" wants this in relation to a future process of making provision, which he is "out for." It is only because the past thing is retained as a possible future thing that this retention is a structural element of desire. The role of mnēmē in access to what is desired teaches us, ontologically, that all being "out for" something is the business of the soul. The soul's distinctive capacity is to have, on its own, a vision of things that are not present.

Section 8: Desire and Anticipatory Enjoyment (35d–36c)

So the outcome of this analysis is a fundamental overcoming of the initial characterization of corporeal pleasure and displeasure as the sensation of something present (a state of one's body). Plato suggests this overcoming by assuming, alongside these two affects of pleasure (as the sensation of satisfaction) and displeasure (as the sensation of emptiness), an intermediate condition within the state of emptiness itself: this combines, at one time, the pain of bodily emptiness and the retention of something pleasant whose appearance would remove this pain. This retention itself is pleasure, and thus man's overall condition is something intermediate between pain and pleasure; which, however, means *one* mixture of both which presents itself now only as pleasure, now only as pain. (On this, compare 46c3, 47d3.) But this unitariness of the "mixed" state forces us to go beyond its ontic characterization as a simultaneity of pain and pleasure. Understood ontologically, no particular state-of-mind (*Befindlichkeit*) of Dasein is such a mixture. Whether by confidence in the speedy arrival of what is desired (*en elpidi . . .*) or, conversely, by certainty that it will not come (*anelpistos echei . . .*), Dasein's state-of-mind is determined *uniformly*, in each case, as pleasure or as the opposite. If one sits down to a meal hungry, one does not simultaneously suffer from hunger and look forward to the meal; rather, one has a *pleasant* hunger. But the same bodily state of hunger can also have the character of displeasure if one knows that there is nothing to eat, so that, instead of being absorbed in one's being toward what one desires, one is abandoned to the present pain of the hunger. So in both cases the hunger, as pain or pleasure, is not simply defined as the sensation of something present, of a bodily state, but is determined by a being toward something that is not present: toward the meal.

Furthermore, desire as such does not primordially involve either a pleasant anticipation of something or the painful awareness that what one desires cannot be procured. Nevertheless, it is by its nature a desire for something pleasant, and precisely as such it is a precondition for a thing like emptiness being felt as painful. "Emptiness" is, after all, the state of something's being missing, and insofar as this missingness is felt, one *is without* that which is missing—but only insofar as one is oneself directed at the absent thing. Thus all feeling that something is missing presupposes a retention of the thing that is missing as something whose presence is expected and habitual. Of course, this missing thing need not be discovered as a particular kind of thing. One can lack something without one's knowing what it is that one lacks. But insofar as, when one lacks something, it is always *something* that one lacks, this awareness does nevertheless presuppose a memory of something. The fact that something is felt as missing is part of the essence of desire itself. Thus the displeasure that the present state causes does not have the character of a feeling of something present but, rather, of an awareness of something which one desires being missing. More precisely, what one desires is not adequately characterized as something that is missing in the sense of not being there. It is something that *I* lack—that is, the missing thing is something that I need. Only in this way is the discovery of its nonpresence a being without it. Only insofar as I desire something that I do not have but which I need or think I need—that is, only in *returning* from what I am already with, in my desire—am I aware of my present state as being without something, as pain.

So it is not at all the case that a bodily state that "in itself" causes pain necessarily—by the mere presence of the painful thing—determines a person's condition as one of suffering. Instead, what is constitutive for the suffering is that the person's natural "being out for" something pleasant is obstructed or, more precisely, that the felt pain—say, hunger—brings the soul back from its already being with what remedies the pain. Of course, in this state of being brought back from the desired thing, the latter continues to be seen as well, but only *as* something that is lacking. That is, in suffering, Dasein places itself entirely within its being without the pleasant thing—in other words, within the presence of the pain—and closes itself against its already being with the pleasant thing. So the phenomenon of desire that Plato has in view here is not really constituted as pleasure or pain by the hopeful or despairing anticipation of what is desired. It is true that desire, as a being out for something (in Aristotelian terms, as a kind of *orexis*), is directed at the procurement of the desired thing; but this is in such a way that this directedness does not depend upon the *actual* possibility of procuring it. In desire, one is not with the desired thing in such a way that one constructs an opinion about its coming into being and, on the basis of this opinion, either rejoices over it in hope or suffers doubly in desperation. Instead, one's being with the desired thing is pleasant prior to the adoption of any attitude regarding the possibility of its reality; and the reverse also holds, that being without something does not mean that one is without hope that what one desires will appear, but only that Dasein is brought back from the desired thing to its present need. So the state of desire is not the kind of mixture of pleasure and pain that presents itself uniformly as pleasure when hope is predominant or uniformly as pain when one is without hope; rather, what is characteristic of desire is that it continually comes back to itself.

Strictly speaking, then, desire is not only temporally *prior* to the decision as to whether one can hope for the desired thing or not, but is fundamentally *independent* of this decision. A thirsty person does not cease to desire water (and to feel pleasure in this desire) when he sees that no water is available; nor, conversely, does he cease to be brought back again and again, by thirst, to his present state of being without, even if he can count on being able to drink soon. Thus it is necessary, in connection with the state-of-mind of desire, to grasp the "fore-" character of desire, together with the character of being without, as structural elements of a specific primordial state-of-mind. This latter can in fact be described—precisely by contrast with the forms of anticipation which Plato does not distinguish from it—as a mixture of displeasure and pleasure for which, however, it is essential that this mixture does not present itself uniformly as pleasure or as pain but *vacillates* between the two. By contrast, the various specific forms taken by the general "fore-" character of the soul, in forms of anticipation, constitute states-of-mind each of which is uniform and different from the one just described.

If Plato does not distinguish here, but characterizes the condition of desire as a mixture composed of bodily displeasure and the pleasure of anticipation, he is operating under the assumption that what is present in the sense of present-at-hand must help to constitute the person's state-of-mind. This assumption reveals itself in two ways. First of all, insofar as in desire, which is understood as happy anticipation, one's state-of-mind is a happy one, despite the fact that part of what is felt in anticipation is the absence of something—insofar as this is the case, the pain in such a case is simply *covered up.* So the fact that the pain is not *felt* characterizes Dasein's "being ahead" with the expected thing as a process of covering up. Moreover, Plato characterizes Dasein's being ahead with the desired thing as pleasure *or* displeasure, because in his interpretation what is desired is discovered in an anticipation that is more accurately characterized as hope or (as the case may be) as hopelessness. The decisive thing here is that in such an interpretation what one desires is always already thought of as a possible or (as the case may be) impossible reality (present thing). This representation of the desired thing as something that is to be expected or is not to be expected defines the state of the desire as pleasure or as unpleasure.

Thus the pleasure of desire is *anticipatory enjoyment,* a mode of being toward future things which does not leave them alone in their futureness but reaches ahead and shifts them into the present. Accordingly, as I said, in Plato's view the pain of the desire which is understood as anticipatory enjoyment consists in the fact that in this already being with what is desired, the latter's not yet being present is manifest at the same time, if only in the mode of the covering up of the fact that it is not yet and thus the covering up of the pain. But one's being with the desired thing, which shifts it into the present, and the manifestness of the desired thing's being not yet do not really constitute a discordant state-of-mind, a simultaneous pleasure and pain. The anticipatory enjoyment does not shift what does not yet exist into the present in the sense that it does not have the latter's not yet existing in view at all. It is perfectly possible for anticipatory enjoyment to be characterized by the fact that one looks forward to something that is to come, without thereby being in a state that would allow one to be glad about it now, if it were already present now. So the fact that the object does not yet exist certainly is something of which one is aware in one's anticipatory enjoyment. But it nevertheless does not constitute a displeasure as part of the anticipatory enjoyment. In being glad about something, Dasein's awareness that the thing does not yet exist has not really led it to conclude that the pleasant thing is not now—that is, it is not *going without* the pleasant thing. In looking forward to something, it has transported itself so much into its future that it takes the present, its current state-of-mind, with it into this future. Anticipatory enjoyment is present enjoyment precisely as the enjoyment, in advance, of future enjoyment of something.

In any case, the positive outcome of Plato's analysis of the soul's anticipatory character is as follows. Insofar as Dasein is always "out for" something—which means that it is already with things that are not present—the pure givenness, as sensation, of bodily pain is not enough to constitute Dasein's state-of-mind. For it cannot be taken for granted that while this pain exists, it is in it that Dasein is perceptible to itself—that is, that Dasein, being determined by this bodily pain, really perceives itself as suffering. Instead, Dasein's state-of-mind constitutes itself as a *being toward* itself which is essentially co-determined by a being toward things that are not present but anticipated. Because Dasein (in hope or in despair) is always already toward future things, the present pathos as such is not the sole determinant of how it fares. This being toward future things is a distinctive capacity of the soul; that is, the being of human beings is characterized by the free possibility of, of its own accord, expecting or fearing something. So hope and despair about something are not (as pleasure and pain) simple givens; they are not simply the presence of anticipatory enjoyment or the opposite. Rather, the state-of-mind that they involve constitutes itself on the basis of Dasein's character of being "discovering" (its *Entdeckendsein*). As "discovering," it lets the world encounter it, and this letting-encounter has the character of taking something *as* something.

Section 9: "False" Pleasure as Groundless Hope (36c–41b)

The anticipatory character that Plato has brought out as the soul's distinctive capacity, by contrast with the givenness of the sensations that are bound up with one's bodily state at any given time, puts the phenomenon of hēdonē in an intimate relationship to the discoveredness of the world. Enjoyment is not simply a state or a feeling but a way in which the world is made manifest. Enjoyment is determined by the discoveredness of entities in their enjoyableness. But insofar as entities are discovered as enjoyable *for* . . . , Dasein itself is simultaneously discovered in its being affected by the world. Thus it is through having discovered things that are to be expected from the world that the really psychic kind of pleasure constitutes itself. In this way it enters the same problematic of true (that is, discovering) and deceiving (that is, concealing) discovering that characterizes the phenomenon of doxa (opinion) in general. Pleasure, too, as anticipatory enjoyment, has the general structure of regarding something *as* something.

The guiding concept of the subsequent analysis is that of the *truth* of pleasure. Truth means discoveredness. Pleasure is true insofar as, in it, entities are presumed to be pleasing that are pleasing. Thus the state-of-mind of pleasure is always understood on the basis of its having discovered the entities "in which" one has it. Indeed, this understanding of one's own state-of-mind through what the world presents one with is so central for Plato's approach to the problem of hēdonē that hēdonē *itself* is seen as a way of discovering the world by letting it affect one. Therefore it not only makes sense to investigate hēdonē's capacity for being true or false, but this is the key issue here. This shows, at the same time, that in general the interpretation of human Dasein, for Plato, is oriented toward the fact that Dasein understands itself as being toward the world (in which it is) in the manner of making provision, which is to say that Dasein understands itself *through* the world. Thus there is in principle no place in Dasein for what we would call "mere moods," in regard to which we imagine that Dasein can be aware of itself, in its mood, merely as "existing and being in the world" without being intelligible to itself in the state-of-mind constituted by its mood—that is, without understanding its mood on the basis of its being toward things that it encounters or for which it has to make provision in the world.[17] Hēdonē and lupē are the basic modes of Dasein's state-of-mind, for Plato, because they are the ways in which Dasein understands itself through the world: that is, the ways in which it understands its pleasure and its pain through what they relate to. Thus the affects (*pathē*) have—to use an expression from our contemporary philosophy—an "intentional" character. Pleasure is always pleasure concerning (or about or in) something. It is because, according to Plato, Dasein is manifest to itself, in its state-of-mind, only as delighting *in something* or feeling pain *on account of* something that there is such a thing as "false" pleasure. It is only because the affects themselves have the character of doxa that Plato can use doxa as his guide in investigating the truth and falsehood of pleasure.[18]

17. In sect. 29 of *Being and Time*, Heidegger has exhibited the methodological importance of mood for the problem of ontology.

18. The substantive meaning of this key theme of *aletheia* and *pseudos* is blurred when Richard Walzer (*Magna Moralia und Aristotelische Ethik*

The thesis that pleasure can be "false" seems strange at first. Socrates' opponent admits that doxa can be false: that one can regard something as something that it is not; but he thinks that this is *only* true of doxa[19] and not true of enjoyment, fear, or hope. Socrates pushes this point of view even further. Surely, he says, pleasure in a dream is real pleasure, and not only supposed pleasure. His counter-argument, however, is that this is also true of doxa itself. The act of regarding something as something must be distinguished from the truth of the content of this opinion, and likewise the act of being pleased must be distinguished from the truth of the pleasure. In both cases the act really happens, and yet the doxa—and likewise the pleasure—is not necessarily true. So if only doxa is supposed to be able to be "false," and not pleasure, this cannot be established on the basis of the reality of the occurrence of pleasure. This would be possible only if the sense of hēdonē lay solely in its occurrence as such and was not modified by *how* this occurrence took place. For the reason why doxa is capable of discovering or covering up is that its occurrence is distinguished, as discovering or concealing, by how it happens. For it is by no means the case that there are no distinctions in how hēdonē occurs (there are, of course, for example, great pleasures and small pleasures; see 27e5). In the case of doxa it is clear that if its opinion fails to correspond to what it is about (to what it regards as something), then the doxa itself, despite the fact that it has

---

[Berlin, 1929], pp. 203–204) mixes up the talk of *alēthēs hēdonē* with the Academy's conjectured talk of *alēthēs philia, andreia*, etc.—unless one were to make the attempt (which strikes me as possible) to understand these phrases too with the help of the analogy to *doxa*—that is, with the help of the structure of *supposing* (*Vermeinen*), which, as a result of the Socratic "intellectualization" of the concept of aretē, would apply to these *hexeis* as well. That pleasure can be true and false is, at any rate, a genuinely Socratic thesis. Think only of the Socratic paradox of the *Protagoras*, that succumbing to pleasure (*huph hēdonōn hēttasthai*) is *amathia*—that is, a failure of self-knowledge. Compare p. 62.

19. Here Natorp's account (p. 339) is inaccurate.

occurred, is not what it wants to be: it is not discovering entities as something. Should not enjoyment itself, when it fails to correspond to its object—that is, when one enjoys something that is not enjoyable at all—likewise be erroneous? And such supposed enjoyment of something that fails to be really enjoyable is, after all, common. But in that case—one hears the response—it is precisely this opinion, this judgment which is contained in the enjoyment, that is deceptive and concealing and not the enjoyment itself. This parry is logical. It sets Socrates the task of demonstrating more precisely that the "doxic" element that is contained in the phenomenon of enjoying something is not separable from the pure datum of the feeling of enjoyment—that the enjoyment itself is not unaffected by the supposition that it contains. Consequently, the question initially is why and how pleasure that is based on true opinion differs from pleasure that is based on deceptive opinion. (The opponent, too, must admit that there is in fact a difference.)

A more detailed analysis of doxa makes it clear why this difference between true and false doxa also entails a difference between kinds of pleasure. Every doxa contains, as constitutive elements, mnēmē and aisthēsis. That is, to regard something as something means, on the one hand, to see a "this-here" in the sense of something directly given to the senses; but what is seen in this way is then taken to be something that is already pre-given and contained in the "soul."[20] For example, I see something on the rock there, something that is given to my senses; and I take it (on the basis of my prior knowledge of what people look like) to be a person. Now, this appearance can deceive me.[21] Perhaps it is a scarecrow—something that is not a

20. Regarding 38b13: in *diadoxazein, dia* surely means not "apart" but rather (in the spatial and, based on that here, the temporal sense) "through," as the parallel construction and meaning of *dionomazein* (*Statesman* 26d5) recommends. Stenzel (*Plato's Method of Dialectic,* pp. 113–114; *Studien,* p. 77), is of a different opinion.

21. Regarding 38d: it seems doubtful to me that the usual interpretation

person but is meant to *look like* one (so as to deceive the birds). In the *Theaetetus*, too, Plato presents this interpretation of false opinion as resulting from an erroneous combination of aisthēsis and mnēmē—in that case, with the explicit purpose of explaining the possibility of false opinions, which suppose something that does not exist.

This discussion in the *Theaetetus* has been unjustly neglected, due to the influence of the Neo-Kantian interpretation of Plato (Natorp). If these theses in the *Theaetetus*, even in the sharpened form they receive in that context, are proposals made by one who lacks knowledge and are not fully satisfactory, this does not prevent their content from having positive value. In regard to the *Philebus* and the *Sophist* (compare *Soph.* 264b), both the image of the wax tablet (doxa as *sunapsis* [joining] of aisthēsis and mnēmē) and the image of the pigeon loft (where knowledge has nothing to do with aisthēsis but concerns a pure potential of the soul) teach us something positive about the structure of doxa. It is not the simple, straightforward taking in of something that is present; rather, it always has a synthetic structure, positing the togetherness of something with something, on the basis of a bringing to mind of something that is not present. Thus mnēmē is the fundamental function of the soul, which makes possible such a thing as

---

of the passage, which is based on Plato's use of the terms elsewhere and was first given by Stallbaum, is correct. Someone who sees something appear in the distance (38c5) on a rock under a tree, will not first of all correctly regard it as a person and then arrive at the *mistaken* idea that it is only something sculpted by shepherds. (I clarify what Plato is driving at by speaking, in the text, of a scarecrow, which of course is not what he means by *agalma*.) Rather, the reverse will be the case: first, from a distance, he will mistakenly take the sculpture to be a human being (*epituchōs* [d6] = "on the off-chance" [Schleiermacher]), and then, when he has gone by (this literal sense must be intended by *parenechtheis* [d9] here), he will know that it is only a sculpture. (We must in any case interpolate the participle of a *verbum sentiendi* for d9, *hōs esti.* . . .) This, at any rate, is what the sense recommends, contrary to Plato's normal linguistic usage.

doxa—mnēmē as the capacity to make present, of one's own accord, something that is not present in the flesh. This is the essential insight in the second image as well—the image of the pigeon loft: the fact that something's being known does not necessarily mean a having present, a having the knowledge "on" like a piece of clothing, but rather requires one to lay hold of something spontaneously and bring it forward. (The term used is *analambanein*, the same word used in the *Meno* to characterize the way in which anamnēsis operates [*Theaetetus* 198d].)

This gathering together is articulated in the manner of taking something as something in the *words* (where it does not matter whether this is proclaimed externally by speech or not): "This is a man." What is understood in this articulated way is held fast in the soul like something that is written in a book. This fixing through words is supplemented, as well, by another form of holding fast to what is thought: in inner *images*, which are as though they were painted by a painter. These notations or images are true or false, depending on whether the opinions they "fix" are true or false.

Since the *Seventh Letter* has been recognized as genuine, the universal applicability of this perceptual aspect (*Moment der Anschaulichkeit*) throughout Plato's concept of knowledge has become unmistakable. This perceptual aspect, which Plato assumed to be universally present in doxa, is especially important (as the Stoic doctrine of the affects, later on, still shows) in connection with the affective character of desire or of anticipatory pleasure. There is no being "out for" something in which the object that this being out for is aimed at does not take perceptual form—in which it is not "before our eyes." Aristotle worked out this connection, in *De anima* III 10, as the connection between *orexis* and *phantasia* (desire and imagination). Phantasia, too, can be true or false. Anything that takes perceptual form (that comes before my eyes) can present itself as something that it is not, for example, as "good." Nevertheless, phantasia is not identical with doxa, as Aristotle shows in *De anima* III 3; and this is essentially because *it is up to us* to imagine something—an aspect that is decisively important here in the *Philebus* as well. The doxa that is primarily in question here is the mental image that is part of orexis. For it is precisely with the doxa that aims at things to come that purely psychic pleasure is associated. Purely psychic pleasure was, after all, distinguished by this connection with things to come. It precedes bodily pleasure, as anticipatory pleasure and its opposite. In fact, the notations and images in the soul are also related to future time, for the contents of our mnēmē are not simply retained past things, but also, and more authentically, hopes for the future (compare pp. 157–8 above). Now each person takes pleasure, in the manner of hope, in the notations and images that are held fast in his soul, whether they are true or false. Anticipatory pleasure is true if, in anticipation, it imagines something pleasant as something that will come to be, and the thing will in fact become real; it is false, on the other hand, if it anticipates something that will not come about. Now, this taking something as something that will come to be, which is part of hope and of anticipatory pleasure, is distinguished from doxa (in the general sense) precisely by the fact that it is up to us. What a person hopes for, longs for, and enjoys is determined by his being. Looking forward to something that will come about is what distinguishes the *theophilēs anēr* (man beloved of the gods).

As I indicated earlier, Plato does not distinguish between the phenomena of desire, hope, and anticipatory pleasure. He combines them in their shared character as a doxa that is directed at things to come. But he sees very well what distinguishes these forms of being toward future things from mere doxa (such as we see—developed into a science of the future—in divination). In desire and hope, Dasein understands itself in terms of its potential gain, by opening up future things as things that it can make provision for or hope for. The "truth" of desire and hope and anticipatory pleasure is not simply the truth of an opinion about things to come and a resulting expectation, but a self-understanding of Dasein in hoping for something, and looking forward to something, *for itself*.

Plainly, a thing like hope is not simply an opinion about the future. Understood as such an opinion, hope would be (regardless of all the possible degrees of intensity and certainty within it) an essentially *uncertain* opinion. In fact, someone who hopes does not see what he hopes for as something that he can anticipate with certainty; rather, his attitude is accompanied by a "perhaps not, too." Looked at in this way, hope would be a mode of expectation that is weighted toward uncertainty. For expectation has, primarily, the character of a specific certainty. Expecting something involves waiting for something in which one does indeed see a "perhaps not now, and not soon," but no "perhaps not at all." In the future from which the expected thing is expected, the way is already cleared for the expected thing to be feasible—very much in contrast to the situation with hope. For the latter gets its uncertainty from an awareness of the difficulties that lie in the way of the thing that is hoped for. But is its regarding these difficulties as surmountable (which, of course, is essential for hope to be possible) sufficient to give it the character of hope? Such an opinion about the path by which the hoped-for thing is to be reached is undoubtedly contained in the hope. Part of hope is that one hopes in relation to (with a view to) something that makes the hoped-for thing seem to be possible. In hope, one does not simply leap toward something to come; rather, in being "out for" the hoped-for thing, one holds precisely to something present which gives one hope—be it only the straw at which the drowning person clutches.

However, it is no accident that for hope, and in it, one clutches something that sometimes has the character of the drowning man's straw. *The basis of a hope is essentially different from what justifies an expectation.* Initially it is a basis—a reason—*only for the person who hopes*; that is, the opinion about the future which is contained in the hope is itself founded in the hope and does not in its turn provide a basis for the hope in the way that an *opinion* about the future would. What the hoping person sees as giving him or her grounds for hope does not by any means have to give rise to a corresponding expectation in a disinterested onlooker (unless it is in the sense of a completely open expectation, having the character of an eagerness to see whether the hoping person will be vindicated or not). So, just because hope is a process of wishing something for oneself—a process in which Dasein is turned back upon itself—it discovers in what lies before it things that give it hope for what it hopes for.

And what hope discovers as something to hope for is likewise not discovered in the manner of a prediction and an opinion about the future. Rather, it is pre-given for Dasein, in a characteristic way, by the possibilities through which (as things that can be provided for) it understands itself. What is hoped for is always thought of as "good" for the one who hopes (or for the person *for* whom or *with* whom one hopes). This already being with what is hoped for is the ground of the possibility of either understanding oneself (in hoping) on the basis of one's genuine possibilities, for which one can make provision, or else ridding oneself, in hope, of providing for one's most immediate possibilities. It is on this basis that hope's character as pleasure—anticipatory enjoyment (in the general Platonic sense of pleasure in being toward things to come)—is determined as true or false. Plato expresses this by saying that what the good person hopes for in fact falls to his or her lot by the favor of the gods, and what the bad person hopes for does not. But it is clear that Plato does not intend this as a profession of faith in a just providence. Instead, he means to characterize the fact that the truth or falsehood of hope is not the truth or error of an opinion about the future, but rather, that one's *being* is decisive for what one hopes for and how one hopes, just because hope is always wishing-for-oneself and not merely opining. A "bad" person's anticipatory enjoyment is deceptive because, in it, hope becomes a process of dreaming of pleasant things, which as such directly conceals the possibilities that are given in fact and need to be provided for, and thus sees what is present in each case in a light in which it can never be satisfying.[22] Thus, false anticipatory enjoyment is no less real than

22. Compare Heidegger, *Being and Time*, p. 239; = *Sein und Zeit*, p. 195.

true and looks completely the same as it, and yet it is false, insofar as it is aimed, as enjoyment, at something that will never come about.

In this way, despite all the difference between hope and doxa which was brought out above and is suggested by Plato himself, he interprets the falsehood of the pleasure of hope by analogy to doxa, as an error in opining about something in the future in such a way that the subsequent disappointment devalues, as it were, the pleasure of the erroneous opinion as well. In fact, the disappointment that follows the "untrue" hope is not simply a new experience of displeasure, one which was preceded in time by the pleasant experience of anticipatory enjoyment. For such untrue hope and disappointment are after all rooted in a perversion—which is not limited to a single sequence of experiences—in the person's whole being. Precisely by continually intensifying hopes to unfulfillable levels in this way, this perversion determines the person's overall state-of-mind as one of displeasure. The continually repeated shifting away from what is present and from the immediate future for which one can make provision only strengthens one's dissatisfaction with the present, and thereby one's displeasure. Because in hoping for and looking forward to something, Dasein does not determine itself, in its state-of-mind, on the basis of something given in the present, but rather relates to itself in its being toward future things, being cognitively at home in its possibilities— because of this, it is, in the state-of-mind of hope, *always already related, on the basis of its entire past, to the future*. The fact that Socrates regards these possibilities of being true and false—now, in the case of hēdonē, just as in the case of doxa—as the real forms of being good and being bad (40e9–10) is in accordance with Socrates' fundamental view that all badness is ignorance and all virtue is knowledge. This is based on the ontological insight that Dasein's being is defined by its role of discovering and that this discovering self-understanding understands and misunderstands itself primarily through the world in which Dasein lives.

Section 10: "False" Pleasure as Exaggerated and Imagined Anticipatory Enjoyment (41b–44a)

Socrates' opponent, who sticks to the usual way of speaking of good and bad pleasure, cannot agree here. Socrates takes this as an occasion for pointing out the falsity of pleasure in still other forms.[23] For in the two possible kinds of *pseudos* (falsehood) that follow, the deception no longer consists in the fact that something that will not be is supposed, in anticipatory enjoyment, to be something that will be; instead, it consists in the fact that it is supposed, in looking forward to it, to be something that will be *pleasant*, when in fact it is not pleasant at all, or not to the appropriate extent. (Contrast 40d8: *mē . . . epi tois ousi . . .* to 44a9: *peri tou chairein.*) In these cases of anticipatory enjoyment the doxic element is located even more centrally, in the enjoyment itself. Here something is taken to be enjoyable which is not enjoyable at all: what was anticipated does come about, but the enjoyment is still mistaken, because what was anticipated is not something that is enjoyable, or is not enjoyable in the way in which the anticipatory enjoyment imagined it would be. These kinds of enjoyment are not mistaken in the sense that they take not yet existing things as things that will exist, while in reality they will not; rather, the mistake here consists in the fact that in presenting things to oneself as enjoyable, one takes something to be something that it is not. Insofar as what we have here is a pure representation of the future existence of what does not yet exist, this opinion is true. But this thing that will exist does not have the character with which anticipatory enjoyment presents it to itself (42a–b!). For the anticipatory enjoyment, as a

23. Regarding 41a7: the indispensable and well-attested *eit* (*kat' allon tropon*), which Burnet relegates to his apparatus, must absolutely be inserted in the text. [Wrong! Burnet's indication refers to 41e6! Substantively, too, it does not fit. The *kat' allon tropon pseudeis* picks up 40e9 again: *we* want to deal with the *hēdoneis* that are bad as a result of *pseudos* (i.e., because—*pros tas kriseis*—there may be good ones, corresponding to them, as a result of *aletheia*).]

positive modification of desire, imagines the enjoyable thing to which it looks forward together with the presence of the sensuous-corporeal pain of emptiness (say, of thirst).

It is this coexistence of the two things that creates the possibility of delusion. The enjoyable thing to which anticipatory enjoyment looks forward appears more enjoyable, on account of its contrast to the present painful circumstance, than it is in itself (and more enjoyable than it will prove to be, after the pain is gone, in the enjoyment of that fact). The excessive expectation that this kind of anticipatory enjoyment involves makes it correspondingly deceptive. So this delusion is one that relates to the *extent* of the enjoyment and is made possible by the indefiniteness (which fluctuates in its extent) of hēdonē and lupē. It is comparable to the deception regarding the magnitude of a thing that is seen from a distance and looks smaller, alongside things seen close up, than it really is. Here, too, the possible deception is due to the soul's fundamental capacity for being toward things that are not present. It is only because not yet existing pleasant things are seen together with what is present (or things that can be expected in the distant future are seen together with what is expected in the near future)—that is, because what is present is not the sole determinant of Dasein's state-of-mind at any given time—that a deceptive anticipatory enjoyment, or mistaken pleasure, exists. (42b2: *nun de ge autai dia to porrōthen ti kai egguthen hekastote metaballomenai theōreisthai, kai hama tithemenai par allēlas. . . .*)

It does not have the character of hope, inasmuch as it does not just hope for the arrival of something from which it expects pleasure, but, being confident of its arrival, is already preoccupied with its enjoyableness. But the opinion that is involved here about the enjoyableness of what is expected is not a mere opinion about the nature of an entity either. The expected thing is considered enjoyable because Dasein imports itself, too, into it and reveals itself in it as looking forward to it. Thus anticipatory enjoyment can deceive itself about enjoyableness on account of its present state-of-mind. One's present lack increases one's anticipatory enjoyment of what one lacks and expects to an extent that exceeds the enjoyment that it actually yields. (The fact that, according to Plato, anticipatory enjoyment presupposes the present pathos of lack is due—it should be remembered—to the fact that the phenomenon of desire is not separate from that of anticipatory enjoyment.)

But even if anticipatory enjoyment does not view the expected enjoyable thing in the context of a present lack, it is still capable of exaggerating the enjoyableness of what it expects. There are the cases in which one has looked forward to something so actively or for so long that one is disappointed when it arrives. Plato does not underline this as a distinctive phenomenon. He interprets all disillusionment in terms of a juxtaposition and simultaneity of something that is expected with something that is present or with something else that is expected. An implication of this is that distance as such is deceptive. In fact, this can explain disillusionment in cases beyond that of deception produced by contrast. As something remote, the expected thing is not only seen indefinitely but is also seen—as something one looks forward to—only in its enjoyable character. As something expected, it depends on retention, but through this expectation and retention, everything is forgotten in it that cannot be retained as pleasant. Thus, parallel to enhancement through recollection, we have enhancement through anticipation. Neither of them depends on a mere weakness of recollection (a forgetfulness); instead, this forgetting is motivated by one's being "out for" the pleasant thing that is to be retained—that is, it is motivated precisely by the affective character of this way of regarding the object.

Other varieties of this kind of disillusionment show even more clearly that it is not really an opinion that is disillusioned and that the disillusionment is part of a unified experiential context with the anticipatory enjoyment, so that it can, in fact, reveal a deceptive character in the anticipatory enjoyment itself. This is so not only in the sense that the anticipatory enjoyment expects more enjoyment from the expected thing than the latter can provide, and is in error to that extent; it is also the case that anticipatory enjoyment and expectation can themselves turn the arrival of the expected thing into a disillusionment. For Dasein's state-of-mind, in virtue of which something is expected to be enjoyable, is not itself beyond being affected by the process of expectation. Expectation itself cannot ensure that when it actually arrives, the object of expectation will present itself to the state-of-mind (which is co-presumed in the anticipatory enjoyment) in virtue of which it appears as something enjoyable. It is in principle impossible for me, in anticipating something enjoyable, to determine in advance the state-of-mind in which Dasein will be when the expected thing makes its appearance. For even when Dasein tries to keep itself in a state of anticipatory enjoyment, it tends to fall out of it. Thus the upshot can be that when something long awaited that has already been expected in vain repeatedly finally arrives, it has a disillusioning, disappointing effect precisely because and insofar as Dasein is no longer able to move from anticipatory enjoyment to enjoyment of it. This is the "too much anticipation" effect. Or, on the other hand, Dasein is able to keep itself in a state of anticipatory enjoyment (this, too, is a result of having to wait in anticipatory enjoyment) only by continually increasing the enjoyableness of the expected thing in its anticipation. In this case, waiting leads to extravagant expectations and thus to disillusionment and disappointment. This disappointment is not in fact due to an error—that is, to one's having been able, at a given moment, to make a more correct decision than one did—but to the manner of the expectation and anticipatory enjoyment itself. It is not necessary to restrict the kind of deception that Plato describes here to anticipatory enjoyment (though that is, of course, the case that Plato initially examines; see 41c, *epithumia*). The same deception can also arise in the case of enjoyment of something present, when it is excessively increased by the memory of a pain that is just past (or even by the expectation of such a pain).

Socrates sets alongside this way of being deceived about the *extent* of enjoyableness (which is formulated in a purely quantitative schema: 42b8) a different kind of false pleasure in which something is taken as enjoyable that is not enjoyable at all. The disturbance of the body's natural equilibrium had been defined as pain, and its restoration (*katastasis*: 42d6) as pleasure. Now if we assume that neither of these two events is occurring in the present, we have a state that is neither pleasure nor pain. One must assume—the Heracliteans to the contrary, notwithstanding—that there is such a state of neither-nor. For the issue here is not the cosmological and physiological thesis that everything is in continual flux but, rather, to what extent these continual fluctuations are *felt*. But it is well known that only changes of a certain magnitude are felt, and only these produce pleasure and pain (compare 33d2ff.). So where appearances are concerned, there is a neutral state. It is free of pain and is not pleasure either—and yet, when one is suffering from pain, one will look forward to this state as to pleasure. So here something is felt as pleasure which does not have the character of pleasure at all. This is made clear by the fact that when the same state follows an actual pleasure, it presents itself, on the contrary, as pain, and thus equally "falsely." This case of false pleasure is intimately related to the one discussed previously. This deception is also created by the simultaneous juxtaposition of two opposed affects, of which one is not corporeally present but is expected or else retained; for a present state of freedom from pain can also seem to be pleasure as a result of the retention of a pain from the immediate past (44a4). This false pleasure, too, is not corporeal but mental, because it depends on something's being taken to be something.

Section 11: Mixed Pleasure as "False" Pleasure (Forgetfulness Directed at Displeasure) (44b–50e)

All these cases of deceptive pleasure presuppose a concept of true pleasure, which means not just the reality of the feeling of pleasure but a self-understanding of Dasein which is based on something discovered as enjoyable. The truth of pleasure is constituted by the discoveredness, in its enjoyableness, of something truly enjoyable. All the possibilities of the pseudos which have just been analyzed have corresponding possibilities of truth: deeming something enjoyable contains equally the possibility of not deceiving oneself—that is, of really taking it as what it is. Nevertheless, the anticipatory character (*Vor-Charackter*) of expectation, hope, anticipatory enjoyment, and desire creates an additional possibility of deception, besides that of erroneous opinion. Even when the opinion of affect is not in error, it is not a true enjoyment and does not disclose something truly enjoyable. For since anticipatory enjoyment is ahead of Dasein itself, the latter's present pathos is necessarily also characterized, at the same time, as displeasure, and thus as a mixture of pleasure and displeasure. It was shown earlier that, according to Plato, displeasure can indeed be covered over by the pleasure of being "ahead" but is still there in the sense of actual presence. Therefore all anticipatory enjoyment, insofar as it necessarily presents itself as a uniform state of pleasure, is in truth deceptive. For the enjoyable thing with which it is already occupied is, after all, not present, and its not being there necessarily also points Dasein's condition in the direction of displeasure. But anticipatory enjoyment (at least as long as it is not separated from desire, as it is not in Plato) is pleasure precisely through the covering up of this simultaneously present displeasure. But this means that the enjoyable thing is encountered not only as something through which Dasein understands itself, in anticipatory enjoyment directed at it, as pleasure; it is also, as an object of desire and thus of lack, a cause of displeasure. Thus the search for "true" pleasure becomes the search for something whose character is such that it is never anything but a cause of pleasure, the aim being to discover, in being toward this thing, the pleasure that is pure, unmixed with covered-up displeasure, and thus "true."

So the analyses that follow this are guided by the more radical intention—excluding any kind of mixture of pleasure and displeasure, which would both contain an element of the pseudos and (because of its admixture of displeasure) not be able to vindicate pleasure's claim to be the good—of discovering true (that is, unmixed) pleasure. Socrates takes as his point of departure (Plato says explicitly: to arrive at *alētheis hēdonai* [true pleasures] [44d2]!) the last-discussed form of false pleasure. There, something was taken as pleasure that in reality was not pleasure but only a freedom from pain. Now, there is a theory that positive pleasure does not exist at all—that everything that we are accustomed to call pleasure is in truth only freedom from pain, like this. Thus the advocates of this theory deny that there are things that are enjoyable in themselves.

Here reference is being made to a radical theory of the affects, a theory whose father (Democritus? Antisthenes?) is unknown.[24] The phenomenological core of the thesis that all pleasure is only a flight from pain is the primacy of pain in relation to the affects' function of making Dasein manifest in its being. In pain, more than in pleasure, Dasein's own condition is brought into view. (Whether it was really with an eye to what it accomplishes in this regard that the primacy of pain was put forward by the advocates of this doctrine is doubtful. It might seem as though their unmasking of the pleasures, of which Plato avails himself, arose essentially from an intention of explaining the affects physiologically.[25]) In any case, we can assume that this unmasking of the pleasures was essentially restricted to their corporeal and corporeal-mental forms and perhaps did not even recognize other, purely mental forms of pleasures. For in showing that most purely mental pleasure-affects are also mixed with mental displeasure, Plato dwells on the subject and goes into detail in a way that makes it probable that he had no predecessor here.

If, in fact, in the states-of-mind of pleasure and of displeasure, Dasein is revealed in its being, then it is certainly not in the same way in the two cases. Enjoyment and taking pleasure cause Dasein, in devotion to the object, to be practically forgotten. Dasein is never so surrendered to the world as it is in taking pleasure. Pain,

24. Compare U. von Wilamowitz-Moellendorff, *Platon* (Berlin, 1917), vol. 2, p. 20.
25. Compare the reference at 44b9: *kai mala deinous . . . ta peri phusin.* Understood as a reference to a physiological theory of the affects, such as I mention, this *deinos ta peri phusin* need not speak against Antisthenes (as Wilamowitz [see n. 24] still thinks).

by contrast, brings Dasein back to itself in a certain way: by impeding one's natural intentness on things that have to be provided for, it creates a break in which Dasein too becomes tangible to itself in its continual gravity. Pain is a disturbance. What it disturbs is the Dasein that understands itself in terms of pleasant things. Thus pain is a disturbance of Dasein's self-forgetfulness in being with pleasant things (whether in the pleasure of desire or in actual taking pleasure in present things). Of course it is true of the theory that Plato alludes to here, as well as of his own interpretation of the affects, that it understands pain, too, in terms of something encountered in the world. The basic affect of pain (*lupē*) does not actually reveal Dasein in such a way that its environment of things to be provided for disappears altogether. Pain, too, reveals Dasein in its state-of-mind, in that Dasein understands its state-of-mind in terms of something that the pain is about. All enduring of pain tends toward understanding the pain in terms of a presence, like that, of something that is causing pain. For the only thing that makes it endurable is that—whether explicitly and consciously or not—one hopes for the pain to pass by, which (however) means that one longs for the disappearance of the pain's cause. In suffering one sees, along with the pain's presence, its "not forever, but only now." That is also why Dasein, when it suffers pain, is especially inclined to seek forgetfulness in taking pleasure, and precisely the most intense pleasures—above all the bodily ones—have this anaesthetizing effect. Now, one can indeed also seek forgetfulness of pain in self-inflicted pain (for example, one can numb oneself against a tormenting thought by bodily exertion and even bodily pain). But in such a case the bodily pain has an entirely analogous function to that of the bodily pleasure: in enduring it, Dasein is surrendered to it in just the same way as in its devotion to pleasure, and this surrender to pain does in fact have the phenomenal features of taking pleasure. In any case, the denial of positive pleasure, as it is made in this theory, is based on the insight that pleasure, and especially the most intense pleasure, is always forgetfulness (in this way) of pain and is sought as such.

Now it is true that Socrates does not want to follow these people to their most extreme conclusion, the denial of all positive pleasure; but he does want to go part of the way with them. For their aversion to pleasure allows them, he says, to see the untrue character of certain so-called pleasures. They do in fact have the methodologically correct principle, which is to investigate the nature of each phenomenon not in its most common, averagely modest instances but in its most intense ones. (For in regard to what something is in its nature, it is not so much the forms in which one usually encounters it that are instructive as what it can be in its most extreme potential and how it is then. Hardness becomes really visible in what it is, not in this or that thing of average hardness but in especially hard things, which perhaps are suited, on account of this characteristic of hardness, to serve as tools for something, as, for example, in the case of iron.) Thus Socrates wants to study what taking pleasure really is not in the most common, average pleasures but in the most intense (violent) ones. These are the bodily pleasures and, among the bodily pleasures, especially those of sick people—say, those who are sick with fever, in whom (after all), notoriously, the most intense cravings are found (which has nothing to do with the, in itself, obvious fact that sick people in general experience *less* pleasure than those who are healthy).[26] Ac-

26. A more precise, detailed interpretation of the difficult section 46c– 47c cannot be given here. It seems certain to me that at 46c6 the description of the purely corporeal mixture of pleasure and displeasure begins ("corporeal" with the qualification that results from the psychic character of *all* affects; compare 46c8: *zētōn*)—a mixture that at first presents itself as one of equal parts and then (at 46d7) with a preponderance of displeasure and (at 47a1) with a preponderance of pleasure. Only at 47c does the discussion proceed to the second kind of mixture, that of corporeal displeasure and psychic pleasure, which had already been discussed at 35d8 ff. What all these mixtures have in common is that they have the character of *suntasis*, of tension (46d1 = 47a6). However the shares of pleasure and displeasure may be determined in each case, the presence of displeasure in the mixture in every case causes the

cordingly, the most intense pleasures, too, are not found among temperate people (the *sōphrones*, 45d7) but among those who engage in excess. So the most intense pleasures, in particular (and, indeed, the most intense pains as well), come about where there is a disorder of the soul, just as they do where there is a disorder of the body. The scratching of a person who itches is taken as an example. This is evidently a state (indeed, a bad state) in which pleasure and displeasure are mixed, but in which immoderately intense pleasures occur— and not accidentally, because such maximally intense pleasure is not a pure pleasure; rather, the admixture of pain, in the itching, is a necessary condition of these immoderate and almost unbearably intense feelings of pleasure. They have to be characterized, then, by the forgetfulness that the pleasure of scratching mobilizes against the pain that preceded it and is continually present with it. So the intense enjoyments, in particular, are not pure enjoyments. In them least of all do we find what can truly justify pleasure's claim to be the good.

But it is also true of the mixtures (which were already discussed in more detail earlier) of the bodily pain of lack with the mental pleasure of anticipation that they are neither pure nor true. This mixture does not, indeed, mean a simultaneous presence of two different states, in which Dasein is determined as pleasure and as displeasure in being toward enjoyable or painful things; rather, it means the unity of a state that, when a joyful expectation prevails, may present an extraordinarily intense pleasure but is never *pure* pleasure. So even if such expectation, and the pleasure that consists in it, may be true in the sense of the possibilities of truth and falsehood that were discussed earlier, this "truth" does not come into consideration in connection with the radicalized reflection that is going on here. For in Plato's

---

pleasure to become swollen to an immoderate intensity, because, in order to stand up to the displeasure at all, it has to deafen it. So pleasure here has the character of deafening, of trying to make oneself forget pain. It is in this *active* sense—as the examples show—that the unusual *apophugai* (44c1) is to be interpreted: not as merely being freed from displeasure, but as fleeing from displeasure into the most intense pleasure.

opinion such anticipatory enjoyment is mixed with pain, which it covers up. So the enjoyable thing to which it looks forward is not something on the basis of which Dasein could understand itself as feeling pure pleasure, if it understands itself properly.

But the purely mental affects, too, do not in most cases have the character of pure pleasure but are mixtures of pleasure and displeasure: anger, fear, desire, love, jealousy, ill will, and so on are pain and yet are full of endless pleasure (*hēdonōn mestas . . . amēchanōn*, we read at 47e5). In the course of the investigation of the most intense pleasures we do in fact encounter these [affects], too, as being especially intense: for example, the "voluptuousness" of anger. Here, too, the special intensity of the pleasure is based not on the special enjoyableness of the thing that gives rise to it but on an underlying painful state of mind which is drowned out by it. So these pleasurable affects, too, are not pure but are mixed with pain, from which they stand out.

As an example to demonstrate this, Plato chooses the enjoyment of comedy, because there it seems especially difficult to demonstrate that such merriment is mixed with pain (48b4). The demonstration proceeds by showing that the enjoyment of comedy reveals an element of *phthonos*, of ill will. For ill will is pain caused by the happiness, the good, of one's neighbor and, together with that, enjoyment of his or her misfortune. But this is what one sees in comedy. For the ridiculous thing that we see there is an inferiority that characterizes the people in the comedy: *agnoia* (want of perception, ignorance)[27] or, positively, delusion—being enmeshed in error *about oneself*. Three forms of this kind of delusion are distinguished (corresponding to a classification of goods that can be found elsewhere in Plato as well). They are regarding oneself as richer, as more beautiful and esteemed, and finally (the most common case) as better—above all, as more intelligent—than one is. In order, now, to bring into view the specific

27. The received text has *anoia*, which as far as the substance is concerned does not make a significant difference here.

form of this kind of delusion that is the subject of boundless merriment in comedy, a further distinction is drawn between two forms of this delusion about one's own intelligence. One is the delusion of powerful people. These people are not comic but terrible and to be feared. The other is the delusion of powerless people. One can laugh about them with impunity. Their delusion is the theme of comic merriment. Now, insofar as these deluded people are our friends (and that this is the case follows obviously from the fact that they are after all the comic heroes, with whom we sympathize), this enjoyment of their inferiority is wrong, and our behavior, consequently, is indicative of ill will. The fact that we have ill will, in general, enables us to feel malicious pleasure if the occasion presents itself and thus, in this case, to enjoy the misfortune of friends. But this means that in fact our malicious pleasure is based on an underlying mood of ill will—that is, that it is mixed with pain.

Looked at as a formal deduction, this demonstration might seem inadequate. Certainly someone who feels malicious pleasure does, in this case, also exhibit ill will (compare Aristotle, *Rhetoric* B 9, 1386b34 ff.). But this does not seem to prove that the enjoyment of malicious pleasure is itself mixed with pain and is such an intense enjoyment precisely because it has an admixture of pain. Only a reflection on the facts of the matter teaches us that Plato has seen an important phenomenon here.

It is never one's enemies, but only one's friends, that are the objects of envy and of ill will; for one envies only someone with whom one has something in common. It is true that one's enemy's good fortune causes one pain, and his misfortune, pleasure, but not in the sense that one grudges him his good fortune (or feels malicious pleasure over his misfortune). In this pain one does not think of the enemy at all, in the sense of wanting him not to have something; rather, one thinks of oneself: of the injury that one suffers, directly or indirectly, through the success of one's enemy. Ill will, by contrast, is not pain due to something that injures oneself but rather, independently of that, a pain due to the other person's good fortune in itself. One can begrudge (*misgönnen*) only where one can freely grant (*gönnen*)—that is, where what is in view is the other person and how he fares, viewing that not as something useful or injurious for me, but, leaving me out of account, as something that is good for him. Nevertheless, behind both freely granting and begrudging there is a concern about one's own being in relation to the other person. Both attitudes presuppose that one is, or thinks one is, somehow on a footing of equality with the other person. What one begrudges him and envies him is something that in some way matters to one, oneself. The issue here, more precisely, is not envy—that is, envying someone for something because one does not have it oneself and would like to have it—but ill will. For it is essential to ill will that one is not concerned with the thing that one begrudges the other person, as such (so that it is not important for ill will, either, whether one already has or only desires and seeks what one begrudges the other person—or not even that, if one begrudges someone else something that one does not want for oneself at all); instead, one is concerned that the other person should not get ahead of one or catch up with one by such a success. Thus there is ill will pre-eminently between competitors (for example, between members of the same profession). In general, it is competitiveness—that is, concern about being ahead of others or not being behind them—that characterizes being with one another and thus constitutes the possibility of ill will.

The other side of ill will is, as I said, malicious pleasure (that one gladly grants someone else his misfortune). Malicious pleasure, too, should probably be distinguished from enjoying the misfortune of one's enemy, with whom one does not stand in the positive relation of having something in common or, consequently, in the relation of competition. One takes pleasure in the misfortune of one's enemy because it benefits oneself. Malicious pleasure, on the other hand, has its basis in competition, and this basis is not to be understood simply in terms of the fact that "in other cases" (when faced with a friend's happiness) we feel ill will, and thus now we are (correspondingly) maliciously pleased at his or her misfortune; rather, our malicious pleasure is itself a mode of appearance of the same fundamental concern about competition, which expresses itself in relation to the friend's happiness as ill will. The immoderateness of laughter is in fact based on an underlying feeling of pain—based, precisely, on concern about being ahead of others.

This structure of concern about competition, which underlies equally both malicious pleasure and ill will, is not positively articulated by Plato; but there is no doubt that he has in view just this fundamental affect (which he calls simply, *a potiori*, phthonos" [ill will, jealousy]) when he claims to find in malicious pleasure itself this kind of intermixture of pain.[28] This analysis of the way in which one finds pleasure in comedy is certainly not unimportant in relation to the specific problems of the *aesthetics* of the comic. But in its actual character it is exemplary for the mixture of the affects in the whole "tragedy and comedy of life" and is thus a contribution to the analysis of being toward others. No distinction at all is drawn here between merely being a member of the audience in the theater and, on the other hand, seeing real persons (not played by actors) and their fates; and thus neither is the question raised as to what extent the specifically aesthetic mode of existence of being played by an actor produces a specific modification in the seeing of such persons and events.

The outcome of this exemplary investigation is that impurity—that is, the mixture of pleasure and displeasure—is present even in the purely mental affects. (A more detailed discussion of all the

28. So *phthonos* can be understood in the widest sense as: in being toward others, looking back at oneself and determining one's being toward them on the basis of this concerned regard for oneself. Its contrary can be understood, formally, as the absence of such a regard—not really as the "not begrudging" that looks back just as much but as a being toward something shared which is not contestable (is not withheld from the other person when one possesses it oneself); or, still more exactly, whose possession does not distinguish one of us over the other because it is something in which you and I are *alike*, are *the same* (*psychē, auto*). On *phthonos* and concern for the facts of the matter, see pp. 44–5.

previously named affects[29] is postponed until the following day—which is again one of the moves, pointing beyond the immediate discussion, that are also characteristic of the beginning and the end of the dialogue. But what is postponed here is certainly not identical in content with what still seems to Protarchus, at the end of the dialogue, to remain and not to have been dealt with. In that case the intention is, rather, to point to the essential lack of closure that is a necessary correlate of all progressive working toward a shared understanding.) So the fact that they are purely mental affects is not yet enough to show that one has access, in them, to something truly enjoyable. The enjoyable thing to which one has access in the affect need not be enjoyable at all, or not to the extent that would be in accordance with the vehemence of the pleasure affect. The discovered and intended object of the pleasure is in truth also an object of pain—the supposedly enjoyable thing is also the opposite of enjoyable—and it is only because the affect has, at the same time, the character of displeasure that the pleasure in it is so vehement. The entity that is intended in the affect as the object of anger, of envy, of malicious pleasure, and so forth is not inherently enjoyable; rather, the only reason why it is the object of such vehement pleasure is that, at the same time, it gives pain. So while the pleasure in it is really felt, it is not founded simply in the discoveredness of something—of how it is enjoyable in itself—but rather, the entity is taken to be such an enjoyable thing so that, through the pleasure in it, the displeasure that it gives will be forgotten and covered up in its supposed enjoyableness. Thus, in exhibiting the mixed nature of these affects, Plato also exhibits their pretendedness—the element of the pseudos in them. True pleasure cannot be present in mixed affects like these but only in pure, unmixed pleasure.

29. As is well known, Aristotle gave the analysis of the affects which is called for here in the context of his *Rhetoric*, in the second book—of the affects named at 47e1, *orgē* in the second chapter, *phobos* in the fifth, *phthonos* in the tenth, and *zēlos* in the eleventh.

Section 12: Unmixed Pleasure as Enjoyment of
What is Enjoyable (50e–52d)

Now it is very noteworthy that Plato distances himself from the theory that he has made use of in unmasking the supposed pleasure that is in fact mixed with displeasure. That is, he does not share the theory's general thesis that all pleasure is only a way of recovering from (of unburdening oneself of) pain; instead, he believes in genuine pleasure, which does not get the character of pleasure solely through pain's being covered up and forgotten. Since he interprets all affects in terms of ways of being toward entities, this means he believes that there is pleasure that discovers something as enjoyable which is enjoyable not only as a result of Dasein's circumstances and present state-of-mind, in which it encounters the object, but always and in itself. It is clear that only such unmixed pleasure, which has discovered something that is truly and in itself enjoyable, can justify the claim of hēdonē to be good. For only if the enjoyable thing *always* has the same characteristic enjoyableness can Dasein understand itself in relation to the possibility of discovering this kind of enjoyable thing, and thus to one of its own states-of-mind, as a permanent possibility.

So according to Plato there is unmixed pleasure. He explains its possibility as due to the fact that it can be present when, despite the de facto physiological correspondence between fullness and emptiness, no such correspondence between the pain of emptiness and the enjoyment of fullness is experienced phenomenally. After all, not all emptying-out and emptiness need to be felt, and that which is not felt, not experienced, does permit a filling up that is felt as pleasure. This is pure pleasure, unclouded by pain.

Now, the enjoyment of beautiful colors, figures, smells, sounds, and so forth has this character—but *not* figures like those, for example, of living human beings (for the enjoyment of a human being is bound up with desire, so that he is also an object of lack and thus of pain), nor, for example, the painted figure of a human being (for this pleasure too would contain an admixture of desire, insofar as the painted figure refers one to the model that it portrays and whom, in seeing the picture, one can long to see and possess). Thus pure pleasure cannot, in general, be had in anything living or depicted, since nothing of the sort is seen only as enjoyable in its appearance, but rather wants to be had, to be used, to be put somewhere; and when it is not had, is not available, is not seen in the place where it causes enjoyment, then it does not cause enjoyment but gives rise to a sense of lack or (as the case may be) to a desire which has the character of pain. Instead, we are concerned solely with forms that are not pleasant and beautiful only in some connection or other (which would mean that if they ceased to be or were not seen in this connection, then they would not be beautiful) but are so in themselves, like the straight line, the circle, and the pure geometrical surfaces and bodies that are constructed out of these pure elementary forms of extension. These pure forms, then, are beautiful in themselves and result in a characteristic pleasure (*hēdonas oikeias*, 51d1)—that is, the enjoyment that we have in them is due to a character of enjoyableness that belongs to them by their nature: to the beauty that is inherent in them, is discovered together with them, and does not first accrue to them in some connection or other.

As additional examples of things that are beautiful and thus enjoyable in themselves, pure sounds (notes) are mentioned, and also smells, insofar as they, too, and the feeling of pleasure that they give do not necessarily involve displeasure (that is, a longing for them while they are not yet there). Also included are the pleasures of knowledge, insofar as no hunger for learning—which would be pain—is presupposed here.[30] For the important question is whether pleasure in knowl-

30. Regarding 52a–b: that Protarchus should of his own accord separate *phusei* and *logismois* (a8) and thus refute the objection Socrates has raised against him is hardly in keeping with the role of hesitant agreement that he plays otherwise. It would be easier to believe if the roles were reversed, which would admittedly require divergences from the received text (perhaps reading *ar'* instead of *all'* at 52a3, and giving this to Socrates as a question, and giving a5 as an objection, to Protarchus and a8 ff., together with b1, to Socrates again, who rejects the objection).

edge involves, by its nature, the pain of the thirst for knowledge. The fact that the loss of knowledge, the state of having forgotten, can under certain circumstances (namely, if one has in view a way in which one wants to apply the knowledge) cause pain is not of importance in connection with the question of the nature of pleasure in knowledge. For, after all, one's pleasure in knowledge does not depend on the attractiveness of the advantage that one achieves by applying it. If forgetting as such were necessarily painful, then pleasure in knowledge would indeed not be "unmixed." For that would mean that for every such pleasure of being filled there would be a corresponding pain of being emptied out or, better (since the mixed character of the pleasure would not be due to the *subsequent* pain of having forgotten), knowledge would be pleasure only on the basis of the pain of emptiness, which would constitute the thirst for knowledge—just as taking pleasure in drinking presupposes thirst, which is pain. Instead of this, receptiveness to the pleasure in knowledge is based on knowledge's own nature of being beautiful and pleasant in itself, even if receptiveness to the beauty of knowledge may be present in only a few human beings.

This unmixed pleasure has the character of enjoyment of something. Its purity is based on the fact that no desire, which would have the character of displeasure, of lack, precedes it. Its arrival has the character of something sudden (thus, *Republic* 584e, *exaiphnēs*; *Phaedrus* 258e, *prolupēthēnai*). Likewise, its cessation does not have the character of displeasure. It is not that the entity that is discovered in it is to be anticipated and imagined as enjoyable and constitutes Dasein's state in that way as pleasure; rather, pleasure is given together with and in its being discovered. So this kind of enjoyment *of* something is the sought-after "true" enjoyment. It is the culmination of the truth that it is possible for the affect to have at all. For Plato sees the affects in general as a way of discovering the world. But the discoveredness of the thing that is beautiful and thus pleasant in itself, which constitutes this pleasure in something, is discoveredness in its extreme possible instance, and thus truth. For it contains no possibility of concealment. The thing that is discovered in this way is not imagined to be something; the discovery that is contained in pleasure in something does not at all have the character of opinion that something is something, inasmuch as nothing is seen in it but the discovered present thing itself. It is intuited (literally, regarded: *angeschaut*) in its simple presence. Thus in the interpretation of the affects, too, it becomes evident that for Plato the real truth is the truth of *intuition* (*Anschauung*), and thus entities are understood ontologically as *present* things.

But as enjoyment *of* (*Freude an*) something, this true pleasure is to be distinguished not only from the anticipatory and opinionative looking forward *to* (*Freude auf*) something (from the anticipatory enjoyment associated with desire) but also from enjoyment *about* (*Freude über*) something, even though what one has enjoyment *about* is something present at the time. The fact that enjoyment *about* something really only relates to "states of affairs," whereas enjoyment *of* something also relates to "things," is not the decisive difference. Instead, the important thing is to see that what one has enjoyment *of* motivates pleasure in a different way from what one has enjoyment *about*: namely, through its sheer discoveredness. If I have enjoyment *about* something, then the thing about which I have enjoyment is taken to be enjoyable. But this does not mean that it is the case that whenever this entity, as such, is discovered, enjoyment about it will always and necessarily be present. Under other circumstances, I can also *not* have enjoyment about the same state of affairs. But that means that it is only under certain circumstances that it is encountered as something enjoyable: namely, when it is encountered in a state-of-mind of Dasein in which Dasein is receptive to it. So the fact that one has enjoyment *about* something does not so much say something about the entity, as it is, as it says something about my being toward it.

The situation is different with something that one has enjoyment *of*. In enjoyment of something, Dasein's state-of-mind determines itself immediately, with this entity's discoveredness, as pleasure. Therefore, when it is discovered, it is always enjoyable and gives rise to enjoyment. This is also the reason why, when Plato shows us things that are enjoyable in themselves, he arrives at the same time at proper, "true" enjoyment. This kind of enjoyment of something has a distinctive *permanence*. Not only does it presuppose that the entity of which it is enjoyment endures, as something that is enjoyable in this way, but the enjoyment itself has the character of enduringness—that is, the enjoyable thing, of which one has enjoyment, is not only in fact itself enduring, as the same thing, but it is also seen as such in one's present enjoyment of it. What is involved in enjoyment of something is both having enjoyment of it now and also positing, in this present enjoyment, that one will always enjoy it, as long as it is present at all, insofar as it remains as it is. More precisely, in enjoyment of it one is not directed at all at its temporal duration (at its "now" and "always" = "not not later"); rather, one is absorbed entirely in its presence at the moment, so that one does not reach beyond what is present towards a future thing, even by denying the possibility that the present thing will disappear. Such enjoyment of something is entirely present in the now and entirely enclosed in the absolute actuality of the present thing. It is just for this reason that it is genuinely true. (No doubt it should also be distinguished from the kind of taking pleasure in something present which, in regarding it, cannot see enough of it—inasmuch as such taking pleasure presupposes hunger for the thing and likewise a concern about keeping hold of it and not losing it.) Thus enjoyment of something is itself pure intuition (aisthēsis and *noēsis*), and Plato does not distinguish it conceptually from the pure intuition of perception and thought. (Aristotle—who in other respects agrees with Plato in seeing this phenomenon of pure enjoyment *of* something as the key to the problem of hēdonē—is the first to make a conceptual distinction here, while recognizing the inseparability of the two things as far as appearance is concerned.) So, as the above analysis shows, Plato's "explanation" of this kind of pleasure in terms of the imperceptibleness of the corresponding emptiness does not hit upon the decisive peculiarity of its structure which his analysis of what is enjoyable in itself points to.

The separation carried out in this way between pure (unmixed) and impure (mixed) pleasures is now set in relation to the four aspects of being that were discussed initially. The pleasures that are distinguished by their intensity, the mixed ones, are without inherent measure, by contrast with the pure ones, which are measured. The mixed ones belong to the genus of the apeiron; that is, they can have the characters of "very" and of "intense." The point is that their strength is not determined on the basis of the enjoyable thing to which one gains access in this kind of pleasure and by measuring it against that thing's real enjoyableness; rather, it is determined on the basis of something that is not given with the entity itself and its true nature— that is, on the basis of the contrast with the pain that is mixed in with it. If, then, the pleasure is not bound to the substantive enjoyableness of the entity, its strength remains dependent on the indefinite and (in itself) necessarily fluctuating difference between it and the displeasure that is mixed in with it and is to be covered over—that is, dependent on circumstances that are not located in the entity itself. This kind of pleasure not only is indeterminable, but it positively tends toward immoderateness, because it consists in a forgetfulness toward this opposed displeasure (although it *thinks* that it understands its intensity as a result solely of the so-very-enjoyable character of the entity that it encounters).

Thus the question of the "truth" of impure and pure pleasure answers itself automatically when one understands the structure of impure pleasure.[31] Nevertheless, this question is posed explicitly one more time. It is clear from the analysis of "false" pleasures in particular that the truth of a pleasure is connected in the closest possible way with the *purity* of what is discovered in the pleasure. True enjoyment is the kind that allows one to encounter something that is beautiful in itself, and thus enjoyable, in the enjoyableness that belongs to

31. Regarding 52e3, *krisin*: here, surely, we must read *krasin*, as Badham already conjectured (this is missing in Burnet), taking into account the *krisin* that follows e4 ff.; while at 55c8 *krisin* must be defended, on account of the added *tēn koinēn*, against Schleiermacher and Badham.

it. The essential thing, in this regard, is that the truly enjoyable thing here is enjoyable, when one encounters it, by virtue of itself; and a precondition of this is that this enjoyable entity is only what is revealed in its being discovered (in seeing or hearing or smelling or in intellectual appropriation). Thus the discoveredness of something that is enjoyable in itself presupposes the purity of what is discovered in this way. So even pure white is not the kind that characterizes an entity that has an unusual amount of white, but mixed with other colors; rather, it is the kind that characterizes an entity that has no other color but white. Likewise, even a small (slight) pleasure is truer and better pleasure insofar as it is free from displeasure, which is something great (intense) but not pure.

This analogy makes it completely clear that pleasure is seen as absolutely parallel to intuition. Just as intuition reveals something that is concretely present, so true pleasure, also, discovers an entity that is concretely present. All pleasure, on the other hand, that reveals something that is not present—such as, for example, anticipatory enjoyment, which presents something that does not yet exist in its quality as something that will exist and is enjoyable—remains below true pleasure in terms of purity and truth. It is true that it too, in accordance with its claim to give access, can be true, insofar as it presents something that will be present and as it will be present. Even then, though, it is not a thoroughly "true" pleasure. For insofar as it is desire, the non-existence of the desired thing is, after all, given, and with it, displeasure. But if this desire is seen as a discovering of · something enjoyable (as anticipatory enjoyment), it is untrue. For as a being toward this enjoyable thing, it is determined in its quality as pleasure by the underlying mood of displeasure associated with lacking something—the mood that is necessarily covered over by desire's anticipatory enjoyment. So the general presumption that Dasein's state-of-mind is determined by both the immediate and the represented presence of enjoyable and unenjoyable things ultimately makes us still regard even the kind of pleasure that presents something enjoyable in its enjoyableness as false—that is, as concealing. For as pleasure it conceals the displeasure that is given along with it. Insofar as such anticipatory enjoyment discovers entities as enjoyable in the way that, when they come about, they indeed turn out to be enjoyable, it is true; but nevertheless it is false insofar as, in having discovered enjoyable things that are (in this way) to be expected, it determines as pleasure a state of Dasein which nevertheless also has the character of displeasure. Thus anticipatory enjoyment's truth or falsehood as an opinion about something to come takes second place to its necessary falsehood as constituting a present state-of-mind.

At the conclusion of this whole discussion of pleasure, which was carried out in the form (which I characterized methodologically) of a division into kinds, we find a number of summary arguments that are developed on the basis of the conceptual formulation of pleasure that is common to all its kinds, arguments that clarify pleasure's non-identity with the good on the basis of the ontological characteristics of each of them. For it is common to all the kinds of pleasure that pleasure is understood as a *motion* (*kinēsis* or *genesis*). In this, Plato no doubt follows what was a universal view among his contemporaries. But he takes it as an opportunity to refute all ethical theories that regard pleasure as the good. The "fine people" to whose help Plato here ironically lays claim (as he does with others at 44c; compare 53c6, *au*) are to be defeated with their own weapons. (Since Zeller, it has been considered certain that the target here is Aristippus.) For every becoming is, ultimately, for the sake of a *being*; but that for the sake of which something is, is the good. So pleasure, as a becoming— something that exists for the sake of something else—cannot be the good.

With this argument, not only is the Cyrenaic *theory* identifying pleasure with the good refuted on the basis of its own presuppositions, but the practical *behavior* of those who seek the meaning of life in such pleasures—that is, in becoming—is also reduced to absurdity. They make life a matter of change (for in postulating becoming, one also postulates passing away), and by so doing, they relinquish the only real possibility of understanding their own Dasein—namely, by relating it to enduring being. But this possibility of pure thought is available precisely only in the state of neither-nor, where one is unaffected by pleasure and displeasure.

The whole argument is a polemical excursus and addendum. It does not really connect with the stage in the analysis of the problem which has already been reached. For one thing, it does not take any account of the assumption that the good life is a *mixed* life. In this refutation of the Cyrenaic theory, there is no place for the relative legitimacy of incorporating pleasure into the good. This is polemically motivated; for the Cyrenaics, too, based their arguments on a summary concept of pleasure. (We know from Diogenes Laertius that, like Protarchus at the beginning of the *Philebus*, they recognized no distinctions whatever among pleasures.) Thus Plato can safely deploy the general ontological character of the good against them—a move that implies, at the same time, the affinity of thought to the good. The preceding discussions, which had (after all) revealed a pleasure specific to the life in pure thought, are not drawn on at all here, even though the analysis has long since ceased to be oriented toward an absolute separation between pleasure and thought. Beyond that, however: in his analysis of pleasure, Plato, by discovering things that are enjoyable in themselves, has discovered a true pleasure that cannot appropriately be characterized as motion or becoming. It is only because he (elsewhere) interprets aisthēsis and noēsis, too, as motion, that this interpretation of true pleasure in terms of motion can seem to him to be adequate. In the analysis of this true pleasure itself, at any rate, he has, in substance, gone beyond this characterization and is already occupying the position that Aristotle occupies when he recognizes the inappropriateness of the concept of motion for aisthēsis and noēsis as well as for hēdonē and formulates their existential character in the central ontological concept of *energeia* (actualization).

A further argument, also rooted in the ontological character of the good, is launched against this doctrine of Aristippus: all the virtues, too, have (after all) a claim to belong to the "good"; this is just as much guaranteed by the fact of our preference (*hairesthai*,

55a5), as is pleasure's claim. This shows that with the good, a human existential state is intended, with which the mode of existence of pleasure accords poorly. Part of the meaning of talk of virtue, and in general of any moral interpretation of Dasein, is, after all, that when someone is "good," he or she is not simply good now and then not good, but is good in general or for ever. But the Cyrenaic theory that pleasure is the good would imply that a human being could not be good in this sense at all, but would be now good, now bad again, and would be good only as long as he or she felt pleasure and bad only as long as he or she felt pain.

Part IV

Section 13: The Doctrine of Science (55c–59e)

Now, in accordance with the initial program, the testing and analysis of the kinds of pleasure are followed by an examination of nous and epistēmē as well. They are tested by knocking, as it were, to see if they contain anything defective, so that, for the final mixture of the two, nous also will be available for judgment in pure form. The doctrine of science that is presented here does not have the character of an actual investigation, as the analysis of pleasure does. It only briefly classifies the kinds of knowledge, which are assumed to be familiar from other investigations. (The relative strictness of the dichotomous schema of this presentation could be compared with the freer form of diaeresis that is practiced in the investigation of the kinds of pleasure.) My intention in what follows is only to give a brief synopsis of this presentation, so as to make clear in what sense this "testing" corresponds to that of pleasure and what its object is. (A real interpretation of Plato's doctrine of knowledge could not in any case be developed on the basis of these schematic presentations in the *Philebus* or the *Statesman* but only on that of the detailed treatment of the topic in the seventh book of the *Republic*.)

The viewpoint to which this testing of the sciences is subordinated corresponds completely to the one that plays the guiding role

in the testing of the pleasures. It is that of "purity," or "truth." Just
as the purity of pleasure meant its being unmixed with displeasure—
and as such purity indeed carried with it the genuine truth of pleasure—so in this case purity means the possibility for science, in
discovering entities, to remain unmixed with uncertainty and accident.
Here science is initially divided into two basic kinds: that which is
related to a process of producing something and that which is directed
only at knowledge itself, in the sense of "education." We find the
same basic distinction elsewhere in Plato as well (at *Republic* 525d ff.
the sciences' practical use is distinguished from their purely theoretical
value, and at *Statesman* 258d ff. we find a distinction between *praktikē*
and *gnōstikē*). Both are epistēmē—that is, seeing—and both reveal
entities; it is just that the science that is directed at production is not
an independent seeing but is, as it were, involved in the production
itself and one with it in its execution (*Statesman* 258d9, *hōsper en tais
praxesin enousan sumphuton tēn epistēmēn kektēntai*). In it, entities
are discovered in such a way that it aims at not yet existing entities
precisely in, and for the purpose of, their coming-into-existence and
is itself at an end when the entities have come into being.

These *productive* sciences are examined, to begin with, for
their "truth." For there are manifest differences in scientificness among
them. First of all, in a class by itself, is the science (which plays a
leading role in these sciences) of numbering, measuring, and weighing.
It makes up the truly scientific character of all these sciences. (What
is left over is not worth much: *Phil.* 55e.) But there are also practical
sciences that do not represent any real knowledge but yield only an
essentially practical familiarity with their objects and produce an ability through mere accuracy of aim and routine skilfulness of the senses.
An example of this is music, which restricts itself (at least in its
practical exercise—the Pythagoreans' mathematical music theory was,
as such, not of *practical* importance) in, for example, tuning strings,
to a merely approximate purity, for the ear (compare *Republic* 531a).
The same purely experiential process of practice is also the rule in
medicine, agriculture, steersmanship, and generalship. Such routine

dealing with something, based on mere practice, does not represent science's real potential, insofar as, in it, one never finds oneself in a situation in which the entity is discovered as it is in itself, and thus one never really knows that one can be sure of it; rather, one always has to rely on guesswork (*stochasmos*, 56a). So the important thing in this examination of the productive sciences is to determine their respective degrees of exactness (*akribeia*). The art of building already has more exactness, and thus a more scientific character, than these arts. For it uses the most instruments. This makes it more scientific, insofar as it is not satisfied with mere "visual judgment" but possesses measuring instruments—that is, it goes back at least to imitations of the pure measures, if not to the pure measures themselves. (Compare Iamblichus, *Protrepticus*, ed. Pistelli, p. 55 = Aristotle.) This art, too—like music, on the other hand—is exemplary in its degree of exactness for a whole group of sciences. The degree of its exactness determines the degree of its scientificness. For exact cognition is a way of revealing something which reveals it as what it itself is, in its own substantive definiteness. Cognition of the kind that we find in music is "inexact" because it relies on mere (auditory) inspection. The cognition that is involved in the art of building is more exact because it aids the eye with instruments.

But the science of numbers and measures themselves is superior to both of these. However, these sciences (of numbers and measures) in turn fall into two kinds: the doctrine of numbers, for example, dividing into that possessed by the many and that possessed by the scientists (mathematicians).[32] The first group count unequal

32. Regarding 56e7: here *logistikē* seems to be distinguished from *arithmetikē*, a distinction that does not occur in this sense (between a *practical* doctrine of numbers and the art of calculating) elsewhere in Plato. When Plato explicitly distinguishes between arithmetic and logistic at all (*Gorgias* 451b), the distinction between practical and theoretical number doctrine is not important to him; and when it is important to him (*Republic* 525a ff.), he (in turn) does not distinguish between arithmetic and logistic.

units—that is, they count entities each of which differs, in fact, from each of the others. Insofar as they count these entities, they necessarily see them in their sameness as members of a genus, but in so doing they explicitly disregard the differentness of each from each. Number, in this sense, is the quantity of something; that is, counting gives the *mere* quantity and not the different substantive characteristics that the counted things possess.

Theoreticians, on the other hand, count pure units, without any regard to entities that could be counted with them. Precisely in taking each pure unit for itself, counting in the theoretical sense constitutes itself as the running through of a homogeneous sequence of numbers, in which each unit, as a unit, differs from the others not at all and, as something counted, differs from them only in its position in the sequence.

This difference is once again a difference in "exactness" and "truth," as is explicitly said at 57c9 ff. In fact, only philosophical mathematics reveals its objects in their full substantiveness (*Sachhal-*

What is meant by *logistikē* here can be inferred from the juxtaposition with the art of measurement or (theoretical) geometry. It is evidently distinguished from these by the fact that it does not "measure" but instead uses numbers for "reckoning" (as an architect computes or a business person keeps accounts); the relevant theoretical discipline is, perhaps, the doctrine of proportions (*logos* = relation, proportion; *logizesthai* = to compute). This is consistent with what we find in the other Plato passages: logistic differs from arithmetic in the narrower sense by the fact that it pursues the relations of magnitude between numbers (*Gorgias* 451b = *Charmides* 166a), which means, however, that arithmetic is the knowledge of numbers and of counting, while logistic is the knowledge of reckoning. The connection with geometry, which we find only in the present passage, points to the origin of the doctrine of proportion in geometry. It is natural that Plato is inclined to speak more of logistic than of arithmetic when the philosophical doctrine of numbers is to be contrasted with the practical (*Republic* 525a ff.). For practice in particular—e.g., that of a merchant (*Republic* 525c)—is not satisfied with mere counting; it requires reckoning and computation.

tigkeit), whereas the practical art of reckoning—which by adding them up makes available in their quantity entities each of which is different in itself from every other, as, for example, in the military art the counting of troops (compare here *stratopeda*, 56d11, and *Republic* 525b3 ff.)—must, in counting, disregard the unequalness and substantive differentness of what it counts, and thus does not attain the discoveredness of the entities that makes them available in their true substantive content. The general who distributes his troops according to their numbers and not according to their qualitatively different fighting strength is not sure—in spite of this numerical definiteness—of the correctness of his plans, and thus of success.

This difference coincides, substantively, with the difference that was initially set up between sciences that are related to production and purely theoretical sciences. This becomes still clearer than in the case of arithmetic with *logistikē* and *metrikē*, which on the one hand serve craftsmanship and trade, but on the other hand represent the pure theory of geometry and the higher types of calculation.[33] The position of the art of building might seem unclear here, insofar as, by its use of instruments, it has a relatively high status among the purely empirical arts, even though the counting and measuring themselves that are practiced in it should be considered separately, and in fact are dealt with later when practical and theoretical mathematics are distinguished. Evidently the precedence of the art of building over arts like music is not so much due to the fact that it involves measurement and counting (which music, and practical life in general, also involve) as to the fact that it has created its own instruments for that purpose. A measuring instrument is something that, being already adapted to the substantive content of the thing to be measured, renders the measure perceptible by the senses (and thus, admittedly, also renders it impure), in order, precisely, to correct mere "visual judgment." The fact that the art of building not only "contains mathematics" but has its *own* kind of measures and that a special kind of art of measurement

33. See previous note.

belongs to it is what sets it apart. (Compare Iamblichus, *Protrepticus*, p. 55, where again the relative exactness of the art of building is attributed to its using its own instruments.)

In any case, the pure theoretical sciences of numbers, measures, and weights are superior in scientificness and truth, because they reveal their objects in pure discoveredness. (Accordingly, their value is not a practical one but is based on their discovering effect for its own sake; compare *Republic* 525d2.) Within the practically productive disciplines, on the other hand, the art of reckoning, measuring, and weighing has the character of a relative discovery only; that is, the degree of their exactness is determined for them by the requirements of practical dealings with their objects.

Thus the question that was posed initially—whether there are also differences of purity and truth within the sciences (differences in their scientificness)—is answered affirmatively. Indeed, even where, as in the case of arithmetic, the same name is used, two distinct kinds, differing precisely in their "truth," turned out to be comprehended under this nominal unity. But even higher, above philosophical (theoretical) mathematics, there stands a science that is true to the highest degree: dialectic. (It would repudiate us, Socrates says, if we did not want to grant it the highest status, because it is, after all, dialectic that we continually rely on, by practicing it, in our inquiring discussion.) It is science in its highest possible form, insofar as it reveals entities in their true being: in that which they are always, as the same thing. Its precedence over mathematics is not really argued for here (unless one were, with Stallbaum and Natorp, to regard as correct the manuscripts that give *pasan* at 58a1, which would agree well, substantively, with the *Republic*; but the continuation of the sentence is more in keeping with an *ad hominem* argument: the *pas* is reflected in a3 in *sumpantas*). This precedence is familiar enough from the investigation in the *Republic*. Mathematics, too, is a positive science. It contains assumptions which it does not itself put in question but from which it develops itself. Only dialectic goes to the archai (principles) of what exists, ultimately to the Idea of the Good—that is, to that in relation to which everything that exists is to be understood as remaining unchanged in its being. It represents the most certain knowledge because its object is fully revealed in what it is. Something that is understood as good is understood in what makes it what it is and has to be. So the fact that dialectic is the highest science is due to the fact that its object—the "Ideas"—really is entirely discovered by it. It has disposition over the logos of the thing itself—for example, of the perpendicular: it has disposition over what always and necessarily defines a perpendicular. It does not take something for a perpendicular that is not really one, as the builder who works with a plumb line continually takes something for a perpendicular that is not really one (that is, overlooks the non-perpendicularity of what he arrives at, by means of the plumb line, as a perpendicular.) So it is in general: the dialectical science of the Ideas as the causes surpasses in truth even the "science" of nature and the cosmos, which, after all, investigates how the cosmos came into existence and what constantly occurs in it.

This generalization is entirely in line with the doctrine of science that is sketched here. The investigation of the world of experience as such can never be a match, in terms of truth (that is, the discoveredness and availability of the realm of objects that it thematizes), for dialectic; because in the world of experience something is continually coming into being and changing, while the Ideas, the being of what exists, constantly are what they are. The Neo-Kantian interpretation (Natorp) is mistaken when it sees in this abrupt contrast between the world of experience and the world of the Ideas a forsaking of the "theory of experience" that was still being offered in the doctrine of the dialectic at the beginning of the dialogue. For there, too, dialectic's true object is not the perceptible itself. The music that one hears about there, for example, is not the art of musicians, because the exact knowledge of the tonal system alone would never suffice to "make" music; and yet only the knowledge of intervals and harmonies which is available a priori from the tonal system is true science, and not the practical performance guided by the ear. Of course it is true that the empirical sciences and practical arts also contain an element of genuine science: the science of counting and measurement, which was extracted from them.

As the true science, dialectic is also granted the most honorable name: nous and phronēsis.

Part V

Section 14: The Settling of the Question (The Good in Human Life) (59e–67b)

With that, the testing of the sciences is concluded. On the basis of the analysis of their kinds, hēdonē and phronēsis now stand really ready for the planned mixing. Once again we are shown, by the familiar arguments, that neither hēdonē nor phronēsis by itself could complete the good. Thus for the decision between hēdonē and phronēsis in regard to the second prize, a clarification of the "good" itself is initiated. We already know something about it, which furnishes us with access to it: its site, which is the mixed life. So it will be necessary first of all to undertake the mixture of hēdonē and phronēsis in the finest possible way, so as to gather from it what constitutes the good in it. An unexamined mixing of *all* phronēsis with *all* hēdonē would provide no assurance of the success of a good mixture. For both of them have, after all, shown themselves to differ, internally, in truth. So we will have to put the purest types of each of them—the true types—into the mixture and then see whether additional, less pure types of them will be needed for the life that is worth striving for. Here it turns out that, together with the purest, divine sciences, the less pure, human ones are also indispensable for life. To be able to live, we need knowledge not only of the pure measures in themselves but also of our ("false") *kanōn* and *kuklos* (rule and circle) (which only passes itself off as though it were really a circle). Indeed, even without the music that is based merely on the ear our life could not be thought of as desirable. Thus, in the end, all the sciences are to be admitted, since none of them do any damage.

Of the pleasures, too, only the "true" ones are initially admitted. Together with them, also, all the necessary ones (that is, all those that life cannot do without, such as, for example, moderate pleasure in food and drink, which is indispensable for a healthy bodily constitution). The question, however, is whether we should admit all the other pleasures as well, like the other sciences—that is, whether they are likewise beneficial, or at least harmless. The pleasures and the sciences are themselves supposed to give the answer to this; nor is this accidental, since the reason for the mixture lay, after all, in the fact that each, by itself, could not be without the other if it were to satisfy the Idea of the Good. Dasein's understanding of itself as good does not relate only to the possibility of having pleasure. Neither, however, does it relate solely to the possibility of knowledge, but rather to both, from the start. So the possibility of having both is the important thing. This means that pleasure and knowledge have to be compatible with one another and can be together only to the extent that they are compatible with one another. But being compatible with one another means: of one's own accord, letting the other coexist. This is why pleasure and thought themselves are questioned. Each has to say on its own account which members of the other category it must want to have with it in order to represent the truly good mode of life. Thus the pleasures[34] answer that, for them, being alone is neither possible nor useful and that of most interest to them is the kind of knowledge that discerns themselves, as well as everything else. They have no motive for excluding any form of knowledge. Only the form of knowledge that discerns themselves concerns them at all, and this is the one in which they are interested.

34. That the pleasures answer in the way they do here means that the answer is a product not of their normal self-understanding but of an understanding, gained through dialectic, of their role in the whole of human reality. The *exclusive* antagonism of the "clear" and the "sweet" (Singer) has long since been overcome here. [Presumably the reference is to Kurt Singer, *Platon der Gründer* (Munich, 1927), which the author discussed in his review in *Logos* 22 (1933): 63–79.—RMW]

It is different with the sciences. To begin with, the way in which they are dependent on the co-presence of pleasure is fundamentally different. It is not through pleasure that they first become what they themselves want to be; rather, they merely permit pleasure— out of regard for the ideal of the best mode of life. So for them it is questionable whether they are compatible with all the pleasures. Thus, in the process of admitting the pleasures, they have to examine the different kinds, in order to decide, for each of them, whether they can be with it or not (compare the twist at 64a3, that nous here is supposed to have answered *echontōs heauton* ["having itself"; that is, reasonably]). Now the sciences evidently will not admit the most violent pleasures (which are, above all, the bodily ones), because they are obstructive to the sciences themselves; but they certainly will accept the true pleasures, which, as ways of discovering what is, as it is, are allied to them in nature—and also all those that appear in the train of the aretē of the body (*hugeia*) and the soul (*sōphronein*). They will not allow any of the others to mix in, since that would prevent the resulting mixture from being as "beautiful" as possible. For a mixture in which every component is compatible with every other is "beautiful" [or "fine": Greek *kalos*]. But the strongest and most violent of the pleasures are not compatible with the sciences; they disturb them because they confuse the soul and deprive it of consciousness, not letting Dasein's constitution be the way Dasein understands it to be good.

Now the mixture is complete, except that an explicit emphasis is added that "truth" must inhere in it. For without truth there is no genuine coming into being or being: that which comes into being would never be what it is supposed to be or survive as such. The only thing that can come into being and be is something that is determined and discovered as what it becomes. A mixture that does not have measure (is not available in its definite measure as this mixture) is destructive, and is so in the first place towards itself (61d–e). This is evident in connection with the mixture of phronēsis and hēdonē that was undertaken above. If one mixes in too much pleasure—namely, the violent bodily gratifications, as well—then these destroy the sought-after happy constitution of the soul, by disturbing the nous and thus plunging Dasein into a forgetfulness of itself, in which, since it wants to understand itself as Dasein, it (once again) cannot last. Thus this kind of gratification creates the confusion in which Dasein sees what it orients itself by totter. The correct mixture, on the other hand, which was just undertaken, was not a blind lumping together of pleasure and knowledge; instead, its constituent parts were seen in their diverse substantive contents and were examined for their compatibility with one another, so that it turned out to be beautiful.

Now it is appropriate to ask what determines, in its ontological structure, this new unity that has arisen and as which Dasein understands itself as good—that is, what is the real basis of the beauty of this mixture (64c)? This cause of the acceptability of the mixture must be the good itself. If we have answered the question about the essence of the good, it will also become clear whether pleasure or science is more closely related to this "good." Now the goodness of each mixture is based on measure and measuredness. Without them, there is no true mixture—in which, after all, the constituent parts are determined into a new unity. The image of the drink may clarify this: if one uses too much honey in mixing it, the drink will "taste too much like honey" (will be too sweet to drink); but in the reverse case it will "taste like water" (be watery). In both cases the excess of one constituent part will make that part stand out in the mixed drink—and thus also the lack of the other. It is nothing proper at all, not a beautiful mixture but an unwanted muddle (note the play on words with *sumphora*!): not honey, not water, and not the drink that was wanted.

Thus the correct mixture, by contrast with the muddle that lacks a definite sense, makes the essence of the good visible in the trinity of measuredness, beauty, and truth. These paraphrases of the unified *idea* of the good are, not unintentionally, remote from all ter-

minological univocity.[35] The conscious looseness of the nomenclature
here means the same thing as when in the *Republic* we are given,
instead of the good, its *ekgonos* ("offspring": 506e ff.). "It itself" leaves
both name and image behind it and cannot be captured by the logos.
It is unspeakable.

But beyond this common element, the *Philebus*'s threefold
paraphrases have their own significant determinate sense, which interpretation must comprehend clearly. The cause of the value or dis-
value of a mixture is its measure and measuredness—and with that,
we read at 64e5, the dunamis (power) of the good has taken refuge in
the *phusis* (nature) of the beautiful. It is certainly not unintentionally
that the words *dunamis* and *phusis* are so explicitly and momentously
juxtaposed here. The *power* of the good becomes visible in the growth
(the nature) of the beautiful. The beautiful—appearance and inner
bearing (aretē), including both corporeal and psychic aspects—is not
something other than the good, but the good itself, as it is speakable
and visible. Measure and proportion are fundamental characteristics
of the beautiful—that is, of the way an entity lets itself and can let
itself be seen. But they are also the power of the good: they determine
the entity in such a way that it can be, by virtue of the overpowering
of the unsuitable in it. As a binding measure, the good is something
whose operation in the realm of being comes from somewhere beyond
being. But as something that is introduced as form into being, it
constitutes being's *nature*. The entity is determined by the completed
harmony of a structure that has measure *in itself*: symmetry. But that
is beauty: form that is unified in itself. Thus the good's introduction
of form turns out to be a bringing-out of the beautiful.

So the statement that the good takes refuge in the beautiful
means more than that it is unspeakable. In this taking refuge, the
good withdraws precisely in order to show itself. Its power proves itself
precisely by its being something more than something overpowering:

35. [On this, one can now consult Friedländer, *Platon*, 2:596, n. 1, and
597, n. 4; *Plato*, 3:542, n. 73.]

by its operating in entities themselves *as their own nature*. For that is the essence of the beautiful: to be present not as an additional characteristic alongside other specifiable characteristics in each entity that is beautiful, but as a relation of the whole, in its parts, to itself: a beautiful proportion in visible dimensions, a beautiful demeanor and bearing in human action and being—in both cases a harmony of the entity with itself, a completeness, a self-sufficiency. These features do indeed mark the preliminary concept of the "good."

Thus the good of human life, too, does not confront us as a norm located in the beyond, but as the beauty, measuredness, and truth of human being and conduct. It is not an extra-human or super-human insight that mixes human life together from pleasure and knowledge; instead, man himself, on the basis of his ownmost nature, understands himself in relation to the good by forming himself in the three indicated respects. That is why measure is not a determined feature of man's being, which occurs in it and, stemming from something with greater power, compels it, but is, rather, a way in which it conducts itself: measuredness that holds itself to the measure. That is why beauty is not the magical harmony of an articulated form but is, rather, the express objective of a process of self-formation aimed at being able to let itself be seen in all its conduct. And truth belongs to this human life not merely in the sense that the constituent parts of this life did not mix themselves "spontaneously" (*apo tuchēs*), however it happened, but in a rationally definite proportion. The definite order of the life structure composed of cognition and pleasure results from the *truthfulness* of these life behaviors themselves: that they present themselves as what they are, and consequently can let each other *be*.

Now the claims of pleasure and science are measured against these three considerations; that is, the purpose is to test which of the two is more closely akin to the good.

First of all, in regard to truth. Protarchus now concedes everything without hesitation; pleasure, he says, is least of all true. "Truth," as a constitutive element of being good, means, in itself, the discoveredness, and thus reasonableness, of the proportion in the mixture. So if man mixes himself, from the various possibilities of his existence, into the unity of a lasting and completed mode of behavior, then truth means that the conduct itself is true—that is, truthful. But this means, for each of its constituent parts, that it presents itself as what it really is. Now, pleasure contains in itself a tendency to present what it imagines—and thus itself—as more than it is. The inclination toward this kind of lying (untrue) declaration—for example, of love—is inherent in this affect itself (*alazonistaton* [greatest imposter], 65c5). People who are out for erotic enjoyment are inclined to forget themselves to such an extent as, in the lover's pledge itself, to foreswear themselves. Consequently the gods do not accept such oaths (*Symposium* 183b), or they forgive the perjury, as if the pleasures were irrational children whom one cannot hold responsible for what they say. Nous, on the other hand, is the truth itself; that is, its discovering sees the facts of the matter—human existence—in complete discoveredness, as they are.

This testing has to do, again, with pleasure and knowledge as general categories. Because for it the issue is not, of course, whether pleasures *can* also be true—we know that just those pleasures that belong to knowing and discovering entities, as such knowing and discovering, are (in fact) true—but rather, whether it is part of the tendency of the claim to pleasure, as such, that what is given in it is never only supposed, but true. It is evidently part of the essence of affect that it draws Dasein into itself so much that Dasein cannot regard what it sees in the affect in any way except with the eyes of the affect itself. Of course, on the other hand, pleasure also *takes on* the constitutive moments of the good mixture insofar as it enters into it. When the question is asked, here, how pleasure and knowledge stand in relation to these moments of being good, the question is to what extent they already have in themselves, of their own accord, *before* the mixture—and bring with them into it—what makes it good.

Knowledge is also superior to pleasure in measuredness. Pleasure is in itself unmeasured. For its characteristic tendency is to lose itself in going beyond all limits (*hōs pleiston epirrein, Gorgias* 494b). Philebus had emphasized this from the very beginning, because this is necessarily the way pleasure understands itself if it understands itself solely in terms of its own intention. Knowledge, on the other hand, is measured, in itself, more than anything else is.

Equally clear is nous's precedence over hēdonē in regard to beauty. Knowledge is never in a condition in which it could not let itself be seen. But there certainly are ugly enjoyments, which shun the light.

Thus the kinship of nous with the good is proved. If the moments of the good that constitute this mixture are enumerated now, in sequence, nous must come before hēdonē. (The moments of the good include, as was emphasized earlier, just as much the constituent parts—insofar as they help to constitute the good—as the existential moments of the unity of these constituent parts.) It will not be possible to omit hēdonē entirely from this enumeration, since it does necessarily belong, in certain forms, to that which constitutes the good life.

At the head of the sequence stands the trinity of the ontological moments that are ontologically determining for *every* good mixture. They are then followed by the constituent parts of the particular good mixture with which we are dealing here—that of the existential constitution of the human Dasein. The order, in sequence, of the three universal characteristics of the good is of subordinate importance here. It is, after all, precisely in their unity that they determine the ontological structure of a correct proportion. At the head stands measure itself, for without measure there is no correct proportion. It is what constitutes its *unity*. In second place is the existential character of the proportion that is determined by measure: the beautiful agreement of all the parts *in* the unity. In the third place is reason, or truth: the proportion's conformity to reason, that is, the fact that its determinateness is determined, sayable, and accessible by reason.

It is clear that these three characteristics of the good must correspond to the four kinds of being that Plato set up at the outset.[36]

36. Let me emphasize explicitly that the discussion of this correspondence

Both are, after all, what is required for the being of a good mixture. Measure corresponds to the peras (limit); the symmetrical corresponds to limited being that has come into existence; and nous or truth corresponds to the aitia (cause). But both the absence, here, of the fourth kind, the apeiron (unlimited), and the contrast between the equivalence of the three elements here and their differentiation there teach us that the purpose of the explication of the structural elements of mixture is different in the two cases. The difference between the two explications should not be understood as resulting from the fact that the discussion here does not deal with mixture in general but only, say, with the specific mixture of the human good. For the trinity of these elements here is explicitly described, when it is first introduced, as constitutive for *every* good mixture. And conversely, in the doctrine of the four kinds it is not, say, *every* kind of juxtaposition of different things that is understood under "mixture" but only—there, too—precisely a *good* mixture. (There, too, the mixed is "beautiful.")

What constitutes a correct mixture is, initially, the common theme of both discussions. In both versions the focus is on the phenomenon of mixture as the determination of the proportion or relationship of mixture. But in the doctrine of the four kinds the purpose is a universal-*ontological* one. The phenomenon of determining is the key by which to gain access to the universal structural elements of being. The characteristics of being that become visible as governing, and in, the production of a mixture are brought out as moments of being that determine the whole of the universe, because being is understood as being produced or being determined. In mixing, one assumes, first, the presence of undetermined and determining moments and secondly, the being of the determined thing—its determinateness. And both of these—the existential moments of the not yet determined, to be determined thing, and the determining thing, and the existential moment of the determinate thing—point back to

---

is not intended to extract the univocity of a dogma from the comparison but to mark off the *horizon* of the present explication, by contrast.

the cause, which combines the one, the indeterminate, and the other, the determining, into the third, determinateness. The latter's ontological import is the meaningfulness and accessibility of the determinate thing's unity.

Here, on the other hand, mixture is no longer the key to the analysis of being; rather, the purpose is to explicate, conceptually, the perspective under which entities are produced or understood as things that are produced. For this explication, then, a standpoint within the very intention of mixing is adopted. The mixture is seen from the point of view of the mixer. Its constitutive moments are the structural moments of the good, as it is understood as what the agent of the mixture has in view. To that extent, we are entirely in the category of the "cause" here and do not depart from it at all.

But what is supposed to be explicated here is not what belongs, ontologically, to every mixture, but what the perspective of mixing involves. The result is that nous figures here not *as cause* but as the mixture's conformity to reason—what we miss when we say there's "neither rhyme nor reason" in something. So nous here is a characteristic of the *object*. Hence the playful juxtaposition of nous and "truth" at 66b6. Truth is nous's objective correlate. Here as well as earlier, of course, nous is the agent of the mixture.

It is equally clear that undeterminedness is not something toward which the mixer is oriented in the act of mixing. On the contrary, mixing has the intention precisely of causing the indeterminate to disappear in the determined mixture. Even if, for each determined thing, it is essential (for its own being) that it stands within a circle of possible misdeterminations (*Verstimmungen*), the goodness of the determined thing nevertheless depends precisely on its not being misdetermined, and the intention of determining productively disregards the indeterminate. So the three moments of the good turn out, here, to be the goal that mixing has in view. More precisely, the mixer stands before the completed mixture and accentuates in it the constitutive elements of its goodness. *But in so doing he only makes explicit the points of view that the mixture was implicitly placed under when it was still to be mixed.* After all, truth was the consideration that governed the whole examination of the pleasures and the sciences from the beginning: that the enjoyable thing to which pleasure gives us access really is what it is supposed (in the pleasure) to be, and thus the pleasure is what it presents itself as; and, likewise, that the thing discovered in knowledge really is what it is discovered as, so that the knowledge itself is what it can be, according to its own potential, as a process of discovering. If this standard of truth, which was decisive for the goodness of the mixture, is satisfied, then the other two moments—the measure that knowledge and pleasure themselves set up and their compatibility (their accordance with measure), which they themselves uphold—are also given.

The fact that all the sciences, even the less "true" ones, are accepted, while on the other hand the violent and immoderate pleasures are excluded, can be seen to be consistent when one considers the being of true science and of pleasure. The so-called untrue sciences are not untrue in the same way as the violent, immoderate pleasures are. The false circle with which the craftsman works is not false in the same sense in which the pleasure of the person who scratches himself or herself is false. It is true that in both cases something is taken for something that it is not. But if craftsmen work with something that is only "approximately" a circle, they do not deceive themselves about what it is; they want the thing that is produced with the aid of the circle to be itself only "approximately" correct—that is, to be sufficiently correct to serve their practical purposes. So even in their inferior exactness, the inexact sciences still understand themselves on the basis of science's idea of discovering entities as they are in themselves. False pleasures, on the other hand, not only take something to be enjoyable that is not enjoyable; they are also blind toward themselves: what is taken in them as enjoyable determines Dasein's state-of-mind in such a way *that truly pleasant things cease to be discoverable for it at all.* While the sciences, then, remain oriented toward the idea of truth even when they are, in the indicated sense, "false," the pleasures are not in a position, when they are "false," to understand themselves, by their true means, as less true. Even the true pleasures are, after all, true only by virtue of the fact that they *understand* themselves as pleasure in terms of the idea of something truly pleasant, which (however) means that they have their measure and truth given to them by the sciences, with whose process of discovery they are bound up. That is the crucial point in Socrates' argumentation: the sciences have this advantage over the pleasures—even those that are truly good and belong in the mixture of the good life—that *it is they that understand themselves and pleasure's ability to be part of the good life by having regard to the good itself.* They cannot, of their own accord, be different from what they have to be in view of the good, which means that when they understand themselves and are authentic, they understand at the same time what makes Dasein in general good. The pleasures, on the other hand, are not of their own accord such that they understand themselves in their acceptability in view of the good. Rather, Dasein in the affect is open for nothing but what it aims at. In this abandonment to its object, pleasure makes Dasein forget itself, so that it loses itself immoderately in the taking of enjoyment.

So, as was foreseen, neither nous nor hēdonē has turned out to be "the good" of human life. For neither of them has the characteristic, which is simply definitive for the good, of the *hikanon*: being sufficient to itself. But nous proves to be much more closely akin than hēdonē is to the third thing which is stronger than both of them. This stronger thing is the determinateness, in terms of measure, of the relation between the two, the relation whose structural elements— measure, beauty, and truth—constitute the idea of the good. Nous is maximally akin to these—that is, it is already of its own accord, according to its own being, the way in which it and the whole human life in which it is, have, according to their best potential, to be. *This* component part of the mixture does not first have to be bound to the characteristics that are required by the idea of a good mixture but is already, by its own nature, one of them. So the mixture does not come about by the sciences' being induced (by entering into a relation to the affects) to be something that they themselves are not, but only vice versa: the hēdonai, by entering into the relation of being together with the sciences, are induced by them to acquire the characteristics that constitute the idea of the good. If, then, actual human life, when it is governed by the idea of "happiness" (that is, of its own highest potential), cannot be without hēdonē, then even in the simile of mixture, which places the constituent parts on a par with each other formally, the ontological precedence of understanding and knowledge has become clear. For it is only by being combined with modes of knowledge that forms of hēdonē that are true, and thus good in themselves, are constituted. Dasein *understands* itself in its highest potential, which however means: it understands itself as engaging in cognition. Pleasure and taking enjoyment befit it insofar as it encounters them in this orientation towards its highest potential. Insofar as they claim, on their own account, to be an orienting aim for Dasein, they have the opposite effect of threatening Dasein precisely in its capacity to be oriented and self-understanding.

In conclusion let me suggest in what way the results of this interpretation are significant for the interpretation of Aristotle's ethics.

We saw that Plato's penetrating analysis pushed the problem of the affects so far that one is immediately reminded of Aristotle's fundamental orientation. Plato, also, develops the idea of a "true" pleasure from its being given together with perception and thought. Pleasure is "good" if it does not disturb these activities but is the pleasure that "belongs" to them. In Aristotle's two analyses of hēdonē (*Nic. Ethics* H 12–15, K 1–5) he makes just this characterization the basis of his conceptual clarification of the problem of hēdonē. Of course, Aristotle consciously goes beyond the conceptual framework in which Plato ties together all the phenomena of hēdonē: hēdonē as *motion*. But we have seen that Plato saw, in substance, the peculiar character of motion that Aristotle grasps in the concept of energeia. For the from-to structure—as opposed to a continuous being-toward something—is no more characteristic of true pleasure, "enjoyment of something," than it is of perception and thought.

But Aristotle provided the real scientific problem of ethics with a new basis in the context of his critique of the general ontological position embodied in the doctrine of the Ideas. It is true that Plato, in the *Philebus*, does not deal only with "the good" but also, explicitly, with the "good" of human life. The *Philebus*'s whole inquiry is based on the assumption that we are not divine beings but human ones. This is precisely why the problem of the affects is the focus of the discussion. Despite its allusions to the affectless bliss of divine existence, the investigation is completely committed to the problematic that arises from the exposition of human Dasein. But its general preliminary assumption that real being is the being of the Ideas makes it interpret the good of human life, as well, in terms of an orientation toward the Idea of the Good. The human good is supposed to be determined by reference to the universal structural moments of the good. The unity of the good of human existence is seen as the unity of a mixture. This implies that Dasein has disposition over, and produces itself out of, its possibilities—pleasure and cognition—in the way in which it has disposition over facts that are present-at-hand. Thus the unity of this produced thing is derived from *universal* characteristics of being, which characterize every entity that can be and that does not perish in the continual fluctuation of "becoming." The real problem of ethics—what it is on the strength of that Dasein understands itself as "good"—stands from the very beginning under a privative sign and on a level with the problem of physics. The references to the affectless existence of pure nous show this. Man cannot understand himself solely on the basis of this thing of which nous is capable, although, as pure allowing being to be encountered, it represents, in itself, the highest thing of which existence is capable. Thus the good of actual human Dasein proves to be a modification of what good really is. What the ontological meaning of this modification is, is more veiled than indicated by the cryptic remark about the good's taking refuge in the character of the beautiful. The ontological features of measure, beauty, and truth, which are collected together in a unitary way as the structural moments of the good, are also supposed to provide the basis for the properly human good, which constitutes man's eudemōnia.

Aristotle criticized this idea of the good precisely on account of its ontological claim (*Nic. Ethics* A 4). But his central argument is ethically oriented. Inquiry about the good in man's doing and being finds human Dasein always already confronted with concrete tasks, within which that which is (in each case) the good must be chosen. The answer to this concrete question cannot be found in a universal idea of the good, even if such a thing exists. Insofar as man's choice is always located in the concrete now of a situation, the agent simply cannot be relieved by a *science* (which is necessarily restricted to general and invariable existential relations) of the choice of what is in each case the good. Thus the question is whether science can be important at all for actual Dasein and its moral tasks at any given time.

To know in advance, before the concrete situation of action, what one has to do in order to be a proper human being, and thus to be sure of oneself—no science of human being and action can undertake to fulfil this demand. It conflicts with the fundamental character of human existence. But insofar as this creature who is not the master of his fate and his future understands himself, within his inconstancy (*Unbeständigkeit*), in terms of lasting possibilities of finding a stance (*Standmöglichkeiten*)—and ultimately in terms of the highest possibility, that of knowledge, of theory itself—then knowledge and comprehension have a task within this constraint and on the basis of this understanding: they can investigate and make visible this actual self-understanding of Dasein *in its unchanging averageness*. But that can never be accomplished through an orientation to the universal idea of the good, which as such is emptied of all substantive content (*mataion*, *Nic. Ethics* 1099b20), and which no concrete implementation can ever satisfy (*Nic. Ethics* K 2, 1172b26 ff.).

Appendix:
Analytical Table of Contents
(1931 Edition)

Play. The care that goes with knowledge and determining declaration. Predication and inference.

Section 3: The Motives of a Concern for the Facts of the Matter in a Shared World (Logos and Dialectic)

The claim to understandability and contradiction by the other person. The reflexive effect of coming to a shared understanding. The abstraction of concern for the facts of the matter. Concern for the facts of the matter and refutation. The reflexive effect of contradiction. Coming to an understanding with oneself. Agreement and teaching.

Section 4: Degenerate Forms of Speech

The unsubstantiveness of "envy." Seeming knowledge as cutting off contradiction. Rhetoric. Seeming knowledge as a technique of refutation. Eristic.

Section 5: The Socratic Dialogue

The dialogue form and idle talk. The Socratic premise: the claim to understanding of *aretē*. Socratic elenctic as shaking *doxa*. Hedonism as an understanding of Dasein. Ironic refutation. Sophistic and Socratic eristic. The positivity of ignorance: the pre-understanding of the "good." The admission of ignorance and the search for accountability.

Part II: Plato's Dialectic and the Motive of Coming to an Understanding

Section 6: The Dialectic of the *Phaedo* and the *Republic*

The logos as hypothesis and the demand of accountability. The hypothesis of the *eidos*. The critique of Anaxagoras's *nous*. The "second voyage" and the truth of language. What the hypothesis of the eidos accomplishes. The ascent to the *archē*. The Idea of the Good and the *Phaedo*. The dialectic of the one and the many as the dialectic of aretē. Dialectic as the problem of grounding. The defense against antilogic.

Section 7: The Theory of Dialectic in the *Phaedrus*

The exemplary importance of rhetoric. What dialectic accom-

Part II: The New Posing of the Question (19c–31a)

Section 4: The More Precise Formulation of the Topic (19c–23b)
    A "second voyage." Testing the two theses against the concept
    one already has of the good. The human motivational basis
    of hedonism. Transition to a new problem-level: mixture and
    the status of each of the opponents in it.

Section 5: The Doctrine of the Four Kinds (23b–27b)
    Clarification of the new way of posing the question. The on-
    tological structure of mixture. Indefiniteness. The *peras*.
    "Mixture" as an image of "determination." The linking ele-
    ment: being a unity. The problematic of the peras. The third
    kind. Mean and measure. Mixture as the togetherness of
    things that are present-at-hand, and proportional definiteness
    as a condition of its ability to exist. The "cause" as an ontic
    precondition of production and as an ontological element of
    definiteness (logos).

Section 6: The Application of this Doctrine to the Question (27c–31a)
    Hēdonē and *phronēsis* and the ontological elements of mixture.
    Hēdonē indefinite in itself. *Nous* a cause in itself. The con-
    stitution of the living body and the cosmos by this cause.

Part III: Investigation of the Kinds of Pleasure

Section 7: Corporeal Pleasure and Psychic Pleasure (31b–35d)
    The need to begin a dialectical analysis. Why this beginning
    is not made explicit. Corporeal pleasure. How it is tied to
    displeasure. Psychic pleasure. Its methodological priority.
    Corporeal pleasure and affectless existence in the nous.
    Psychic pleasure: *mnēmē*. *Aisthēsis* and *anamnēsis*. Desire
    and retention.

Section 8: Desire and Anticipatory Enjoyment (35d–36c)
    The psychic aspect of corporeal pleasure. The unitary mixture
    of the pleasure of anticipation and the displeasure of lack. Its

interpretation as desire. The interpretation of the pleasure of desire as anticipatory enjoyment. The soul's anticipatory character and the intentional structure of the affects.

Section 9: "False" Pleasure as Groundless Hope (36c–41b)
Psychic pleasure and truth: pleasure as a way of understanding oneself through the world. How *doxa* can be false. Analysis of doxa. The freedom of *phantasia*. Anticipatory pleasure as hope. Hope and expectation. Hope's falsehood not error, but at the same time falsehood of the way one is.

Section 10: "False" Pleasure as Exaggerated and Imagined Anticipatory Enjoyment (41b–44a)
Exaggerated anticipatory enjoyment as being deceived about the extent of the enjoyability of the expected thing. Its causes: contrast and distance. Imagined anticipatory enjoyment: the supposed enjoyability of the expected thing as a way of relieving pain.

Section 11: Mixed Pleasure as "False" Pleasure (Forgetfulness Directed at Displeasure) (44b–50e)
All anticipatory pleasure false: mixture with displeasure. The weight of pain and forgetting in pleasure. The pleasure of alleviation and of anaesthetization. The mixedness of corporeal pleasure: itching. The covering up of pain in the purely psychic pleasure affects: the enjoyment of comedy. The pain of "envy" and laughter. Such (mixed) pleasure is only supposedly pleasure.

Section 12: Unmixed Pleasure as Enjoyment of What is Enjoyable (50e–52d)
Things that are enjoyable in themselves. Colors, figures, etc. Pleasure in knowledge. Pleasure *in* something: not supposing, but intuiting or regarding. Enjoyment about and of. Conditionally versus unconditionally (permanently) enjoyable things. The truth of pleasure as its purity. Mixed pleasure always

concealing. Addenda: pleasure and motion. Pure pleasure in something is more than motion. The fluctuation of pleasure and the constancy of being (humanly) good.

Part IV

Section 13: The Doctrine of Science (55c–59e)

Practical and theoretical sciences. Differences, in regard to truth, among the productive sciences: building and music. The science of numbers and measures as a practical and a theoretical science. The priority of dialectic.

Part V

Section 14: The Settling of the Question (The Good in Human Life) (59e–67b)

The undertaking of the mixture. Testing the constituent parts. Admission of all the sciences by the pleasures. Selection of only some kinds of pleasure by the sciences. The question of the good as the question of the cause of the mixture's beauty. The moments of the good. The flight of the good into the beautiful. The precedence of knowledge over pleasure in regard to truth: truthfulness; in regard to measure: measuredness; in regard to beauty: being able to let itself be seen. The table of the goods. The three moments of the good and the four "kinds" of being: the changed point of view. Knowledge's proximity to measure, and pleasure's self-destruction through lack of measure.

Conclusion

The problem of the affects in Plato and Aristotle. The idea of the good and the lack that is inherent in ethics and physics. Aristotle's critique and the positive possibility of an ethics.

List of Literature

Works Cited

Editions of the *Philebus*, with commentary:

G. Stallbaum, *Philebus* (Leipzig, 1842)

C. Badham, *The Philebus of Plato*, 2d ed. (1878)

R. G. Bury, *The Philebus of Plato* (Cambridge, 1897)

Translations:

F. Schleiermacher, *Platos Werke* (Berlin, 1817–28), vol. 2, pt. 3, 3rd ed. (1861)

O. Apelt, ed. and tr., *Sämtliche dialoge*, 2d ed. (Leipzig, 1923)

Commentary:

P. Natorp, *Platos Ideenlehre. Eine Einführung in den Idealismus*, 2d ed. (Leipzig, 1921)

Translation Key

A list of translations adopted for selected especially important terms follows. It will provide a rough guide for those who would like to be able to reconstruct the original German to some extent, though they are not always used with complete consistency, as I have also tried to produce something not entirely alien to the author's rather informal, non-technical style. Many of these translations correspond to those used by John Macquarrie and Edward Robinson in their translation (New York, 1962) of Heidegger's *Being and Time*, a book which, of course, was the single most important influence on Gadamer in this work. I have omitted most grammatical variants where the root is evident.

Accountability: *Rechenschaft*
Anticipatory enjoyment: *Vorfreude*
Beneficial or advantageous: *nützlich*
Care: *Sorge*
Circumspection: *Umsicht*
to be Cognitively at home in something: *sich auf etwas verstehen*
Coming to a (shared) understanding: *Verständigung*
Concern for the facts of the matter: *Sachlichkeit*
Declaration: *Aussage*
Definite: *bestimmt*
Discovery, discovered: *Entdeckung, entdeckt*

Enjoyment: *Freude*

Explication: *Auslegung*

Facts of the matter, thing, reality: *die Sache* (see also "Substantive")

Genuine: *echt*

To Give reasons or causes, to ground: *begründen*

Gratification: *Genuss*

Ground: *Grund, begründen*

Involvement: *Bewandtnis*

Make provision: *Besorgen*

"Pathos," passion, receptive state: *Pathos*

Pleasure: *Lust*

Present-at-hand: *Vorhanden*

Pre-understanding: *Vorverständnis*

Reason or cause: *Grund*

Respect, perspective: *Hinsicht*

Science, scientific: *Wissenschaft, wissenschaftlich*

State-of-mind: *Befindlichkeit*

Substantive: *sachlich*

Index

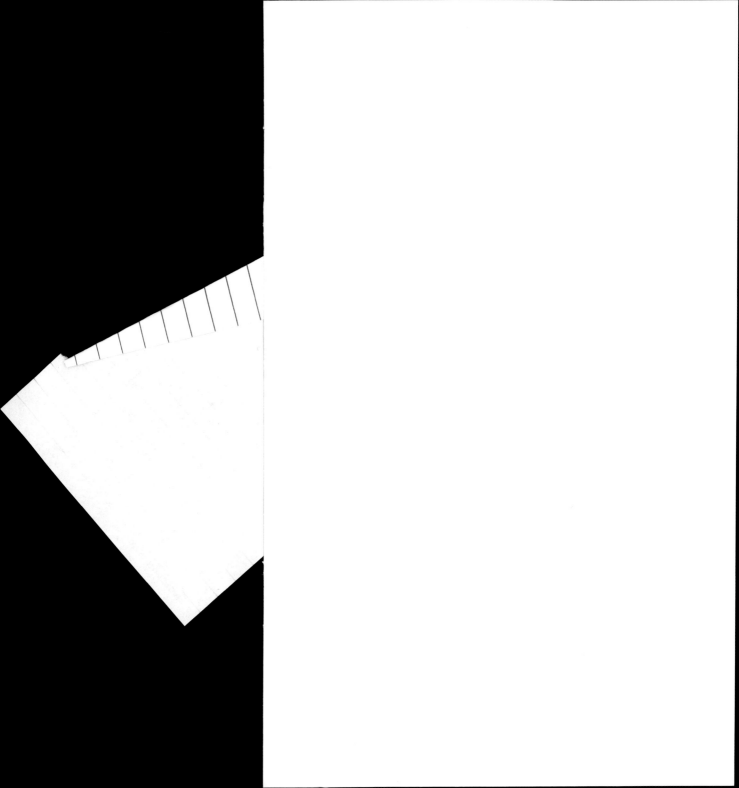

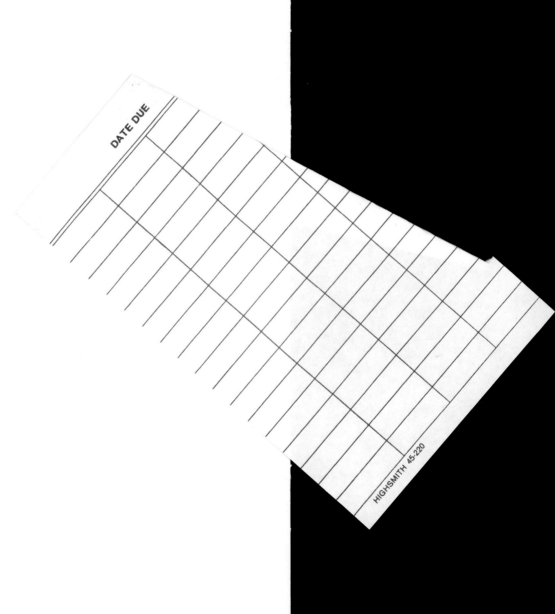

DATE DUE

HIGHSMITH 45-220